BRUCE LEE
DYNAMIC BECOMING

Reflections on the Life, Legacy and Philosophy of the Martial Art Master

by

James Bishop

Bruce Lee:
Dynamic Becoming

Promethean Press
1846 Rosemeade Parkway #192
Carrollton, TX 75007

Manufactured in the United States of America

ISBN 0-9734054-0-6

Table of Contents

INTRODUCTION

I am often asked to explain the philosophy of Bruce Lee. People expect that I can sum it up in a few words. In truth, I have a better chance of sprouting wings than I have of being able to put Lee's philosophy on a postcard.

It is human nature to try to define something. However, when we look at things deep enough, we realize that we are not trying to define so much as we are trying to make definitions as a tool to enhance our understanding. That's the ultimate goal: "understanding" Bruce Lee's philosophy rather than defining it.

Bruce Lee was a singular individual. He seemed to be the type for whom the term "individual" was coined. There were (and are) none like him. Lee's philosophy was predicated on a sense of individuality. It was a philosophy preserved in the catacombs of one man's mind, full of twists and turns and dead ends. Like a fine suit, it was tailor-made to Bruce Lee's specifications, and fit no other person. This is an important point that has been missed by many fans and practitioners of his martial art, who have spent many fruitless years chasing the will o' the wisp that is the essence of Bruce Lee.

At the Jun Fan Jeet Kune Do Nucleus Seattle[1] seminar in 1999 I saw a lot of people who were trying to "be Bruce Lee". They were imitating everything he did in the movies, such as the little hand gesture he made in his movies with his pinkie and thumb extended, the head movements and facial expressions, even the vocal noises, doing imitations that would have put an

---

[1] A little terminology: *Jun Fan Gung Fu* is what Bruce Lee originally called his martial art when he began teaching in the United States; *Jeet Kune Do* is the name he gave to it in its later stages. The *Jun Fan Jeet Kune Do Nucleus* (which became the *Bruce Lee Educational Foundation*) is a group of Bruce Lee's original students, friends and family who established an organization to preserve and promote the martial art of Bruce Lee. *Jun Fan Jeet Kune Do* (also known as "Original Jeet Kune Do") is the name they gave to the art as he practiced it during his lifetime, to make the distinction between it and other interpretive versions of the art that have evolved since his death.

Elvis impersonator to shame. I thought it was particularly sad and disappointing because they were mimicking Bruce Lee (or what they thought was Lee from watching his movies) instead of trying to be themselves and see what Lee left as a legacy that could be of value to them in their own personal growth as martial artists and as people.

Jeet Kune Do was Bruce Lee's personal expression of his martial art; whenever another person tries to follow him, they are doing their own interpretation of Jeet Kune Do. It's rather like Shintoism. Shinto is really tied into being Japanese. For that reason, a German, for example, may apply and study some of the aspects of Shinto, but they can never really "be" Shinto, because they just aren't Japanese. In the same way, we can practice the techniques that Bruce Lee passed on in Jeet Kune Do, but only Lee could truly be called a practitioner of Jeet Kune Do, because Jeet Kune Do meant Lee's personal expression. What Bruce Lee would best appreciate from us would be if we looked at what qualities he had as a human being which made him so successful (his motivation, his inquisitiveness, his self-reflection) and developed those qualities for ourselves to make our lives better and maximize our potential, rather than trying to make our bodies look like Bruce Lee, or copying his war cries, to name just a few; yet, people continue to look to Bruce Lee as the unquestionable truth in martial arts and all things. There is no single truth. The truth exists only in relation to the person that perceives it.

Bruce Lee believed that there is no such thing as a "best style". Lee didn't even like the term style, because to him "style" was a cage. That doesn't mean that you can't look at the overall performance of a "style" and see that it has efficient means for fighting or, in a philosophical context, that it has meaning that rings true for you. Nonetheless, it is not *the* art itself, because no such thing exists. What works for one person may not work for the next, or what works in one moment may not be what works in the next. There is no such universal standard. That exists within you to decide. As Bruce Lee said, "I cannot teach you, only help you to explore yourself."

Bruce Lee's philosophy has experienced an uphill battle since before he died. It faces difficulties on many fronts. For one, few instructors in Bruce Lee's martial art of Jeet Kune Do teach the philosophical concepts. That is partially because the instructors lack a working knowledge of philosophy. It is much more difficult for an instructor to delve into the philosophy in detail when they don't have the background to interpret and explain it. Some instructors also have no interest in it, and don't even think of helping their students explore themselves. Several Jun Fan Jeet Kune Do Nucleus members have been fairly vocal about their disdain for the philosophy of Bruce Lee. I know of at least one Nucleus member who has dismissed it as "psychobabble". On the other hand, there are plenty that do a fine job of conveying all the aspects of Bruce Lee's martial art and philosophy.[2]

Another reason is that people have a hard time getting past the image of Bruce Lee as a chop-socky movie actor. Many of them are strongly opposed to the idea that the man who made films like *The Big Boss* and *Fist of Fury* could be such a reflective and rationalizing man. Mainstream philosophy, which is infected with academic snobbery and Western arrogance, has equally underestimated his value. This is especially distressing to me because Bruce Lee is a wonderful ambassador for philosophy. He reaches an audience, nay, *creates* an audience, which would not otherwise be there.

"For me, Bruce Lee's onscreen presence was made possible because of how he managed to achieve goals from within," notes fan Neil Cozens. "I always think that what goes on inside a person first and foremost is the most important because this is what shapes the outward projection of the person."

Finally, the perpetuation of Bruce Lee's philosophy faces a most difficult opponent in the form of his own estate. Never before has someone been promoted as a philosopher while simultaneously subject to the restrictions that come with being a media commodity. On the one hand, his estate wants to promote him as a philosopher. On the other hand, the estate wants to closely control all dissemination of information related to Bruce Lee with a proprietary interest. The two are mutually exclusive, diametrically opposed goals. If Plato's estate had chosen to exercise the same kind of proprietary control over his philosophy because he was a famous wrestler, we wouldn't be remembering him now. But then, you won't catch Plato's image on a lunch box or a Pez dispenser. No other philosopher has ever had the

---

[2] The difficulty for many of the torchbearers of Bruce Lee's martial art is that they come from an occidental mindset, whereas Bruce Lee had a very oriental mindset. In the occidental mindset, all things must have clear, neat definitions. There is no duality; things must always be black or white. Some people from the Western world can't conceive of a reality with no clear distinctions that, at times, can even be paradoxical. Eastern philosophy is replete with such paradoxes, and that is the philosophical base of Bruce Lee's art and philosophy.

dubious distinction of being represented by the same media law firm that handles the estate of Elvis Presley.[3]

Yet, while I believe Bruce Lee should be rightfully recognized for his philosophical contributions, I am the first to admit that he was not original. There is nothing in his philosophy that cannot be found elsewhere, as this book itself will attest to. Everything in Lee's philosophy I have found in Humanistic Psychology, Taoism, Zen, and the philosophy of Jiddu Krishnamurti. In that sense, he is no different than the average academic philosopher of today; very few generate original ideas. Where Bruce Lee does differ with that group of people is that, instead of simply analyzing the ideas of other men, Lee was concerned with applying those ideas. Bruce Lee's genius was in finding commonalities and connections with various ideas and disciplines. He weaved a tapestry of personal truth out of the experience and insight of many distinguished minds that came before him.

In the following pages you will find a collection of my articles, lectures and discussions on the subject of Bruce Lee's philosophy. Some have previously been published in the pages of other publications, and a few are entirely new or never published before. All have been revised and annotated. What you will not find are what you have come to expect from a Bruce Lee book: lots of flashy pictures and complex explanations of how to perform the perfect kick. Instead, you will find a serious study of the

---

[3] A prime example of this is evident in the response I got from Universal Studios, which produced the Bruce Lee biography movie *Dragon: The Bruce Lee Story* and also has an agreement to be the official licensing arm of the Bruce Lee Estate. I made a request to use a photograph from the *Dragon* movie to illustrate a passage in my first book on Bruce Lee that expressed the profoundly positive effect that the film had on me. In response, I received the following: "Please be advised that all material contained in and relating to the above-referenced Universal property is copyrighted and we control all rights. Therefore, under no circumstances are you to use any materials of any characters from the films, the titles, or make any references to the property for any purpose whatsoever." Beyond the fact that I had a first amendment right to mention and write about Bruce Lee that they were ignoring (a right which I exercised), Universal's admonishment underscores the paradoxical effort of the Estate to promote Lee as a philosopher and as a merchandising commodity.

On the other hand, Dr. Wayne Dyer, a prominent humanistic psychologist and self-help author/lecturer, is an example of someone in the media's eye who is a messenger first and a marketer second. Dyer has made millions of dollars from his many books, audio tapes, videos, and lecture tours. Dr. Dyer was a special guest at a recent pledge drive for a public broadcasting station in Dallas, Texas, where they presented one of his many self-help videos on television. While he was there to promote the pledge drive and bring attention to his work, he suggested to the viewers that those who purchase his videos make copies and give them to their friends. The fact that Dr. Dyer would not receive royalties from bootleg copies of his videos was of little concern to him; spreading his message was his main concern. An attempt to do a similar thing with Bruce Lee educational materials would likely get you a harshly-worded letter from the Bruce Lee Estate's attorneys.

philosophy of Bruce Lee, his influences, and its parallels in the areas of psychology, philosophy, sociology and theology.

I am amazed at the impact that Bruce Lee's philosophy has had and continues to have on so many people. I am gratified that the work my colleagues and I have pursued over the past few years has borne such satisfying fruit. From Texas to Ireland, from Seattle to Madrid, we have been able to accomplish some very positive things, both publicly and personally. It's a testament to Bruce Lee that he lives in the hearts of so many people.

The Philosophy of Bruce Lee

The following chapter is adapted from my book *Remembering Bruce: The Enduring Legacy of the Martial Arts Superstar*. It gives a basic overview of the philosophy of Bruce Lee and how it impacted his friends and students.

Bruce Lee's martial art could not have been as successful and complete without the deep philosophical base he gave it. Martial arts, by nature, are a reflective practice where the practitioner must examine not only the issues of life or death but also the nature of the self.

One of the biggest influences on Bruce Lee, philosophically, was the Brahmin philosopher Jiddu Krishnamurti. Krishnamurti was born into poverty in 1895 in southern India. He was an unusually compassionate and intellectual boy, and at age fourteen was recognized as the pre-destined "World Teacher" by the mystical Theosophical Society, which adopted him and sent him to England and France to be educated and eventually assume his role as their leader. However, in 1929 at the age of 34 he shocked the Theosophical Society by renouncing his role as the World Teacher, arguing that religious doctrines and organizations stood in the way of real truth. "Because you have placed beliefs before life, creeds before life, dogmas before life, religions before life, there is stagnation. Can you bind the waters of the sea or gather the winds in you fists?" Krishnamurti then went on to become a very influential motivational and philosophical speaker until his death in 1986.

Lee found that Krishnamurti's viewpoints on life ran parallel to his own. In his book *Freedom from the Known*, Krishnamurti writes: "You cannot look through an ideology, through a screen of words, through hopes and fears. The man who is really serious, with the urge to find out what truth is, has no concept at all. He lives only in what is." Lee adapted this idea in forming his martial art philosophy: "You cannot express and be alive through static put-together form, through stylized movement. The man who is really serious, with the urge to find out what truth is, has no style at all. He lives only in what is."

Bruce Lee defined his Jeet Kune Do thus: "Jeet Kune Do is training and discipline toward the ultimate reality in self-defense, the ultimate reality in simplicity. The true art of Jeet Kune Do is not to accumulate but to eliminate. Totality and freedom of expression toward the ever-changing opponent should be the goal of all practitioners of Jeet Kune Do."

"A classicist or traditionalist will only do what the teacher tells him and that's it. The teacher is pedestalized, you do what he says and you don't question him," says John Little, the former director of the Bruce Lee Educational Foundation.[4] "But Bruce was drawing from some very diverse sources, such as gestalt therapy, Krishnamurti, etc. Not that these people were necessarily creators either, but they saw a certain truth that they wrote about. Bruce saw that same truth, and he saw its application to martial arts."

"The amazing thing about Bruce was that he was able to bring in things from (what we would think) is outside and make it a part of the Jeet Kune Do concept," says Leo Fong, a former Bruce Lee student.

Bruce Lee's Los Angeles Chinatown student Bob Bremer remembers Lee relating to him the story of the "Chinese Woodcutter":

> "The old Chinese woodcutter was out in the forest chopping wood," said Lee. "He's chopping the wood and chopping the wood, and pretty soon the bushes start rattling and the trees start vibrating. He looks over there, the bushes part, and out steps a dragon. The Chinese woodcutter says to himself, *Golly! I always thought they were just stories! This is real! If I could capture it or kill it I could be famous! I wouldn't have to cut wood anymore!*
>
> "So he took his ax and takes a step toward the dragon. The dragon turns and says, 'Oh oh oh. You son of a bitch. I know what you're thinking. If you take another step toward me I'm going to breathe fire all over you and burn you to a cinder.'
>
> "The woodcutter thinks, *He can read my mind! He knows what I'm thinking before I even do it! It's hopeless! I might as well go back to chopping wood!*
>
> "So he goes back to chopping his wood, and he's chopping and chopping. In the middle of one of his swings the

---

[4] *The Bruce Lee Educational Foundation* was an organization founded by a group of Bruce Lee's students, friends and family to preserve his art. It was formerly known simply as *Jun Fan Jeet Kune Do*.

ax flies out of his hand and hits the dragon right between the eyes. Kills him."

"Bruce never told me what he meant by that story," says Bremer. "For months I was thinking, *What was he trying to tell me? I'm going over there to learn a physical thing, and he's messing with my mind! What the hell is going on?*"

Lee was trying to instill in his students the natural spontaneity of combat, to reach a point where the action becomes thoughtless, where there is no separation between the fighter and the fight. Where there is no intention to act there can be no expectation of action. This is where the importance of wu-shin, or "no mindedness", comes into play. Also called *mushin* by the Zen masters, wu-shin is the art of detachment, wherein a person learns to let his mind wander free of thought on no particular thing. In this way the mind can be most efficiently responsive to what ever comes. Like an echo or a reflection in the mirror, the reaction is instantaneous and without conscious thought. Said Lee: "The great mistake is to anticipate the outcome of the engagement; you ought not to be thinking of whether it ends in victory or in defeat. Let nature take its course, and your tools will strike at the right moment."

Bruce Lee believed that he could not teach his students so much as point them in the direction of knowledge. "I cannot teach you, " Lee mused to James Franciscus in the television series *Longstreet*, "only help you to explore yourself."

"He actually was one of the very few that applied the philosophy to the art," said Dan Inosanto. "Everything he taught was like 'Be soft yet not yielding. Firm yet not hard.' I was thinking, *what the hell does that mean?*"

Inosanto was not alone when it came to being confused by Lee's philosophical nature. "He often spoke in parables," says author Joe Hyams.

One of Lee's favorite parables was the story of the western scholar who came to Japan to learn about Zen from an old Zen master. As the story goes, the two sat down to introductory tea, and it became evident after a few minutes that the western scholar was more interested in telling the Zen master what he knew than learning anything from him. As the Zen master poured the tea for his guest, the scholar continued to ramble on. The tea began to spill over the edges of the cup; the Zen master continued pouring. "Sir!" said the western scholar. "The cup is over-full!"

"Yes," replied the Zen master, "and like this cup you too are over-filled with your own ideas and opinions. How do you expect to learn if you are not willing to empty your cup?"

Bruce Lee would often quote this parable to his students. He encouraged them to speak up if they had a difference of opinion in his teachings but, if pushed too long, he would say, "At least empty your cup and try." Lee believed that you should not dismiss something out of hand without first investigating it for yourself.

Bruce Lee also believed in Goethe's dictum: "Knowing is not enough; you must *apply.*" It was his opinion that knowledge is useless if it is not put to good use. More importantly, one can never determine the *value* of knowledge if it is not tested. To quote Lao Tzu: "Tao people never try. They do."

Lee embodied the Taoist concept of *tzu jan,* or honest self-expression. Because he refused to subordinate himself to one style of fighting, he was free to be open and critical of all fighting concepts, including his own. This part of Lee's character caused the greatest conflict between himself and others, especially martial artists who are often trained to accept the teachings of their instructor without question. Indeed, the term *master*, used in many martial arts styles to denote the teacher or leader of the school, implies absolute and unquestioning authority. As the ancient Greek philosopher Socrates first explained, the best way to knowledge and wisdom is through the dialectic, or the process of placing ideas in open discussion so that the inherent weaknesses of the ideas can be discovered. This Socratic Method is now used, not only in philosophy, but also in the scientific method of examination, wherein a researcher will first formulate a hypothesis and then try to prove or disprove it. The science of martial arts should be no different.

Bruce Lee's personal expression of martial arts was something that he believed was unique to him and him alone, because it was the product of his personal attributes and deficiencies. Among his physical "quirks" were poor eyesight, being short and lightweight, a bad back, and one leg that was shorter than the other. What he lacked in these areas he made up for in speed, timing, and strength. Dan Inosanto, his protégé, said, "The total picture Bruce Lee wanted to present to his pupil was that, above everything else, he must find his own way. It is important to remember that Bruce Lee was a 'pointer' to the truth and not the truth itself."

For Bruce Lee all knowledge led to self-knowledge. Lee placed a great deal of emphasis on this belief in his teachings. It was one of the most important concepts he derived from his study of Krishnamurti. As Krishnamurti said: "We must first understand ourselves in order to know anything and to understand and solve problems." Lee felt that, for a person to grow and evolve, they must come to know themselves through whatever medium they choose: dance, music, art, or martial arts to name a few.

Bruce Lee believed in our inherent right to question the status quo and to pursue knowledge with a critical and investigative eye. How can a person honestly expect to prosper in a society in which they allow someone else to make the decisions and draw the conclusions for them? Partake of the wisdom of others but think for yourself. No one respects a mind that cannot be independent.

Bruce Lee also believed that an inner change was needed for society to evolve. Social change outwardly will always fail so long as there is no inner change, no revolution within each and every one of us. That is why communism failed, and why such progressive social changes will always fail, so long as we remain the same. Ignorance and stupidity often breed much faster than wisdom.

In Plato's *Allegory of the Cave* the philosopher describes a dark cave where people have been chained up since childhood. They are forced to face the wall of the cave, and have never seen the fire burning behind them or the people passing by. The only knowledge they have is of the shadows cast against the wall. These prisoners are forced into a state of perpetual ignorance.

Bruce Lee felt that people in today's society were experiencing a similar sort of bondage. "Styles tend to separate men, because they have their own doctrines and then the doctrines become the gospel truth that you cannot change!" In our world today we simply accept what we are told to believe at face value without examining its root or the ideology and motivation behind it. Too often we are getting a partial or imperfect piece of the "truth" that excludes something vital.

"A lot of things you take for granted," says John Little. "There's so many; his (Bruce's) teachings cover such a broad field. The whole idea of not accepting tradition for tradition's sake. Accept it if there is a reason for it, but you must know what the reason is; not to be part of a herd mentality, which is very important. Development of the individual character, as opposed to meek complacency."

Most importantly, Lee teaches us that we are only limited by how much we believe in ourselves. You may set out on the same road with a greater distance to cover than someone else, but you may both reach the same destination, if you are willing to work for it.

"As I look back, I realize what Bruce imparted in me was not totally about physical combat, it was about *life*," says Leo Fong. "I get a sense that what he said had martial arts implications, but the bottom line was that it went beyond that. It went deeper. Anyone who can break through the boundaries of physical combat will understand that Jeet Kune Do has to do with handling life's situations. I got a glimpse of that when he said, 'I practice martial arts so I can knock the hell out of my fears and insecurities.' The insightful person will see the spiritual and mental dimension of the Bruce Lee concepts. It's easy to punch out an attacker. It takes more than physical skill to overcome the loss of a loved one to terminal illness, facing death, divorce, and other adversities. What Bruce showed me and taught me was the need to develop inner strength and self-reliance.

"In an excellent article written in the September 1971 issue of *Black Belt Magazine*, titled 'Liberate Yourself From Classical Karate', Bruce talked about confinement. He said, 'One cannot express himself fully when imprisoned by a confined style. Lacking boundaries, combat is always fresh, alive and constantly changing.' After going into details about Jeet Kune Do and how much different his approach is compared to the classical styles, Bruce said, 'At this point you may ask *how do I gain this knowledge? That* you have to find out all by yourself. You must accept the fact that there is no help but self-help. For the same reason I cannot tell you how to gain freedom since freedom exists within you.'"

Leo Fong paused a moment to reflect, then shook his head. "It is my belief that the highest compliment we can pay to Bruce Lee is not to try to be a clone of Bruce, but rather take that which is good, which he had left to us, and discover the truth within."

"There's nothing that Bruce Lee accomplished that is beyond the realm of anyone if they are willing to put forth the will to do it," says John Little. "You don't know what your limitations are. That is something that can only be accurately accessed in retrospect, so you never know how good you're going to be or what you can accomplish until you put forth the effort to try it."

Whereas other celebrities were more concerned with getting a bigger swimming pool, Bruce Lee was concerned with getting the bigger picture. He was intent on doing more than become a successful movie star. Bruce Lee wanted to change the world.

Taky Kimura sees the effect Bruce Lee has had on people every time he goes to Lakeview Cemetery to tend to Lee's grave. "I go up to the cemetery all the time, and I see these people up there. Many of them aren't even martial artists, but they're up there. They're up there looking for something within themselves. When you look at all these people out there who claim that they aren't role models, they are role models because they are in the limelight. But Bruce is a guy that, twenty-six years later, that cemetery is so trodden that they just put new sod up there. You watch; in a few months it will be worn out again. When I go up there, I usually bump into somebody, and I try not to be forward but I usually introduce myself. I ask them why they are up there, and they tell me these things, you know, and it's just incredible the inspiration Bruce is creating, aiding these people."

Perhaps in the end it will be the philosophy of Bruce Lee, not his martial art, which has the greatest importance in a historical perspective. Lee has influenced generations since his passing with his concepts of liberation from classical thought, bending to adversity, economy of action, and openness to learning. These are concepts that will greatly benefit people of all doctrines, disciplines, and vocations.

ON TOTALITY

The following chapter is the essay I wrote which earned me the top collegiate level award for writing in the Bruce Lee Educational Foundation's First Annual Essay Contest. I say "first annual" with an inner chuckle, because none ever followed it. In the months after I received the award, John Little left the foundation and any serious effort to promote the philosophy of Bruce Lee and do something positive with it followed him.

I received the award at the Jun Fan Jeet Kune Do Nucleus' Annual Banquet in Las Vegas on April 29, 2000. It was presented to me by John Little, then director of the Bruce Lee Educational Foundation, and given to me by Shannon Lee, Bruce Lee's daughter. The moment was especially memorable because, as I was leaving the podium, I was stopped by Linda Lee Cadwell, Bruce Lee's widow, who took me aside and expressed to me how much she enjoyed my book, *Remembering Bruce*. She then took to the podium, announced that I had written an excellent book on Bruce Lee, and recommended it to the entire audience.

The directive for this paper was as follows: "Using the scope of Bruce Lee's thought from axioms through to aesthetics, explain the moral and philosophical meaning of the following quote: 'There is no such thing as an effective segment of a totality.'"

One of the most profound statements attributed to Bruce Lee was his belief that, "There is no such thing as an effective segment of a totality." It is a cornerstone of Lee's personal philosophy and is a running thread found throughout his martial art teaching and in his personal and business relationships.

Understanding the meaning of this statement is no simple feat (or is it?). There are its applications in combat; its meaning as pure philosophy; its applications to man's relationship with the world around him. For the sake of discussion, the meaning of the statement will be addressed in this essay on three fronts: the three basic aspects of man, which are mind, body and spirit. Like three rivers pouring into the same sea, these three come together and express themselves in man's thoughts and actions.

Mind

Bruce Lee believed that for cultivation of the mind, for true learning, the one that is in the process of learning must be emancipated from all forms of conditioned education. For Lee the conditioned, classical education, with its dogmas and its unassailable truths, worked against the goal of true learning. "You can't organize truth," he said. "That's like trying to put a pound of water into wrapping paper and shaping it." Drawing upon influences in the works of Lao Tzu, Krishnamurti, and Carl Rogers, Lee believed that a person must be completely open and receptive in the learning process, free of the intellectual chains of custom, classical education, and authority. Only in a state of total freedom can we form our own opinions about the information we receive, which is essential to the real learning process. Without this, we do not come to an understanding of what "is", but instead we come to learn another person's concept of what "is". In the education system as it stands today, what we receive as knowledge is filtered through the partialized and fragmentary worldviews of our educators, who often are more concerned with passing on their personal dogmas to their students than opening their minds to knowledge and allowing them to form their own critical opinions. They demand that it be accepted at face value. As Bruce Lee said: "True observation begins when one is devoid of set patterns." Only when we can approach learning unburdened by the shackles of our own or other people's prejudices can we be free to see things in their totality. Interestingly, the Chinese term for master, *tzu*, means "child-like". By this the Chinese recognize that the child has true freedom, in that it is devoid of the partiality that comes with conditioning, and is therefore most open to the learning process. So, in a sense, to refer to someone as "tzu" is a recognition that the individual has found that child-like freedom, again. "In order to cope with what is," said Lee, "one must have the awareness and flexibility of the styleless style. When I say 'styleless style,' I mean a style that has totality without partiality. In short, it is a circle with no circumference where every conceivable line is included."

Body

The concept of totality found its physical expression in Bruce Lee's martial art. The historic fight with Wong Jack Man was a watershed event in Lee's life: he realized that his rigidly adhering to his Wing Chun[5] style had limited him in his ability to win the

---

[5] *Wing Chun* is the style of martial art in which Bruce Lee formally trained in Hong Kong as a teenager.

engagement. He also realized that conditioning of the body was an aspect of the problem that could not be ignored. Said Lee: "To me, styles that cling to one partial aspect of combat are actually in bondage. You see, a choice method, however exacting, fixes its practitioners in an enclosed pattern. Actual combat is never fixed, has no boundaries or limits, and is constantly changing from moment to moment." To Bruce Lee, blind adherence to a "style" of fighting limits the individual's freedom of expression, and deludes him into thinking of it as the truth in combat. "In other words," said Lee, "once conditioned in a partialized style, its practitioner faces his opponent through a screen of resistance." Bruce Lee's Jeet Kune Do was based on the idea of the totality of physical expression, of finding the simplest and most efficient way of doing things that was not influenced by a stylistic preference. "Jeet Kune Do uses all ways and is bound by none," said Lee, "and likewise uses any technique or means which serves its end. Efficiency is anything that scores." As such, Lee was open to being critical of other arts and techniques, and open to criticism of his own, both self-criticism and the criticism of others. By doing so, he was able to refine his fighting ability and maximize his potential.

Spirit

Bruce Lee's monistic worldview was something that he brought to his personal relationships and to the expression of his being. On the union of marriage, Lee said that husband and wife are not individuals, but two halves of a whole that, like the tai chi, exist in a complementary and necessary relationship.

Bruce Lee believed that, on a greater scale, all people are united by their humanity and that prejudice and isolationism are counter-productive to the continuing growth and cultivation of the human race. "Under the sky, under the heavens," he said, "there is but one family. It just so happens that people are different." Lee recognized that institutionalization, nationalism, and the race and gender problems of our century were illusions that blinded the individual to his greater connection to the world around him. A fine example of this is the work of Sifu[6] Martin O'Neill, an Irish Jun Fan Jeet Kune Do teacher in Belfast, Northern Ireland. Sifu O'Neill has been able (through his teaching of Bruce Lee's martial art and philosophy) to unite Protestants and Catholics who have

---

[6] *Sifu* is a Chinese term that denotes a teacher or instructor.

been at war with each other for several generations-something that years of political and diplomatic processes have been unable to do. Lee understood that relating in totality meant transcending groups, transcending ideologies, and transcending ego. He came to recognize that his friend's problems were his problems, that his society's problems were his problems, and that it required him to take a pro-active approach to relating to them, so that he became known as a very giving friend and someone who tried to teach as well as entertain. By the same token, Lee could rejoice in his friend's triumphs as well as be compassionate in their tragedies.

Bruce Lee said that man is in a constant process of relating. "If one is isolated he is frozen and paralyzed. To be alive is to be related." There can be no object without the subject, and vice versa. One cannot exist without the other.

In the end, no words can adequately encapsulate the full meaning of Bruce Lee's "totality" statement, for once you attempt to classify and codify its meaning, you lose sight of it. Any attempt to completely define it is ultimately self-defeating. By trying to define what it is, you define (by inference) what it is not. That is not "totality". So the purpose in such an endeavor is not really to define but to come to a greater understanding of "totality" through the process of examination.

THE TAOIST CONNECTION

The following chapter is the first article I ever wrote about Bruce Lee. It was actually an assignment I completed for my Eastern-Asian Philosophy class. As a professional writer attending college, I had a real philosophical problem with writing a paper for which I would not get paid. I learned to resolve the dilemma by writing essays that I could then sell for publication. When the Eastern-Asian Philosophy assignment came up, I used the *Tao* connection to make it a Bruce Lee article, which I then sold to CFW publications. They, in turn, published it in the February 1999 issue of *Inside Kung Fu* magazine.

The article caught the attention of a publisher in California who contacted me and asked me to write a book about Bruce Lee, which ultimately became my first book, *Remembering Bruce: The Enduring Legacy of the Martial Arts Superstar*.

Incidentally, if you are wondering, the professor gave me an "A".

He is considered by his peers to be the greatest fighter of the twentieth century, and quite possibly ever. To the world he was an action movie star. To his students and disciples he was a teacher who was gifted with an extraordinary philosophical mind that he brought to bear, not only in his martial arts training, but also in his life and how he lived it. Though he was well studied in all aspects of Western and Eastern philosophy, the Taoism of Lao Tzu played one of the largest roles in his fighting and living philosophies, the two of which could not be separated from one another.

Bruce Lee was born in San Francisco in 1940, in the Chinese year of the dragon. His father was a Chinese actor touring with the Canton Opera. As a child growing up in Hong Kong, Lee was exposed to Tai Chi Chuan by his father, who practiced it for his health. Though he learned very few fighting skills from his father, this was the first exposure Bruce Lee had to Taoist concepts.

By his teenage years Lee had begun to get in trouble. The streets of post-war Hong Kong were rough, filled with gangs and violence. Triads were a constant threat. After several serious incidents, Lee's parents agreed to enroll him in gung fu[7] classes.

---

[7] *Gung fu* is the Cantonese spelling of the Mandarin *kung fu*, and was the preferred form of usage for Bruce Lee.

At the age of thirteen Lee was accepted into the kwoon (training hall) of renowned Sifu Yip Man, the head of the Wing Chun school. Under Yip Man's tutelage, he began to study the Wing Chun style of fighting as well as its philosophical underpinnings, which Yip Man greatly stressed.

Wrote Lee's widow, Linda: "If there is anything that Yip Man gave to Bruce which may have crystallized Bruce's direction in life, it was to interest his student in the philosophical teachings of Buddha, Confucius, Lao Tzu, and other great thinkers and philosophers. As a result, Bruce's mind became the distillation of the wisdom of such teachers, specifically, but not exclusively, the deep teachings of the yin/yang principle."[8]

After four years of training in gung fu with Sifu Yip Man, Lee had reached an impasse. When engaged in sparring he found that his body would become tense, his mind perturbed. Such instability worked against his goal of efficiency in combat.

Sifu Yip Man sensed his trouble, and approached him. "Lee," he said, "relax and calm your mind. Forget about yourself and follow the opponent's movements. Let your mind, the basic reality, do the counter-movement without any interfering deliberation. Above all, learn the art of detachment."

Bruce Lee believed he had the answer to his problem. He must relax! Yet there was a paradox: the effort in trying to relax was inconsistent with the effortlessness in relaxing, and Lee found himself back in the same situation.

Again Sifu Yip Man came to Bruce Lee and said, "Lee, preserve yourself by following the natural bends of things and don't interfere. Remember never to assert yourself: never be in frontal opposition to any problem, but control it by swinging with it."

Sifu Yip Man told Bruce Lee to go home for a week and think about his words. Lee spent many hours in meditation and practice, with nothing coming of it. Finally, he decided to go sailing in a junk (boat). Lee would have a great epiphany. "On the sea, I thought of all my past training and got mad at myself and punched the water. Right then at that moment, a thought suddenly struck me. Wasn't this water the essence of gung fu? I struck it, but it did not suffer hurt. I then tried to grasp a handful of it but it was impossible. This water, the softest substance, could fit into any container. Although it seemed weak, it could penetrate

---

[8] Source: Page 27 of *The Bruce Lee Story*, by Linda Lee, published by Ohara Publications, Santa Clara, California, 1989.

the hardest substance. That was it! I wanted to be like the nature of water.

"Therefore, in order to control myself I must accept myself by going with, and not against, my nature. I lay on the boat and felt that I had untied with *Tao*; I had become one with nature. I just lay there and let the boat drift freely and irresistibly according to its own will. For at that moment I had achieved a state of inner feeling in which opposition had become mutually cooperative instead of mutually exclusive, in which there was no longer any conflict of mind. The whole world to me was unitary."[9]

Lee had not only discovered the state of wu-shin, or no-mindedness, but he had become immersed in the Tao itself. Later, in his film *The Big Boss,* Lee would exemplify the nature of wu-shin in his battle with a large group of attackers. As he is surrounded he enters a state of calm, detached awareness, with his mind resting on no one thing and aware of everything in its totality. Lee would try to express some aspect of his philosophy in every one of his movies.

At the age of eighteen, Lee's parents sent him to America to get him away from the gangs and violence of Hong Kong. Lee settled in Seattle and stayed with family friend Ruby Chow, who owned a restaurant. They often clashed, as Lee refused to show Chow the elder piety that she felt was due her under Confucian tradition. While working at her restaurant, he attended Edison Technical School and earned his high school diploma.

He quickly developed a reputation for his gung fu skills and soon had many people wanting to study under the gifted nineteen year-old. One of those people, Taky Kimura, a thirty-eight year-old Japanese-American, had been in the United States internment camp during World War II, and suffered difficulty in getting a decent job afterward, under the shadow of post-war anti-Japanese sentiment. Demoralized, Kimura was seeking something to give him back his self-confidence. He found it in the young Bruce Lee, who became his mentor, spiritual guide, and best friend.

Lee went on to the University of Washington at Seattle where he majored in philosophy. His grasp of Eastern concepts was so profound that he became in great demand as a lecturer on Eastern philosophy. It was during a lecture he gave at Garfield High School that he first saw Linda Emery, who would one day become his wife.

_____

[9] Source: Page 39 of *The Bruce Lee Story,* by Linda Lee, published by Ohara Publications, Santa Clara, California, 1989.

Lee had avoided setting up a kwoon of gung fu in Seattle because he wanted to focus on his education. But, not liking the jobs he had to do to support himself, he finally opened one near the university in late 1963. As he had never achieved instructor rank in Wing Chun gung fu, he christened his school the Jun Fan Gung Fu Institute, after his Chinese name.

Bruce Lee was already beginning to feel discontent with "styles" of fighting. The idea did not follow the Taoist concepts of harmony and formlessness. On the separation between hard and soft styles of gung fu schools Lee said, "It's an illusion. You see, in reality, gentleness/firmness is one inseparable force of one unceasing interplay of movement. We hear a lot of teachers claiming their styles are either soft or hard; these people are clinging blindly to one partial view of the totality. I was once asked by a so-called 'kung fu master'-one of those that really looked the part with the beard and all-as to what I thought of Yin and Yang? I simply answered, 'Baloney!' Of course, he was quite shocked at my answer and could not come to the realization that 'it' is never two."[10]

Lee understood the false division that so often traps students of Taoism, the false division in recognizing Yin and Yang as opposites, and not as complements. The *Tao* is the undivided path.

Bruce Lee quit the university and married Linda Emery. After the wedding the two moved to California, where Lee opened another school. Within a short time Lee had caught the attention of San Francisco's Chinatown. They were upset by Lee's practice of teaching the arts to non-Chinese. For his part, Lee believed that all humanity was a totality, and did not make the distinction between races. "Under the sky, under the heavens, there is but one family."

As Lao Tzu wrote:

To live in harmony is to follow Tao.
To follow Tao is enlightenment.
Competitive struggle
Is contrary to the Tao.
Whatever violates Tao
Will not endure.[11]

---

[10] Source: Page 43 of *The Bruce Lee Story,* by Linda Lee, published by Ohara Publications, Santa Clara, California, 1989.
[11] Source: Verse 55 of *The Tao Te Ching* by Lao Tzu. Shambhalla Publishing, Boston, Massachusetts, 1961.

One day a group of Chinatown Kung Fu men appeared at Lee's kwoon demanding that he stop teaching the "gwei-lo" or foreign devils at once or he would have to fight their top fighter, Wong Jack Man. Thinking him a paper tiger, they were startled when he accepted. When they tried to impose rules and a date for the fight Lee became angry, saying the fight would take place immediately and without rules. His opponent had no choice but to agree.

Lee and Wong Jack Man then formally bowed and began to fight. Lee fought in strict Wing Chun style and, combined with Wong Jack Man's own style, the two seemed to cancel each other out. After three minutes, Lee finally managed to put Wong Jack Man on the floor and forced him to submit.

Though Lee's victory ended his problems with the Chinatown community, he was very unhappy with how the fight went. He found that his style of fighting had held him back; a fight he should have won easily in a few seconds took three minutes and a narrow victory. He realized that he must continue to evolve. The idea of styles of fighting had come into conflict with his Taoist beliefs that the way of fighting is formless and all-encompassing, and that styles separate the fighter from the truth.

It was at this point that Bruce Lee's expression of martial arts and philosophy, *Jeet Kune Do*, was born. Its chief principle of "having no way as way" borrowed heavily from Lao Tzu, "This is called shape without shape, form without object."[12]

Soon Lee began to study other styles; he adopted footwork from fencing and some hand strikes from western boxing, to name a few. His philosophy was to "absorb what is useful, discard what is useless, and add what is essentially one's own." By November 1966, Lee had a clear idea of his new vision for fighting. In 1967 he coined the name *Jeet Kune Do* to represent his personal expression of the martial arts. He then designed a symbol for Jeet Kune Do that consisted of the Tai Chi symbol with two arrows around it moving in opposite directions. This implied the constant interchange between yin and yang. Within a few years he was the top martial artist in the world, attracting as students top fighters such as Chuck Norris and Joe Lewis; and such celebrity students as Steve McQueen, James Coburn, Blake Edwards and Kareem Abdul-Jabbar.

---

[12] Source: Verse 14 of The Tao Te Ching by Lao Tzu featured in *Source Book in Chinese Philosophy* by Wing Tsit Chan, 4th Edition. Princeton, New Jersey, 1963.

Lee did not believe in learning by accumulation, but instead believed that the highest form of mastery was one of simplicity, of "stripping away the inessentials", much like Lao Tzu believed in the need to disband all schools of formal learning. Indeed, Lee disbanded his own school system shortly before his death, lest his way be taken as "the Way".

Soon after Lee got his own break in Hollywood as Kato on the *Green Hornet* series. It earned him great popularity but folded after only one season.

An offer by Raymond Chow's Golden Harvest Studio in Hong Kong brought Lee back to Asia to make the movie *The Big Boss.* When the movie came out, Lee became an overnight sensation throughout Asia. Two more films followed: *Fist of Fury* and *Way of the Dragon.* In the movie *Way of the Dragon,* Lee demonstrates the Taoist principle of adaptability in his climactic fight scene with Chuck Norris. Having fought to a virtual standstill, Lee begins to adapt his fighting method from one of rigidity to one of pliancy, and emerges the victor.

His fourth picture was intended to further expound upon the Taoist theory of flexibility as means of survival. Entitled *Game of Death,* the movie, as conceived by Bruce Lee, would have begun like this: "As the film opens we see a wide expanse of snow. Then the camera closes in on a clump of trees while the sounds of a strong gale fill the screen. There is a huge tree in the center of the screen, and it is all covered with thick snow. Suddenly there is a loud snap, and a huge branch of the tree falls to the ground. It cannot yield to the force of the snow so it breaks. Then the camera moves to a willow tree which bending with the wind. Because it adapts to the environment, the willow survives. What I want to say is that a man has to be flexible and adaptable, other wise he will be destroyed."[13] Though the movie was begun, Lee never finished it, and the *Game of Death* that reached theaters bore little resemblance to Lee's original vision.

In 1972 Warner Brothers approached Lee to make a movie for American audiences. In the movie, *Enter the Dragon,* Lee tried to express some of his Taoist philosophy. In an early scene in the film he discusses a sparring match with an old Taoist priest. When the priest asks Lee what he thought of his opponent when he was facing him, Lee replies, "There is no opponent. Because the word 'I' does not exist." The priest is very pleased by his

---

[13] Source: page 138 of the book *Words of the Dragon,* edited by John Little, Published by the Charles E. Tuttle Publishing Company, Boston, copyright 1997 Linda Lee Cadwell.

answer. This scene was cut out of the American version because the producers thought American audiences would be turned off by all the philosophy mumbo jumbo.

But through it all Bruce Lee was still teacher and guide to his friends. At the time he was filming *Enter the Dragon*, Lee's friend Taky Kimura called him from the United States with a personal crisis: Kimura's marriage was falling apart and he was despondent and suicidal. "I lost two brothers a month apart and then my wife left me," said Kimura.

Lee told him, "Taky, I haven't met your wife but I've counseled you before. You must do everything in your power to solve the thing but, at some point in time, you may just have to walk on." Lee was saying that if nature dictated that the marriage was over, going against it would only bring further unhappiness. Lee was expressing the Taoist philosophy of *wu-wei*, or following the course of nature without resisting it. "Walk on," he told Kimura, "walk on."[14]

"Life is an ever-flowing process and somewhere on the path some unpleasant things will pop up-it might leave a scar-but then life is flowing on, and like running water, when it stops, it grows stale. Go bravely on, my friend, because each experience teaches us a lesson."

On July 20, 1973, Bruce Lee died of a cerebral edema, three weeks before the opening of *Enter the Dragon*, three weeks before he would gain worldwide fame.

Bruce Lee was buried at Lakeview Cemetery in Seattle, Washington. The casket was covered in white, red, and yellow flowers making up the yin/yang symbol. Among the pallbearers were Steve McQueen, James Coburn, Lee's brother Robert, and one of his top students, Dan Inosanto. At the graveside James Coburn had the last words: "Farewell, brother. It has been an honor to share this space with you. As a friend and a teacher, you have given to me, have brought my physical, spiritual, and psychological selves together. Thank you. May peace be with you."

On his tombstone was engraved the message: "Your inspiration continues to guide us toward our personal liberation." Lee's gravesite has been faithfully cared for by his friend and student Taky Kimura for the past twenty-five years.

---

[14] "Walk on!" was a phrase that Bruce Lee picked up from Zen, likely from the book, *Walk On!*, by Christmas Humphreys. Writes Humphreys: "Life is a bridge -- build no house upon it; a river -- cling not to its banks;....a journey -- take it, and walk on!"

In the period since his death an argument has arisen concerning the evolution of his martial art. Dan Inosanto, his chief student, quietly continued to cultivate his fighting system, saying that Jeet Kune Do is not a style but rather a concept that can be applied to all aspects of life. Lee's older students, his wife included, have tried to preserve it as it was at Lee's death.[15] Though it is essential that Lee's body of knowledge and experience be preserved and passed on, it is equally essential that Jeet Kune Do continues to grow and evolve (as Lee undoubtedly would have had he lived). The continual process of evolution is at the heart of all Taoist beliefs, and it was this message that Lee tried, more than anything, to impart to people through his teachings, writings, and films. As Lee stated: "I do not believe in styles anymore. Styles tend to not only separate man-because they have their own doctrines and that doctrine becomes the gospel truth that you cannot change. But if you do not have styles, if you just say, 'Here I am as a human being. How can I express myself totally and completely?' Now that way you won't create a style, because a style is a crystallization." The Way is a process of eternal growth.

Today, Bruce Lee's Jeet Kune Do concepts are practiced by thousands of martial artists and non-martial artists worldwide. A historical society called the Jun Fan Jeet Kune Do Nucleus has been formed in the United States by his students and family, in an effort to preserve his legacy. Radford University in Virginia offers a lecture course in Jeet Kune Do concepts. His philosophy has also been the part of college curriculums in Seattle, Washington and Dallas, Texas. The legacy of Bruce Lee and Jeet Kune Do continue to grow and evolve.

Clearly, Bruce Lee was deeply influenced by the Taoist theories of Lao Tzu. As Diane Dreher wrote in her book *The Tao of Inner Peace*, "Unlike Confucius, who upheld tradition, Lao Tzu appeals to progressive individuals who think for themselves, depart from convention, and seek the higher truth. He knew that new solutions rarely come from old leaders, entrenched in the status quo. Often they come from ordinary people who believe in the power to make a difference."[16] Though Bruce Lee was far from ordinary, he represents the perfect example of the modern Taoist, a twentieth century representation in physical and spiritual exercise of Lao Tzu.

---

[15] This is known as the *Jeet Kune Do Concepts* versus *Original Jeet Kune Do* dispute.

[16] Source: Page 269 of the book *The Tao of Inner Peace* by Diane Dreher, HarperPerennial, New York, New York, 1991.

INTERVIEW WITH PATRICK STRONG

The following is an interview I conducted with Patrick Strong, a student of Bruce Lee's. Strong studied with Bruce Lee both in Seattle and later when he moved to California. After Bruce Lee's death, Strong trained in Wing Chun Gung Fu with Hawkins Cheung, a friend and martial art classmate of Bruce Lee. He also trained with the Gracie family, Brazilians who dominated no-holds-barred fighting tournaments in the 1990s, revolutionizing the martial arts industry in much the same way that Bruce Lee did in the late sixties and early seventies. Strong went on to become a Hollywood screenwriter and bit actor and choreographer. He choreographed the fight scenes in the "Fistful of Yen" segment of The Kentucky Fried Movie, *which was a parody of Bruce Lee's last film,* Enter the Dragon.

While this interview may be lengthy with explanations of martial artistry, it does give the reader a unique glimpse into the way in which Bruce Lee applied philosophy to his martial art.

James Bishop: When did you first meet Bruce Lee?

Patrick Strong: I believe it was late 1960 or the beginning of 1961-right in that wintertime. A friend of mine was training with Bruce, Doug Palmer. Doug was a very good friend of mine who lived down the street. He had told me about Bruce Lee earlier. Then one day somebody else mentioned Bruce and I went to watch a workout. I was boxing at the time and so I went down to see what was going on.

James Bishop: What was your initial reaction to Bruce Lee the man?

Patrick Strong: He was a young, good-looking guy. He was really handsome and had a very pretty girlfriend. You know, I was boxing at the Cherry Street Gym which had some professional fighters - Archie Moore used to come in there every once and a while, up from California, and hang around a little bit - and I thought I had seen some really fast guys. But when I saw Bruce I had never seen anything like that before. *Blinding speed.*

James Bishop: What was it like training with Bruce?

Patrick Strong: You know, I've trained in martial arts ever since then (and with a lot of different people) but what probably struck me most about Bruce Lee (other than his blinding speed and effectiveness) was that he could express himself with martial arts as in philosophy. His philosophy was an extension of his art. For example, he would teach the ton sao, which is the palm-up hand in Wing Chun, and in that hand is another principle which is called the immovable elbow principle. He would describe that elbow, that it would fit one fist's length away from the body, and if that elbow were ever pushed in any further than that then your structure would be destroyed. It was the holding place - the place that you held - and under no circumstances would you let that be compromised. And then he would turn around and apply that to things in life: there is a point that you will not go beyond, that you will not give beyond. For example, in business negotiations, there might be a point where you know you are going to hold firm, you're not going to go beyond that point, and so you hold there; once you go beyond that point then you lose, you lose what you set out to accomplish.

So he would do that all the time. He would describe his art in philosophical and in meaningful terms.

Then, in that same hand (the palm-up hand) he would describe the arm as neither bent nor straight. To bend it would have been an extreme, as in too much yin. To keep it straight would have been too much yang. So it was neither bent nor straight. When I was a young fellow, and he would be talking like this, I didn't know what he was talking about. I was seventeen or eighteen years old, and here is some guy describing an arm that is neither bent nor straight: it is both bent and straight. If it's straight the structure is destroyed. If it's too bent the structure is destroyed.

James Bishop: And, as an eighteen year-old, you really couldn't grasp the full meaning of it.

Patrick Strong: Well, it was the first time I had heard anybody talk like that. When I went off to college, the first courses I signed up for were philosophy. Then the stuff started making a lot of sense.

But I spent a great deal of time listening to Bruce. I listened and hung on every single word that he said, and some of those terms have gotten lost over the years. A few years ago I was up in Seattle and I was visiting with (fellow Bruce Lee student) Taky Kimura. I started talking about non-intention and Taky didn't know what I was talking about. I said, "Don't you remember how Bruce was talking about how you arrive at non-intention by being like a set of keys that lie on the top of a table. The table moves, the keys fall. They don't intend to fall - they just *fall*." And he goes, "Ah! I forgot!" So what has happened over the years is that everything has gone toward non-telegraph. But Bruce's key was non-intention. Non-telegraph and non-intention are not the same things.

James Bishop: Tell me more about the difference between non-telegraph and non-intention.

Patrick Strong: Non-telegraph is not to send a message to the opponent that you are about to move and/or strike. You don't dip the shoulder, you don't make an expression, you don't pull the hand back, you don't set up your pace - your set pace - as though you are about to hit. You don't send a telegram that you're about to strike. Non-intention, on the other hand, is that you strike without the intention to strike. You strike without intention - you eliminate the intention.

If Bruce were to telegraph his strike to you, he could still hit you with ease before you could react simply because his physical initiation would have been executed with non-intention. Non-intention is the "thing" deeper than non-telegraph. It would be impossible to be as fast as Bruce without non-intention.

To know non-intention is to do more than just execute; it is also to be able to see the intention in your opponent. His intention will show before his telegraph. If you read his intention, he's yours. If you read his telegraph, he may still hit you if his intention is concealed within the movement of his telegraph, providing he is fast.

So when they made *Enter the Dragon* the editor noticed, when he was running the film over and over again (particularly the scene with Bruce and Bob Wall where they would touch in cross-hands position and Bruce would move in with a pak sao and hit Bob

Wall), that no matter how much he slowed that film down there was absolutely no preparation from Bruce at all. In other words, there was absolutely no telegraphing. Well, the way that he achieved zero telegraphing was through zero intention, non-intention. There was no intention to strike. So the editor said, "Well, there wasn't like you could see a place where he began to make his movement. He was here one second and the next second he was there. There wasn't anything that precipitated that movement at all. It just happened.

To strike as a result of reading telegraph is slow compared to striking as a result of reading intention. The mere fact that Bruce could strike with non-intention at reading the intention sounds amazing, but is really very simple. Also, keep in mind that a telegraphic move may be nothing more than a fake by your opponent, but he will not be able to fake his intention.

James Bishop: That reminds me of a quotation I once read attributed to him. Someone asked him if he were forced to kill someone in self-defense, how would he justify his actions to a court, and he said that he would say that he didn't do it, that *"IT"* did it.

Patrick Strong: I think you probably read an interview on me, because I said that. That's a story that he told me.

It's an interesting concept, because when he was doing *Fists of Fury [The Big Boss]* there is a point where he is fighting the fellow in the ice factory. He hits the man in the abdomen and then he grabs his fist and looks at it like it was this thing that was unleashed, like it did it by itself. He didn't really hit the guy, but it was like the fist had done it - the weapon used itself. It just happened. And so he grabs his fist and he looks at it, almost in a horror as to what it just did. That's the idea of non-intention exactly.

When you're driving down the street and a child runs in front of your car - your foot just goes to the brake. You don't intend to put your foot on the brake, you don't prepare to put your foot on the brake, it just happens - BANG! No intention.

And that is what he meant by that thing that if the judge asked him if he would plead guilty or not guilty, he would of course plead not guilty because he did not kill the man - *it* killed him. It's just like, when you hit the brakes were you guilty of hitting the brakes to stop from hitting the child? No, you had no intention; there was no premeditation. It wasn't you that did it. *It* did it. "It" being the ultimate innocence.[17]

James Bishop: I recognize part of what you are talking about as the scientific principle of kinesthetic imprinting.

When you move, your nerves direct your muscles to contract, pulling on bones and tendons, which causes joints to move. Though in most instances this is a result of a conscious impulse sent from your brain, the way in which you move is directed by nerve impulses that travel from the peripheral nerves to the spine and then back to the muscles, independent of conscious control. This information has been learned, by the muscles and by the nervous system.

When you touch something hot and your hand jerks back, your body has acted independent of conscious control, with nerve signals being sent to your spine and action taken immediately, based on muscle memory. This is necessary because in such an instance there is not time for the brain to receive the sensory information, analyze it, and then decide on a course of action. So too is there not enough time in a fight to think about what you will do.

When you practice these techniques your muscles and nervous system are "learning" these movements in a process known as kinesthetic imprinting. The techniques are programmed into your nervous system and muscles, which will execute the techniques independent of the brain when your body recognizes the necessity.

---

[17] Bruce Lee took the concept of "It" from Eugen Herrigel's book, *Zen in the Art of Archery*. Wrote Herrigel:

> "One day I asked the Master: 'How can the shot be loosed if *I* do not do it?'
> 'It shoots,' he replied."

and:

> "It is as if the sword wielded itself, and not just as we say in archery that 'It' takes aim and hits, so here 'It' takes the place of the ego, availing itself a facility and a dexterity which the ego only acquires be conscious effort."

When your skill level has risen, you will perform without thought. Conscious attention to your actions will diminish. Your movements will become more harmonious and automatic, and your mind is freed to become more aware of your surroundings. You will develop an animal-like grace and quickness.

Developing grace and precision in your movements will give you increased control and make better use of energy. This efficiency ensures that you minimize wasted effort and that your muscles do not work against each other. It will also circumvent the problem of the sympathetic nervous system's "fight or flight" response. Essentially, the "fight or flight" state causes your nervous system to revert to an instinctive reaction, which, if you have reached that level of kinesthetic imprinting, would be your techniques.

Patrick Strong: Well said. Once you understand a few principles you can look to Bruce's notes in the *Tao of Jeet Kune Do*. It is fraught with information about this matter. The problem is that Bruce was simply taking notes, rather than writing a book. He wasn't writing a thesis or a book that would have explained the concepts in far greater method and detail. Beware: the *Tao of Jeet Kune Do* is incredibly incomplete.[18]

However, there is value in the *Tao of Jeet Kune Do* for those who understand the roots of Bruce's methodology. Understanding those roots is the key to understanding Bruce, if you are so inclined. Where do you get that understanding? You get it through research and your own self-examination.

Bruce used this analogy to explain it: "Pretend that a young man wants to learn to fight, and I let him fight one of my students, instructing him to fight the best way that he can and with everything he's got. At this point, he knows very little about fighting. When he fights, he just fights from his instincts: punching, kicking, elbowing, whatever. He is 'innocent'. [Bruce used this word, "innocent". It is a key word.]

---

[18] Not simply *incomplete*, the *Tao of Jeet Kune Do* has faced considerable criticism for being unoriginal. The book was a selective collection of Bruce Lee's personal notes, which in many cases turned out to be quotations and tracings from other sources, among them the book *Aikido* by Kisshamaru Ueshiba, the United States Army Boxing Manual, and various works by Krishnamurti and other writers.

"Now I teach him a new way to stand, move, punch, kick. He can hardly walk let alone fight. And when I tell him to fight he is far worse off than before. Nothing seems to work. Everything is mechanical. He is trying to use the way. He is limited.

"And yet, he continues to train until, one day, everything becomes natural once again. Only, the way he stands, walks, punches, kicks, and uses his elbows are very much different. His movement is more efficient. He is faster and more powerful. He is no longer 'stuck' in his movement." Once again, he is "innocent".

To be "innocent" is to use no way as the way. To be "innocent" is to have no limitation. In other words, you are no longer constipated and restricted by your method. You are no longer limited by those imposed limitations. Instead, you are instinctive. You are self-expressive. Your body of martial knowledge is no longer in your head, it's in your nervous system and muscles.

Bruce advocated "instinctive economy". This means he developed and used movements that are instinctive.

The instinctive reaction is what you do in an emergency, or when startled. For instance when your hands fly up to protect you, instead of your trying to high block, inside block, outside block, or low block.

By training your instinctive reaction movement you are training your nervous system. This is "key". You train the nervous system with thousands and thousands of correct movements. The movements are as close to instinctive reaction as possible. This was one of Bruce's greatest secrets. To begin the movement simply and on the eccentric action, takes away the decision or "intention" to move.

In the film, *Enter the Dragon*, Bruce slaps the young student on the forehead and says, "What was that, a demonstration?" A second slap and he says, "Don't think. *Feeeeeel*".

This scene, as well as other scenes in Bruce's films, give many keys to his personal art. He said, "feel".

This is the way that Bruce trained himself. He paid attention to his feelings. He looked inside of his structure. He felt the small things. The tiniest of things. Not only in his punch, but all of his structure, tools, and movement. Why do you think that Yip Man made him do the sil lum tao so painfully slow? So that he could properly train his nervous system and properly construct the proper neuro-pathways, and "settling" of his structure. This is what is meant by "shedding away and getting rid of the non-essentials." You are ridding yourself of any excess muscle involvement or improper neuro-responses, not just simplifying technique by streamlining the movement.

Unfortunately, too many people believe that "no way" means the absence of correct principles and mechanics, as though reacting and initiating were nothing more than a range of the momentary expediency. Nothing could be less true. This is simply not what Bruce meant at all.

James Bishop: So you think that non-intention was one of his best secrets to speed?

Patrick Strong: It was *the* secret to his speed. At the time I didn't know exactly where it came from, I learned it years and years later.

Bruce used analogies to explain his non-intention -- one was in describing bamboo. "What makes the bamboo dangerous" said Bruce, "is that if you bend and suddenly release it, it will snap back. The bamboo is 'innocent'. It doesn't have to think or decided to strike."

When he studied Wing Chun, Bruce Lee learned some principles, which dictated his martial art and the rest of his life. He adhered to many of those principles and he expounded off of them, built off of them, and he modified things around them yet those same principles he held dear. For example, in chi sao[19]: if you and I are doing chi sao (that's the sticking hands technique) and my hands touch your hands, what happens is that my energy goes toward you and your energy goes toward me. If I suddenly move one of

---

[19] *Chi sao*, or "sticking hands", is a sensitivity drill in Wing Chun gung fu in which the two practitioners maintain constant physical contact with each others' arms as they execute flowing drills. The idea is to maintain control over the opponent's arms, preventing them from being used as weapons while preparing for your own opening for attack.

my hands, if I suddenly get it out of the way, you don't *intend* to strike me - what happens is your hand just comes in and hits me. It's because when my hand is against your hand there is a pressure built up, and when I release my hand your pressure just shoots in like a spring. It would be the same thing as if you took a spring and you compressed it in your hand and you release the spring, what is it going to do? It's going to pop open; it's a *spring effect*. It's not going to get ready to pop open, it's not going to get set to pop open, it's just going to pop open. In chi sao, when I am touching your hand and putting pressure on you and you suddenly move your hand and make it weak or anything, my pressure will go straight in like water rushing through a dam. There's no intention to that. So with chi sao that idea of the *spring effect* was already built in. What Bruce did is to take that same idea and apply it to off-fighting, meaning that you are no longer in contact or touching. So what happens now is that instead of the spring effect being the servomechanism it now becomes gravity. Simply by dropping will give you the same effect as though the spring shot forward. Do you see the connection?

James Bishop: Yes, I can.

Patrick Strong: One thing developed out of the other. In the origin, you have the chi sao and the idea of chi sao is to fill the gap. What happens is if you and I are doing chi sao and I get weak off of my right hand, your left hand will come crashing through. You don't think about hitting, you don't see that I moved my hand, you just feel it. By the time you feel it it's too late because it is already gone. It was a spring effect.

Now that spring effect comes from the structure of the hips, and that structure is learned in the sil lum tao, Wing Chun's very first form. It sets up a bow action of the hips. The way that the tools work in that form is by setting up the pressure. So once the pressure is released, it just goes.

So what happens then, going back to the chi sao, the first thing that's going to go is my hand. This was Bruce's big secret, to move the hand before the body, which is just the opposite of karate.

So, if I have the spring effect, and we are both pushing against each other, if you take your hand away real fast then my hand just shoots in - it doesn't shoot in before my body, my body didn't have the time to shoot in. There are big, big muscles groups in the body that could never react that fast. What happens when my hand shoots in is that my center of gravity will change and my body will follow my hand.

Bruce took the off-fighting and took the very same principle (and the same principles found in fencing and other directional arts). By dropping that hand it lowers the center of gravity so that the hand is in the dropping phase and then by the time that hand goes and the body catches up to it and when the hand hits and the arm is extended it is backed by the body and the new principle now becomes the pole principle. It's the body driving the punch through. That gives the punch deeper penetration, rather than hitting like, for instance, a karate blow, which hits more on the surface. A pole effect punch goes very deep into the body. If Bruce hit you in the body you felt it everywhere, such as in the one-inch punch.

James Bishop: It's amazing how much scientific thought he put into it.

Patrick Strong: He was developing his art as he went along and he was experimenting and learning as he was teaching, putting things together. So it was like the layers of an onion: as you go deeper you find something else.

James Bishop: Let me ask you about the Wong Jack Man fight. You've said before that you spoke to Bruce Lee about it shortly after it happened.

Patrick Strong: That fight happened in Oakland, California. After the fight Bruce came back up to Seattle and we went to dinner and he talked about that fight. It has always amused me because that night when he was talking about the fight he was very excited about it, very animated. Wong Jack Man, he said, was spinning and moving. He was very hard to hit, hard to keep up with, because he was running. But Bruce just chain-punched him, he kept going, and finally he threw him down and beat him up. Bruce was very excited about it.

Later, his story changed, evidently, to other people, because now he thought that he wore himself out and got really tired and he wasn't in the right kind of physical conditioning for it. And he felt limited in his Wing Chun.

James Bishop: Do you feel that he just wasn't prepared to admit that at that moment?

Patrick Strong: Well, I can tell you that if I go out and I am going to fight somebody and I do the chain punches I would be exhausted after a few seconds. You can't throw those things with that kind of power and go go go go go - boy, they take you down fast! You have to nail the guy right off the bat. You can't chain punch for that much time, not in a real fight. You'd be exhausted.

James Bishop: And according to the official account, Bruce Lee chased him around the room for three minutes like that.

Patrick Strong: I mean, it is just exhausting! Now Bruce wasn't in the greatest physical condition but he was in very good condition. The exercises that we used to have to do, the workouts we did, would make some of the guys faint and throw up because they were hard, hard workouts.

I was getting bigger because I was lifting weights. One day Bruce wanted to see what weightlifting was all about so I took him down to the gym. He got in there and just had a ball with it; he discovered then that there was ways of getting bigger. Evidently, after that, he started training with weights for strength and all that. He got into the fitness thing because James Lee was a very strong guy and bodybuilder.

But still Bruce wasn't someone that ran a lot, but he could still do bunny-hops around the floor. For short distances, he could move faster than anyone I have ever seen in my life. He was great at that - he just didn't have the endurance for going out and running and running and running. He did that later.

James Bishop: I read an article today on the Wong Jack Man fight in which Wong Jack Man was interviewed. Wong Jack Man stated that, when he fought Bruce Lee, Bruce was repeatedly attempting to *bil jee* (gouge) his eye. Then you tell me that it is the technique he favored, so it makes a lot of sense.

Patrick Strong: Yeah, it was. What Bruce told me was that Wong Jack Man was moving away and spinning, which makes it hard to land the strike. To really get that type of accurate, Wing Chun strike you need to hit the guy dead-center.

James Bishop: And he has to be stationary for at least a split second.

Patrick Strong: Bruce Lee was so fast that, if the guy were standing there, he would get his eyes. But if the guy was running and spinning it was not so easy. Bruce said he would hit Wong Jack Man and the guy would spin, moving his body in such a way that the blows would roll off of him. But Wong Jack Man wasn't making a fight out of it; he was basically running, according to Bruce. Had he turned to fight he would have had to turn and square off with Bruce, which probably would have changed things really fast.

James Bishop: What's your take on the whole Concepts versus Original Jeet Kune Do debate?

Patrick Strong: I don't see anything wrong with fighters taking Bruce Lee's concepts and principles and applying them to their arts. That's basically what happened later, anyway. Then go out and learn other arts, learn anything that you can, and then work in those principles that Bruce had and modify it and make it work for you so that you have your own expression. I do that myself. I don't call it Concepts, but I have been very much involved in Gracie Jujitsu[20] and I have other fighting backgrounds in Shorin Ryu karate, Tae Kwon Do and a bunch of other stuff.

In my art I do a lot of groundfighting and I take Bruce's stand-up principles right to the ground. In fact, I use his principles for shooting in, the non-intention to shoot in for single-leg takedowns. I apply the very same principles of non-intention. Then I use a lot of the Wing Chun defense moves, I had to create new moves to do that, but I used the principles to stop the groundwork from coming in. And then when I go to the ground, I use the traps and Wing Chun punches from ground positions from mounted

---

[20] Gracie Jujitsu is a martial art style that gained popularity during the 1990s when the Gracie family dominated no-holds-barred fighting events.

positions, because the mechanics of hitting out of rotation don't work very well. Too slow.

James Bishop: So is it a case of what Bruce referred to as "flowing"?

Patrick Strong: Well, flowing means to be able to move from one position to the next without getting jammed up. Bruce's biggest problem that he saw in karate tournaments was with their forms. It wasn't that he was against forms - he learned using forms. Bruce was great at doing gung fu forms - I mean, he was *fantastic* at doing them; and they helped develop his structure and performance. But what he didn't like in a form was when you get stuck in the movement. Block, punch, kick. You get stuck in the movement. Start over again. Block, block, punch, punch. Start over again.

So what happens is the karate guy gets out there and he fights in simple contact sparring. He goes in and punches one time and then takes a pose again. One kick, one punch and then he has to start over again. He can't flow; he gets stuck after two or three moves.

Well, in chi sao that would be very low level, to be stuck in one or two moves. You have to be able to flow from one thing to the next and break up the rhythms and do a lot of things without getting paralyzed or frozen in your movements, not knowing what to do next. So Bruce described sparring in tournaments like two chickens fighting. They stand out there, face each other and *peck! Peck!* Then the other goes *peck! Peck!* And it goes on and on as they take little pecks at each other. That's how he described it.

Bruce took the highest from of his art from the chi sao, which means to flow with your opponent and create the lines. But not just to get one punch, but to go through and make one and move to what's next and after that. Most people who do chi sao can't get past two moves. They come in with one move, the guy checks that; they go to a second trap and then it's all jammed up and stuck. But a really good chi sao practitioner goes from one to the next and keeps going. That's the highest form of the art when you are the total complement of the opponent. You are one with him.

He gives you and creates his mistakes and you take them without the intention.

This is very difficult and takes a very high degree of skill. It was an ideal that was very early on adopted by Bruce as a criteria for high standard. It would remain the highest standard and ideal for all of his future martial art. It is the crux of Jeet Kune Do. At least, it was meant to be. Kali people call it *flow*, to be able to move and fit in with the opponent.

To fit in with the opponent was a core principle in Bruce's methodology, as it is in all martial arts. Again, consider the boxer, grappler, karateka, fencer, etc. At what level would any of them be? For that matter, consider any contact sport.

James Bishop: Tell me more about fitting in.

Patrick Strong: To fit in with an opponent means to become one with him. While this may sound highly high-minded and somewhat out there on the fringe of Zen it is, in truth, a highly pragmatic approach to what Bruce considered the highest level of martial art. It is the essence of his personal art - the way he did things.

Becoming one with the opponent is no different than becoming one with the horse you are riding. In grappling, you are entangled with your opponent and your sensitivity reads his every move, which helps you to defend and attack. You attack against his weakness and take what he gives you.

In boxing, you fit in with the opponent's timing and distance.

In Bruce's art, you do both of the above.

Chi Sao taught Bruce how to develop sensitivity to his opponent so that he could marry into his center of gravity, thereby becoming a single unit with him. However the opponent moved, Bruce would move naturally move with him without thought or intention. He had learned how to maintain his structure at all times while, at the same time, moving to destroy his opponent's structure.

He became one with his opponent in the way the water becomes one with the wall of the dam, so if the dam weakens or breaks, the water rushes through instantly and forcibly.

Likewise, if Bruce's body sensed a weakness in his opponent's structure and defense, he would move through the weakness or opening without thought, plan or intention.

In off fighting, Bruce applied the same principles, only replacing the spring effect to the absence of pressure to the effect and sensitivity to a shift in his center of gravity.

Bruce took this Principle a lot further than most, and he gave it a great deal of thought both philosophically and pragmatically. Philosophically, he found its essence in the Yin and Yang, while pragmatically he understood it mechanics. He applied both.

James Bishop: How do you respond to those people who have criticized him for not entering tournaments and "proving himself"?

Patrick Strong: At his time, when he was in the no-contact era, his stuff would never even have been counted as points. It was like poison hand techniques. A bil jee would never have counted as a point; a low kick to the knee would never have counted as a point. So his thing didn't even compare to that. It was apples and oranges.

Later, when it went to kickboxing, *that's* the time that Bruce should have been around. But by that time he was gone: he was in Hong Kong making movies and then he was dead. His art was more toward something that goes in based on contact, not on point karate. It wouldn't work, because to do point karate you have to have a clean shot in and out that the judge sees. That's not Bruce's method. Bruce's method is to jam the guy down and repeatedly blast him with punches that do not go all the way in like reverse punches and snap back to the hip. It didn't make any sense for Bruce. Bruce would not have worked well in a tournament like that.

James Bishop: I heard that Bruce Lee referred to them as "contests of ego".

Patrick Strong: Yeah. He was very down on that type of fighting because he thought tournament fighting and point karate were ridiculous.

That's why he was so interested in boxing, because a boxer does not get stuck in his movement. A boxer ducks and weaves. He's not just punch, punch, punch. He's ducking, weaving. He's dynamic all the time. He's not getting stuck in his movement, standing there in a fancy pose facing an opponent, looking bad. He's in there moving all the time and that's what Bruce saw in boxing that he liked so much. He saw the reality in that.

He saw that in Muhammad Ali. He was studying Muhammad Ali in the early sixties. What he noticed in Ali was in his timing. Now, this is very important - once again, Bruce's home was Wing Chun. In chi sao you have all of these timing mechanics. In the very beginning when two people start to roll it's beat, beat, beat, beat... Pretty soon you learn how to slip in between the beats. So Bruce had all these ideas of how the beat worked, how to work in half-beats and how to work in slip-beats. He had all that from Wing Chun. When he watched Ali fight he recognized the same thing. So he immediately picked up on that and, as early as 1963, we were doing the drills that became the Jeet Kune Do drills. He immediately knew what it was looking at and began developing drills for its development. It was the same bones, just different meat.

He noticed that Ali wouldn't have to step back to avoid a punch; he could be there and when the guy punched he would bend at the waist. When he bent back at the waist the guy's punch didn't reach him. So that punch snaps and is on its way back. In between that second and when the next punch from his opponent comes Ali would follow the punch back in and hit in between the timing. So the secret was that Ali wasn't moving his feet. He wasn't stepping out which would have meant he had to step back in again. Instead, he was bending at the waist to get out of the way and then followed the punch back in and got him in between his beats. Bruce had that in 1963.

At the time Muhammad Ali fought Sonny Liston, Bruce developed his timing drills and strategy that are in Jeet Kune Do to this very day. Actually, this was really nothing new to him because he already knew this stuff from Wing Chun chi sao, where beats and half-beats are the crux to the timing. It's just that he was now able to see it in another fighting form, along with other things that he liked very much.

James Bishop: Every few years in the martial arts magazines they will come out with some article hypothesizing what a fight between Muhammad Ali and Bruce Lee would have been like. Do you know of Bruce ever considering such a thing?

Patrick Strong: He may have, but not that I know of. I did an interview once with a writer who is very close friends of Ali's daughter and he told her that Bruce had patterned a lot of his stuff from Ali's movement. She told her father and Ali told her that he was so flattered that Bruce Lee would have done that - that it was really an honor that he could teach someone like Bruce Lee, whom he thought was a great fighter.

James Bishop: From every thing I have read about them it seems clear that they both had a great deal of respect for each other. The thing about Muhammad Ali and Bruce Lee is that, not only were they fighting geniuses in their own ways but, as human beings removed from the fighting aspect of their lives, they showed a great deal of courage and leadership.

Patrick Strong: Yes. I think now is a good time for people to take a look at Bruce's art because today the martial arts is evolving and you have a lot of cross-training now. There is no-holds-barred fighting and people are becoming very conscious today of what works and what doesn't work, and there is some very valuable things that can be gleaned from Bruce's research. One of those things is speed: how to hit a guy so fast that there is no escape. Another is how important it is to hit dead-center in the body, how to set up a guy so that you can hit them dead-center. How to set up rhythms to keep the flow going, how do you develop a standing base so that when you find yourself in a clinch with a guy that you can create the distance to be effective and take away his ability to be effective - the same strategy that is used in groundfighting. All of those things work for no-olds-barred fighters; all of those guys can take Bruce Lee's concepts and principles and apply them to what they are doing and what will you have? You'll have the "Concepts" method. That's why I say I have no problem with the Concepts method. I do it myself.

James Bishop: Basically, they are now doing what Bruce Lee did, and that's adapting.

Patrick Strong: Exactly.

James Bishop: Did you attend Bruce's funeral?

Patrick Strong: No, I didn't.

James Bishop: What are your memories of the day you heard that Bruce had died?

Patrick Strong: I was with Joe Hyams, the author of *Zen in the Martial Arts*, which was dedicated to me. Joe Hyams was a private student of Bruce's.

James Bishop: Yes, I've had the opportunity to speak to him before.

Patrick Strong: Joe and I heard it at the same time. Joe Hyams was one of Bruce's private celebrity students and when Bruce went over to Hong Kong I took over teaching him. I was up at his house and we were working on a story that we were writing together when either Ed Parker or one of those guys called up to the house and gave us the news. It just stunned us both.

James Bishop: Some people have belittled Lee since his passing. Bob Wall[21], for instance, has made a minor career out of bad-mouthing Bruce Lee. People seem reluctant to give him his due. Why do you think that is?

Patrick Strong: There are a lot of people who view Bruce as a movie actor and the stuff that he did on film was not his fighting art. That stuff was film choreography. It wasn't what his fighting art was all about.

Bruce became the greatest fighter in the world without ever becoming the greatest fighter in the world. He did it through movies. So there are a lot of people, and rightfully so, who would question that. I mean, whatever made Bruce Lee the greatest

---

[21] Bob Wall was a martial art tournament competitor in the 1960s whom Bruce Lee used in two of his movies, *Way of the Dragon* and *Enter the Dragon*.

fighter in the world? The only people that knew how good Bruce was were the people that worked with him, who stood on the firing line with him.

Bob Wall has been on the firing line with Bruce. Chuck Norris has been on the firing line with Bruce. In Chuck Norris' book he writes about being up at Bruce's house up on Roscomare Road. They were up there sparring and Bruce could not stop his spinning back kick. That was Chuck's best kick. So they start talking about that kick and Chuck explains something about that kick and then from that point on Chuck could not land that kick again. That doesn't take anything away from Bruce to say that he couldn't stop a kick that was Chuck's best tool. Once he learned *how* to stop it, then it didn't work against him. He was a phenomenal martial artist, but to say that he was the greatest martial artist in the world - that's a real stretch.

Rather than say that Bruce was the greatest martial artist in the world, I would rather say that he was a great innovator and researcher; he had an unquenchable thirst to learn. I mean, he was a research scientist in this stuff. He was forced to do it. He left Hong Kong at an early age, so he didn't have the big instructors to guide him through the thing. He had to go out with what he knew and piece it together and figure it out for himself and he did that by lots of researching and testing. That's not to say he wasn't really good - Bruce was *amazing*, just flat out amazing, but not everyone will buy the notion that he was the world's greatest martial artist.

James Bishop: And it can never be proven.

Patrick Strong: No, it can't. In my estimation he wasn't the greatest. I couldn't imagine him going up against (Brazilian jujitsu stylist) Rickson Gracie or any of the Gracies. But if you talk to other guys they would say, "Oh well, Bruce would take their eyes out." That's because they don't know that the Gracies have a defense against that. They would not be so susceptible to losing an eye and if they did it would not matter to them. If you take Rickson Gracie's eye out of his head and he has a hold on you, it's not going to matter. That won't stop him.

James Bishop: What do you think Bruce's greatest legacy will be?

Patrick Strong: I think his legacy now, to the young people, is that he was the greatest martial artist who ever lived. I don't believe that. He's certainly one of the great ones, but I can only say that because I knew him. But I don't know all the other great ones. I've known some of the great ones, really great ones. In many ways, Bruce is right there with them.

A personal legacy for people who knew him was that his martial art and his philosophy were one and the same. His philosophy was an extension of his martial art. The tools of his martial art such as the ton sao, the bon sao all apply in some way to his philosophy. Like the immovable elbow: don't let it give too much and destroy your structure. If that elbow gives away too much, it could mean that you lose your character. It represents your honor: if you give way on your honor you lose your integrity; you lose yourself as a person. Bruce Lee could talk like that, he could make the comparison between the immovable elbow holding the position for a tool and your honor that cannot be relinquished, or should not give way; should not submit.

James Bishop: What's your fondest memory of Bruce?

Patrick Strong: I was a lifeguard in Seattle, and once and a while he would drive out to the beach and visit with me. That always touched me.

Bruce had a saying about fighting that became very famous: that it's impossible to learn to fight without sparring, that it was like, "trying to learn to swim on dry land."

One day I was teaching swimming lessons and he was watching me. I had the kids up on the dock and they were practicing their dog paddle, before we got into the water. Just before I put them in the water I said to him, "Well, we can learn to swim on land but you can't really 'learn' to swim until you get into the water." That night in gung fu class he used the same analogy for a fight.

The best times were after class, when we all went out to dinner. That's when Bruce would start to talk. In my case, I learned a lot more talking to him, hearing him talk about his gung fu and his theories, than I ever did in class. In the class you got to learn the techniques and stuff, but you can't just learn techniques - you need more than that. What Bruce was really great about was his ability to talk about his art, the philosophy and about what makes those tools work.

James Bishop: So do you think that his philosophy will be his greatest legacy?

Patrick Strong: If you only know Bruce Lee's footwork, if you only know his kicks, if you only know his punches, what you have is kickboxing. There is a lot more to it than that. There's the philosophical code that makes all of that stuff work in your personal life.

JEET KUNE DO IN IRELAND

The Third Annual Jun Fan Jeet Kune Do Seminar and Annual Meeting was held April 23-25, 1999 in Seattle Washington. I was fortunate to have the opportunity to attend the event, and these are my experiences at the seminar.

I arrived on Thursday April 22, the evening before the event began. Shortly thereafter I met up with Sifu Lamar M. Davis II, a Jeet Kune Do instructor and his entourage. I had come to know Sifu Davis via phone and e-mail while doing research for my book on Bruce Lee, but it was our first face-to-face meeting. He was as genuine and outgoing in person as he was in our correspondence, and an immediate friendship was solidified.

One of the members of his entourage was Sifu Martin O'Neill, a Jeet Kune Do instructor from Belfast, Northern Ireland. I was very excited to meet Sifu O'Neill since I am of Irish heritage and I was eager to discuss with him the culture and people of Ireland.

The next afternoon we loaded onto the buses and began our tour of Seattle, which included the important places that Bruce Lee lived, worked and taught martial arts. On the trip back to the hotel I sat next to Martin O'Neill. We had a wonderful conversation about life in Ireland: its culture, political ills, and its natural beauty. I think he was impressed with my knowledge of the island, considering I had never been there. We developed a good rapport on that bus ride.

Later that evening Sifu Davis, Martin O'Neill and I went to dinner. Along the way we encountered Leo Fong, a Methodist minister, film actor, director, and martial artist, who was friends with and studied under Bruce Lee. Fong and Sifu Davis were friends, and he joined us for dinner. I was amazed at how open, honest, and insightful Leo Fong was. He had a keen mind that was able to combine years of martial arts training with a Christian sensibility, and at the same time have a profound grasp of Eastern philosophy. In the course of conversation, O'Neill mentioned, just as an aside, that he was having great success in bringing Catholics and Protestants together at his school in Belfast. I immediately recognized the value in what he was doing and committed myself to write an article on him.

This interview was conducted the night of April 24, 1999 in Seattle Washington, after the Jun Fan Jeet Kune Do Nucleus' third annual memorial banquet. It appeared in the March 2000 issue of *Martial Arts Presents* magazine.

"It's a society at war with itself," says Martin O'Neill about his country. The Jeet Kune Do instructor from Northern Ireland has grown up in the heart of the country's troubles, witnessing and experiencing the pain and violence of sectarianism and political persecution.

O'Neill, who is also a senior social worker near the city of Belfast, says that the division between Protestants and Catholics on the emerald isle is deep and centuries old. "There's a lot of hatred that goes on in society here. In many ways it knows no bounds, and it's a very sad indictment of our inability to live together."

The conflict in Ireland dates back to the year 1169 when Anglo-Norman troops invaded Ireland at Bannow Bay in County Wexford, cementing a British presence on the island that has remained until this day. With the succession of Protestant Queen Elizabeth I to the British throne in 1558, persecution of Irish Catholics began to grow. Oliver Cromwell's attack on Ireland in 1649 resulted in Irish massacres and the forced resettlement of thousands of native Irish citizens. By 1691 the Protestant British had acquired absolute authority over the island. Four years later, British rulers imposed a series of severe restrictions on Irish Catholics. The laws (which came to be known as the Penal Laws) prevented Irish Catholics from bearing arms, restricted their rights to education, banned them from holding any political offices or becoming lawyers, and prevented them from voting. Though some of those rights were restored to the Catholics over time, the deep hatred and mistrust that Catholics and Protestants in Ireland felt for one another remained. British political control over Ireland became official with the passing of the Act of Union in 1800, which joined Ireland and England as one. In 1845 famine swept the country for three years. More than one million people starved to death and hundreds of thousands immigrated to America.

The beginning of the modern era of the Irish conflict began during Easter 1916, when Patrick Pearse and 1,500 Irish volunteers declared an independent Ireland, an act of open rebellion against British rule. Four hundred people died over the four days of the rebellion and 2,500 were wounded. Although the rebellion failed, the subsequent executions of its chief architects helped to activate Ireland's desire for independence. The Irish Republican Army's ambush of British forces at Soloheadbeg in County Tipperary in 1919 officially began the "War for Independence." The country was partitioned in 1921 with six counties remaining under British rule and the remainder forming the Irish Republic.

The conflict continued sporadically until 1969 when the current phase started, which itself was marked by regular violence until the recent cease-fires. Most of the violence is concentrated in Northern Ireland and, in particular, the city of Belfast. It is here, at ground zero, that Sifu Martin O'Neill makes his contributions to the peace process in Ireland through his efforts as a senior social worker and by sharing Bruce Lee's martial art and philosophy with his countrymen.

O'Neill comes from the town of Lurgan, near Belfast. "I grew up in a working class estate," says O'Neill. "I was one of five children. It was pretty much an ordinary happy kind of upbringing until I was just barely in my teens and the conflict in Northern Ireland started up again. That was the end of childhood as such."

The violence and hatred that surrounded O'Neill in his teens made life very difficult for him as a young man. "It was very different then because the society was torn apart by what was basically a civil war.

"I left school when I was sixteen, with no qualifications. I went to live in Dublin (in the southern part of Ireland) because I couldn't get a decent job in Northern Ireland, which, I think, was due primarily to sectarianism. Catholics found it very difficult to get a job in that environment. I suppose it has parallels to some of the kinds of racism we find in other societies, and I think America has its fair share of that. John Little's book *The Warrior Within* had a chapter on racism, specifically Bruce Lee's experiences with racism, which I related to in terms of the experiences I had of sectarianism (which is like a parallel of racism). In my society you are condemned and labeled as an accident of birth, whether you were born a Protestant or Catholic."

It was in Dublin that Martin O'Neill would first become involved in the martial arts. "I had been interested in martial arts since I had seen the movie *Fist of Fury* (called *The Chinese Connection* in the United States). I saw Bruce Lee's performance on screen and was very impressed. I wondered what it was that he did. I really wanted to have a go at whatever it was, and so I went and found a karate school and thought that was what Bruce Lee did."

O'Neill began his martial arts training in Wado Ryu in 1976. "I remember when I first went to the karate school it was really scary. I was very nervous. I stood outside the dojo door for a while, thinking, *Have I got the guts to go across this door?"* *(O'Neill laughs).*

"It was scary for a while, but I enjoyed it. It was quite a tough variant of Wado Ryu, a lot of full contact fighting. I received my black belt in 1980. I also got into other styles, Kobudo, etc., and did that for about ten years."

During his Karate years O'Neill competed in semi-contact and full-contact tournaments and bouts. "I won the Irish karate title,

51

and I lost some bouts," O'Neill says, honestly. "It was, however, an enjoyable experience, very challenging."

Martin O'Neill moved to London where he went to college and obtained a B.A. Honors degree in social science and social work. He worked as a probation officer for a time, as well as in family childcare. Eventually, Martin moved back to the area of his upbringing. With the martial arts still a large part of his life, O'Neill decided to open up a Wado Ryu school.

"I was allowed by my sensei to open up a school and to teach classes under his guidance," says O'Neill. "That went very well. We had a big class. We were the first karate school in that area, and some days we had maybe forty people training there. We ran a tough school. It was good fun: bumps, bruises and black eyes were given out on a regular basis!"

In the meantime, Martin O'Neill's knowledge of Bruce Lee's martial art was growing. "I had heard about Jeet Kune Do and read about it. I bought the book *The Tao of Jeet Kune Do*. I thought it was interesting but confusing. I couldn't understand what it meant. I couldn't fathom some of the concepts behind it. For instance, he talked about boxing: in some ways it seemed like boxing and kickboxing, but in other ways it seemed very different."

O'Neill soon got the chance to experience Jeet Kune Do first hand. "I had an opportunity to go to a seminar by Sifus Steve and Mike Krause, two Scotsmen who are instructors under Sifu Dan Inosanto. They were in Ireland demonstrating the art of Jeet Kune Do. Needless to say, I was very impressed with what I saw, and I enrolled with them as a student. Soon after, they took me on and made me an apprentice in Jeet Kune Do concepts and Filipino martial arts."

O'Neill studied under the Krause brothers for about six years, attending their instructor's course and regularly traveling from Ireland to Scotland for training. One of the highlights of his time with the Krause brothers was the opportunity to meet and train with Dan Inosanto himself. For O'Neill, meeting with Inosanto was a very memorable experience. "I found him to be an excellent instructor," remembers O'Neill. "He is a walking encyclopedia of martial arts. He has pursued his own path in the martial arts, and he has paid tribute to Bruce Lee through that. I think he has found his own way, and I respect that, totally."

Four years ago, Martin O'Neill's own path of martial arts evolution took him away from the concepts approach and into the original Jeet Kune Do arena. "After being with the Krause brothers (who are excellent instructors) for about six years and becoming reasonably proficient in JKD concepts, I started to become concerned that my knowledge of Bruce Lee's art was deficient. This, however, may have been my own fault for not looking hard enough. I read an article by Sifu Lamar M. Davis II in a US magazine and was very impressed by what he had written. I wrote to him, and he wrote back. Then I got one of his videos.

"Before I had seen his videos, I thought I knew something about Jeet Kune Do. I thought I knew something about trapping. However, after buying one of his trapping videos I realized I knew little about trapping and even less about Jeet Kune Do."

The two developed a good friendship based on their correspondence and eventually Martin O'Neill got the opportunity to come to the United States and train with Sifu Davis. "We corresponded a bit, and he invited me over to Alabama to train with him in his kwoon during his summer camp. I took the chance. There was some anxiety, I must admit, because I had never been to the United States before and I was going to be traveling on my own, but I couldn't have been more welcomed. He was very friendly and his students were great to work with. I was just thoroughly impressed with his friendly approach. He has a wicked sense of humor! He knows Jeet Kune Do thoroughly and is very demanding, yet at the same time he is able to inject humor in the training so that people can enjoy themselves. His training sessions are very hard but in the middle of them he will crack a joke and make it easier to get through them. I was used to the Japanese instructors who would shout and bellow at the class and stuff like that."

The week that Martin O'Neill spent at Sifu Davis' summer camp was a watershed event in his development as a martial artist. "It was the hardest training I had done in a long time, and there were no excuses taken about jet lag, but I really enjoyed it and it opened my eyes in terms of what Bruce Lee's art was all about. What I could see in Sifu Davis was the ability to functionalize *The Tao of Jeet Kune Do,* someone who could actually interpret it both physically and philosophically and teach it in a way that I could understand it. So I've been studying under him ever since."

Shortly after O'Neill began training under Sifu Lamar M. Davis II he decided to open up a Jun Fan/Jeet Kune Do school in Belfast. "I had always had a group training with me," says O'Neill. "Even in the concepts time, I had a group of people I trained. When I switched from the concepts group to the original system I lost some people who didn't make the switch. But I still kept some of the core people and we have maintained a small but dedicated group training in my hometown of Lurgan. Then about three years ago I opened up my school in Belfast. These were the first Jeet Kune Do schools in Ireland!"

The response to Martin O'Neill's Jeet Kune Do school has been positive, albeit slowly growing due to Ireland's lack of knowledge about Jeet Kune Do. O'Neill knows that it will continue to grow with time. "It is going reasonably well. Most people don't understand that what I offer here is Bruce Lee's authentic art, but the word is getting out. Traditional martial arts are very strong in Ireland, generally speaking, and few really understand what Bruce was doing. It's only when they come and see and get a sense of what it's about that they get a chance to really experience it."

After O'Neill opened up his school in Belfast Sifu Davis traveled to Ireland to teach a seminar at his student's new kwoon. Like O'Neill in America, it was Sifu Davis' first visit to Ireland. Unlike, O'Neill's trip, Sifu Davis was entering a world of political and social turmoil.

O'Neill says Sifu Davis' visit was made with some trepidation from his family and friends at home. "He came and he didn't know what he was coming into. Some of his friends were a wee bit worried about him coming to Ireland because Northern Ireland and Belfast have a reputation for indiscriminate violence. It didn't stop him from coming over, however, and I think he had a good time. Certainly, the people who met him enjoyed training with him."

Sifu Davis did experience some degree of culture shock while he was in Ireland, but, as O'Neill says, "He took it all in stride, though he was a bit taken aback by some of the things he saw, such as people marching around the streets armed to the teeth! People here take it for granted because they are so used to it, but he was surprised by how acceptable it was. We don't have the kind of ordinary law and order that you enjoy in America. It's a different situation."

It is that situation that Martin O'Neill hopes to help change with his Jeet Kune Do school. And to date, the school has been able to do something that 800 years of fighting and thousands of hours of political peace negotiations have been unable to do: it has begun uniting Catholics and Protestants.

O'Neill believes it is the philosophy behind Bruce Lee's art of Jeet Kune Do and the charisma of its founder that is bringing the two sides together. "In Northern Ireland people live separate lives and a separate existence. It's hard for Americans to understand that. Many Protestants and Catholics live in separate areas, which is very sad. I think that Bruce's art gives us an opportunity to bring people together because his art transcends color or creed. It gives people an opportunity to come together and train and build friendships. That's what's important, I think. Here in my school they come together and, through the example of Bruce Lee, discover that they have much more in common than they have in differences."

In Martin O'Neill's Jeet Kune Do school Catholics and Protestants train side by side and are immersed in the principles of Bruce Lee's personal philosophy, including the most important one: "Under the sky, under the heavens, there is but one family." They begin to understand the deeper meaning of Bruce Lee's words and soon come to the realization that they are a part of a greater whole called humanity and not simply an isolated sub-group who can afford to ignore the rest of society. They begin to see people in terms of the bigger picture.

O'Neill had his own glimpse of the bigger picture when he recently attended the third annual Jun Fan Jeet Kune Do Seminar in Seattle, Washington. He was deeply moved by the gathering of so many people of different backgrounds and ideologies for the common cause of perpetuating Bruce Lee's teachings. "Being at the Jun Fan Jeet Kune Do annual meeting had a profound effect on me. It has been a lifelong ambition of mine to meet and train with Bruce Lee's original students, so I thoroughly enjoyed the experience. I think that it's a great idea to perpetuate and promote Bruce Lee's teachings. I believe they were in danger of being lost.

"I applaud the work that is going on by the board of directors of the Nucleus and, in particular, Linda Lee Cadwell. I think she is marvelous and such a strong woman. We had a bus tour of Seattle during the seminar, and she was the tour guide. At her late husband and son's gravesite, she was giving a commentary on her life with the two of them, and it was so moving to listen to her. My own sister lost her son a few years ago when he was sixteen. It broke her heart. So I have some idea of how Mrs. Cadwell must feel. I think she is very courageous."

Another person O'Neill had the opportunity to meet at the seminar was Sifu Taky Kimura, Bruce Lee's best friend. "I talked with him at Lakeview Cemetery," says O'Neill. "He spoke to me the way you speak to a friend. He's a very open person and one who cares a lot. I met some of his students and trained with them. They are a credit to him; they're lovely people. They have no egotistical hang-ups, and they were very friendly. They want to share the knowledge."

Martin O'Neill believes people can benefit from learning Bruce Lee's martial art. "I hope that it grows and more people get access to it. It's starting to become more accessible, and there are now more people being authorized to teach it. Certainly, the Nucleus has done their part, as well as the publication of books on Bruce's contributions to martial arts, to health, and to philosophy. I think that *that* influence (philosophy) is going to be profound."

O'Neill is also able to bring the principles behind Jeet Kune Do to his job as a senior social worker, where he currently works in community development. "It's a varied job where you're constantly dealing with people's problems; you're dealing with humanity. You're working with the feelings of people who are facing up to the difficulties they have found in their lives. In this, I think Jeet Kune Do can help people through its very positive philosophy of life. That's one thing that I have found in being in Jeet Kune Do, through the friendships that I have developed with people in America and the support I have received from my sifu and other people that are involved with Bruce Lee's legacy. So, it all can have a very positive influence, I think, in Ireland. It's a challenge working in the field of social work, but I think that Bruce's art gives support to me because it assists me in life. When you feel strong within yourself then you can reach out and help other people. Some of Bruce's sayings that have been published in books have very important meaning to me. One of his sayings is: 'There is no help but self-help.' You have to sort your own life out first before you help anybody else. That's very important, Life is a journey rather than a destination. The destination is when we die. But certainly, my journey in life has been enriched by having the opportunity to train in Bruce Lee's art."

One source of great strength for O'Neill has been his family. "I've been supported over the years by my parents, my wife Bernie, and my two beautiful daughters Sorcha and Meabh. They're just wonderful and the light of my life. My wife has been very encouraging and has helped to make it possible for me to do this."

When asked if his children have followed him down the path to martial arts, O'Neill replies, "Not yet. My oldest girl has done a bit of pad work with me, but I'm trying to get her more interested in self-defense. The younger one, I think, has a good future in martial arts because she has a wicked temper and is very skilled at low-line kicking against my shins!" *(Laughs)*.

Martin O'Neill remains hopeful that Ireland's future will be brighter than its recent past. And there is a strong possibility that his hope is justified: In 1994, the British government, Sinn Fein, Loyalists, and other political parties finally began to meet and discuss the possibility of peace. In May of 1998, voters throughout Ireland approved the historic Good Friday Agreement, which established a new form of self-rule for embattled Northern Ireland. In addition, it gave minority Catholics a greater voice while also meeting the Protestant demands that the island remain a part of Britain. With that behind it, Ireland has now turned its attention to the more difficult task of disarming the two sides so that they can finally live in peace.

"I hope that, with the help of God, we get peace," says O'Neill. "I hope that the cease-fires in Ireland continue and we reach an agreement that everyone can approve of. It is my hope that we can move into the next millennium with no one being shot because of their religion or their politics."

A positive step toward that end was the establishment of a power-sharing government that would have allowed Ireland to enjoy a greater measure of autonomy. Unfortunately, Britain suspended the weeks-old home-rule government after the two sides failed to come to a resolution about IRA disarmament. Once more the future is in doubt.

In the meantime, Martin O'Neill will continue to do what he can toward the path of peace. "All I can do is make a small contribution to that, and I do it through my community relations work and also my involvement with Jeet Kune Do by saying that Jeet Kune Do is open to anyone who subscribes to the basic rules and regulations; and that the door is open and people can come in and learn and grow together. It's not going to solve the social and political ills of my country, but it helps me to know that not only am I making a contribution to the peace process but also that Bruce Lee's art is making a contribution. I think he would have liked that idea."

DIALOGUE WITH JOHN LITTLE

Perhaps no one in recent memory has been more important to Bruce Lee's legacy, nor more maligned, than John Little. Little is the man responsible for creating the renaissance that Bruce Lee's legacy enjoyed in the 1990s. He compiled and edited the Bruce Lee Library Series for Tuttle Publishing, which released, for the first time, thousands of pages of Bruce Lee's personal writings for the viewing public. In addition, he released the only book to date that focused on Lee's philosophy, as well as a book of interviews with Lee.

Little scored a major coup when he located the master copy of what came to be known as the "Lost Interview", a televised interview with Bruce Lee conducted by Canadian Pierre Berton at the height of Lee's popularity in Hong Kong. It remains the only surviving video of Bruce Lee being himself in front of a camera, commenting on his life, stardom, and philosophy. Until he located the master and released it to the public, the interview was only known to a select few, passed around in poor quality, incomplete bootlegs.

Little also took the body of private film and audio recordings in possession of the Bruce Lee Estate to produce the authoritative video on Bruce Lee's martial art, *Bruce Lee's Jeet Kune Do*, which contained home footage of Bruce Lee demonstrating his techniques and teaching his students, narrated by Bruce Lee himself.

Little's documentary, *Bruce Lee: In His Own Words*, was featured on the 25th anniversary video release of *Enter the Dragon*, the film that made Lee a star in the United States. The documentary featured the human side of Bruce Lee, with Lee discussing his life, and included poignant film footage of Lee with his family. The documentary won the Toronto Film Festival's top honors.

Little was instrumental in the development of the Bruce Lee Educational Foundation. It was his vision that, for a short time, allowed it to reach out beyond the martial art focus of the Jun Fan Jeet Kune Do Nucleus to the non-martial art fans of Bruce Lee, previously only marginalized.

Little's final work in the name of Bruce Lee was the film, *Warrior's Journey*. This was another coup on the part of Little in which, for the first time, he presented the uncompleted footage Lee shot for his final film, *Game of Death*, as Lee envisioned it, based on his handwritten script notes and choreography layouts. The film also included a documentary outlining the philosophical story behind Lee's final film.

John Little and I shared a vision of a socially productive approach to Bruce Lee's image and philosophy. Like me, Little believed that Bruce Lee's celebrity and ideas could be used to fight prejudice and help people discover their potential. Like me, Little faced an uphill battle, fighting both the fans' preconceived notions of Bruce Lee as well as the direct students of Bruce Lee, who felt their little fiefdoms, carved out of the Bruce Lee legacy, being threatened by this new group of which they had no knowledge and, more importantly, no control. Efforts seemed to be made to discourage this philosophical line of work. In one (in my opinion) very suspicious example, the *Bruce Lee Magazine* that Little edited and in which appeared our philosophical writings developed some rather *unusual* layout and printing problems for several successive months. The publisher, CFW Enterprises, assured Little that it was a machine-related problem, but I remain unconvinced, considering that their other martial art magazines were being produced by the same machines, at the same time, and with none of the problems. The published result of the *Bruce Lee Magazine* was such a product of such gross incompetence that it defied a random explanation.

John Little has been resented by those who knew Bruce Lee because he took the spotlight away from them and resented by the fans because he was in a position they would have died to be in. Yet, when Little broke from the Bruce Lee Educational Foundation in the spring of 2001, the world of Bruce Lee lost one of its best spokesmen, and the fans lost one of their greatest advocates.

Little is currently working to preserve and disseminate the writings and teachings of the Pulitzer Prize-winning philosopher Will Durant, recipient of the Presidential Medal of Freedom. The following dialogue was conducted in 1999 and published, in part, in my book, *Remembering Bruce*.

James Bishop: Your interest in Bruce Lee dates back to your childhood.

John Little: I have been an ardent, zealous fan of Bruce Lee since I was twelve. I used to read everything about him I could get my hands on. I remember I'd go down to Chinatown in Toronto and pick up all the Chinese language magazines that would come across to Canada in the mid-to-late 1970s. Then I would take them back home and get Chinese friends to translate them and look at the pictures. I even snuck into a screening of his films with a hand-held 8mm camera and filmed them. Then I would go back and watch them on a viewer. It was great because watching Bruce and the way he moved his body and the way he executed his techniques allowed me to practice that through the aid of that viewer and a mirror. When we actually had a karate school that opened down the street from me a year or so later, I was able to advance to green belt within about a week because of the dexterity I had gotten from imitating Bruce.

I was fascinated with Bruce, always was, but as you grow older you begin to think that it's time to put away childish things and become a man. You get married. You have responsibility. You attempt to justify what could be viewed as adolescent hero worship. But it always struck me that Bruce Lee had more to offer.

Bruce wasn't just a guy who could throw a baseball with great velocity, a person who was a onetime heavyweight champion, or, in my case living in Canada, a guy who could put the puck in the net. He had a philosophy, and it was the philosophy I found myself getting more and more fascinated by. And as for his physical fitness, he was a man who was just in awesome physical fitness! His physique was tremendous!"

To me, when I was growing up, Bruce represented the perfect male: he was tremendously well built and a good-looking guy. He was intelligent, and he had a philosophy. He was successful. He was married and had children. He was doing work that he loved. He had a creative vein, and I decided that was it! That's what everybody should aspire to! But none of the books that came out had any information on how he trained or how he built his body. That led to my own (sort of using Bruce's philosophical principles) researching the science or the facts of Bruce's physical fitness and muscle physiology. Long story short, that (in turn) took me to California where I got to meet Brandon Lee.

It was like he ripped a veil off of past memories and brought it all back. I realized that Bruce and Brandon's philosophy dealt with what Brandon called 'real world applications'. It had to be truthful; it had to be real. It couldn't be artificial or pragmatic. So, it was hard for me to leave that mindset and go back to interview a champion bodybuilder who was going to tell me why it was life and death to have twenty-inch arms, you know. I couldn't square it anymore. It just didn't make sense.

Anyway, I was with *Muscle and Fitness* magazine when I did the article on Bruce. The nice thing about working for (Joe) Weider at the time was that it gave me the opportunity to speak to people and pursue areas of fitness that previously might not have been open to me. And certainly the first opportunity I had to flex my muscle in that domain was to do something on Bruce Lee, and that was his training methods.

James Bishop: How did your involvement with the *Bruce Lee Library Series* come about?

John Little: The Bruce Lee Library Series came about as the result of a friendship I developed with Linda Lee Cadwell, who is Bruce's widow and a terrific lady. She invited me up to Idaho to look through Bruce's papers, initially with the idea of doing a book on his training methods, which has since become *The Art of Expressing the Human Body*. But while I was there I was just stunned at the wealth of material, particularly the non-martial art material. It just opened up a whole new vista of perspective on Bruce Lee for me because, like most people, I knew he was intelligent and I knew he had a philosophy, but from my perspective it was a philosophy that dealt solely with the martial arts. Well, how wrong I was! He was a philosopher first and the martial arts were but one expression of it. His filmmaking was another expression of it. His interaction with people and friends, his business dealings were others, as was his training and physical fitness methods. I was just delighted; I was like a kid in Aladdin's cave, being able to see papers that nobody but Bruce Lee had seen, in some instances, since he wrote them, such as annotations in the margins of his books, little philosophical jottings that he had done enclosed within the pages of a book. There was everything: correspondence, daytime diaries, the whole bit. It was like going to Bruce Lee University and learning all these different courses that were the 'totality' of the man. And it was something that's great because I learn something new about him everyday.

I was surprised by so much of it because it was new and personal. I guess the most striking thing about it was how prolific a writer he was. Again, here's a man who passed away at the age of thirty-two and did the bulk of his writings during an eight year period. And yet, my first time returning to California from Boise, from visiting with Linda, I returned with sixty pounds of photocopied material! I had to make a subsequent trip and I came back with about 30 pounds worth! This is not an ordinary martial artist! To have over 2,500 books as he does in his library, the bulk of which are philosophy books, just shows that his martial art wasn't created in a vacuum. It was created out of much thought, and that's philosophic method. That's mind training. I think that his mind was certainly the organ Bruce Lee trained everyday. That's what gave birth to his art.

James Bishop: On a philosophical note, was Bruce Lee influenced in any way by the Positivists?[22] Though they seem to

---

[22] Positivism was a school of philosophical thought developed in the 19th century that held the view that the only true knowledge comes from science. They believed that since theology and the metaphysics of philosophy could not be verified, the "knowledge" that comes from them should be ignored.

swing to the extreme on the scientific side of thought, I have recognized some similarities in their work and in Bruce's approach to his art.

John Little: It is interesting but I cannot find any evidence that Bruce was influenced directly by the Positivists. There is nothing in his writings (nor his philosophy notebooks from college, which contain the broadest reference in his writings to specific "Western" philosophers) of Auguste Comte or, further back, Francis Bacon (considered one of the forerunners of what became known as Positivism). There is -- looking into the 20th century extension of Positivism to the Vienna School and beyond -- not much apart from (and this is admittedly reaching) a book or two of Bertrand Russell's (*Wisdom of the West*) -- which, admittedly, had little to do with his "logical atomism", and A.J. Ayer's (whom I twice heard lecture at McMaster University) tome, of Logical Positivism, *Language, Truth and Logic*. There is no Wittgenstein, for example, and, even in Ayer's book, there is no underlining, which indicates either Bruce bought the book but did not get around to reading it, or he read it and felt nothing in it necessary to underline.

However, I agree with your observation that there are some "similarities in their work and in Bruce's approach to his art." Every philosophy student at some time picks up Antony Flew's book "A Dictionary of Philosophy" and, on page 264 under the heading of "Positivism," Flew writes:

"All genuine human knowledge is contained within the boundaries of science, that is to the systematic study of phenomena and the explication of the law as embodied in therein. Philosophy may still perform a useful function in explaining the scope and methods of science, pointing out the more general principles underlying specific scientific findings, and exploring the implications of science for human life. But it must abandon the claim to have any means of attaining knowledge not available to science. Whatever questions cannot be answered by scientific method we must be content to leave permanently unanswered."

Later, Flew cites a quotation of Comte's: "Science whence comes prediction; prediction whence comes action," which is not that dissimilar to "Knowing is not enough, we must apply" -- Bruce's dictum. As science can be equated with "knowledge" and, from the Positivist's perspective, it is the only means by which we can know anything, and then follows "action" or the "application" of this knowledge.

Bruce, of course, was a firm believer in the scientific method in not only his philosophy, but also its application to combat. He once said in an interview:

"We should regard our martial art training as scientific and every energy and capacity can be explained by science. It is not mystical at all. Therefore, everything should logical."[23]

And:

"In any physical movement there is always a most efficient and alive manner to accomplish the purpose of the performance for each individual. That is, in regard to proper leverage, balance in movement, economical and efficient use of motion and energy, etc. Live, efficient movement that liberates is one thing; sterile, classical sets that bind and condition is another."[24]

The first quote in particular could have been taken from a textbook on Positivism (i.e., "every energy and capacity can be explained by science") -- and yet, Bruce was not a Positivist.

James Bishop: It's interesting that you mention Ayers' *Language, Truth and Logic.* One of my philosophy teachers made the interesting point that Ayers and those of his movement tried to eliminate the philosophical and religious ideologies, yet were in fact creating there own metaphysic.

Clearly Bruce was not a Positivist, though he did seem to be something of a metaphysical minimalist (speaks of chi, yet denies existence of a "god"). I think the thing is that, as a thinker, Bruce may have developed some independent views about things that are similar in thought to other schools, without ever having studied the others' philosophical traditions.

---

[23] Source: Bruce Lee quoted in the article entitled "Interviewing Bruce Lee: Bruce Lee Tells Us The Secrets of Combat," published in *Bruce Lee & Jeet Kune Do Magazine*, No. 10, 1977.
[24] Source: Bruce Lee's handwritten essay entitled "Toward Personal Liberation (Jeet Kune Do)" circa 1971, Bruce Lee Papers -- also published in *Bruce Lee: Artist of Life*, Charles E. Tuttle Publishing Company, 1999.

John Little: It's a phenomenon of Bruce that while his thought is reflective of many different "isms", he, himself, cannot be pigeonholed. And, in my opinion, this is because the "truth" that these various modes of thought or schools of philosophy come to see are not true because they see them, but rather, they see them because they are true. And, therefore, it is a "vision," if you will, that is not the exclusive property of any particular school, method or (in martial art parlance, "style"), but of human beings -- presuming of course that they are sufficiently motivated to seek it.

At times I see Bruce as a:

Confucianist
Taoist
Buddhist
Positivist
Existentialist
Gestalt psychologist
Nietzschian (although I have no evidence that he ever read Nietzsche)
Empiricist
Rationalist

Classical Liberal (ala Herbert Spencer/John Stuart Mill)
Objectivist (although he never read Ayn Rand)
Atheist
Pantheist
Mystic
Platonist
Aristotelian

All of these, I think, are elements within the human psyche that are called by different names and identify different prisms through which we, at various times in our development, come to view and understand life. None of these positions are fixed; all are dynamic as, indeed, all living entities must be (perhaps I should also add that Bruce was Heraclitian in this respect as well).

Nevertheless, Bruce's viewpoint of the metaphysical nature of human beings as a combination of "natural instinct" (intuitive, emotional, artistic, spiritual) and "control" (reasoning, scientific, linear) is in some respects an attempt to synthesize the Platonic with the Aristotelian elements of our nature and, in truth, to recognize the fact that in human affairs it is not "either/or" -- it can be both, always and forever, although we often become enamored with our "personal fancies" or beliefs or filters through which we feel comfortable looking at life through to the point where they become a crutch or security blanket for us, and we refuse to let go of them when it is time to move on in our evolving state of consciousness (from cradle to crematorium, from child to adult). As Bruce said, "we are constantly learning and when we stop learning, that's when the coffin lid is closed." And not just linear learning, but learning in all aspects of our humanity. Perhaps Bruce was also something of a Shakespearean, recognizing that "each man in his lifetime plays many different parts."

I think this is how the more enlightened and more fully human among us get through life and grow from the experience.

James Bishop: I have also found similarities between Hegel and Bruce Lee. Both believed life was a natural process of growing self-knowledge (though in Hegelian thought it is more oriented in the entire world-spirit than in the individual).

John Little: As to Hegel, I also agree with your observation as an extension of the reasons given above. Hegel's dialectic, which begins with a "thesis" by which a principle of negativity moves to its opposite, called an "antithesis," and then -- the forces of the two in position clash, producing an emergent reconciliation of the two which, though new and different, share aspects of both thesis and antithesis called a "synthesis" -- is simply another way of stating that that reality is a dynamic (not static) process, which also might explain why truth proves to be such an elusive quarry to us all.

Recall Bruce's statement that "in the contrast of comparison some new thing might grow", coupled with his statement about "natural instinct " and "control" -- this is very Hegelian as it speaks to the entire dialectical process of Hegel (e.g.: "thesis" or "natural instinct" meets its opposite, "anti-thesis" or "control" which leads to a "synthesis" or "a successful combination of both" and "out of this contrast of comparison, some new thing grows").

James Bishop: Among your points you stated that a great deal of "isms" could be applied to Bruce but that it would be incorrect in doing so, as it would pigeon-hole him. I agree, totally. That was one of the most important points that I have absorbed through his words and the words of Lao Tzu and Krishnamurti: that truth is formless--as soon as you try to shape it you lose sight of it; that it is subjective, constantly changing and, in many ways, ineffable. I am reminded of the anecdote Krishnamurti used to tell.

"You may remember the story of how the devil and a friend of his were walking down the street, when they saw ahead of them a man stoop down and pick up something from the ground, look at it, and put it away in his pocket. The friend said to the devil, 'What did that man pick up?' 'He picked up a piece of Truth,' said the devil. 'That is a very bad business for you, then,' said his friend. 'Oh not at all,' the devil replied, 'I am going to let him organize it.'"[25]

John Little: I, too, particularly like Krishnamurti's anecdote of the devil and the "piece of truth." You see the application of this in so many attempts to "arrest" or "fix" something into a doctrine or organization.

James Bishop: I think the reason that many in the United States have trouble studying Bruce Lee's philosophies is that they have this concrete, analytical, black-and-white mindset where everything has to be clearly defined, that it is simply impossible to perceive of a "circle with no circumference". Which is not to say everything is clear to me, but once you recognize the idea that things can have a duality of being, such as the Tao, to truly understand that it is not a black and white existence but a black/white existence, you can go along way toward understanding Bruce Lee's mindset. Once you can learn to accept such seemingly contradictory statements, as are a part of much of the Eastern philosophical tradition, you finally have your "foot in the door". But it's hard to give up this conditioned mindset, and I guess that is what Krishnamurti was getting at when he talked about "freedom from the known".

I am curious to know if Bruce Lee's script for *The Silent Flute* will ever be published.

John Little: We have considered publishing Bruce's script for *The Silent Flute* along with his notes on choreography and minutes from his meetings with Coburn and Silliphant. However, there is some question over copyright as both Coburn and Silliphant's estate are involved in the final product. The good news is that Bruce also wrote a script that is *very* much like *The Silent Flute*, several months before he died, and we are actively pursuing its

---

[25] Source: speech by Jiddu Krishnamurti in Ommen, Holland, August 2, 1929.

development, which, if successful, would represent Bruce Lee's purest expression of his martial philosophy. Unlike *The Silent Flute*, which required compromises to a certain extent from Bruce to Coburn and Silliphant (the co-writers) in order to keep them involved in the project, this other project is PURE Bruce and by far the best work he has ever done.

James Bishop: An interesting aspect of Bruce Lee's thought: I was amazed to find that many of Bruce's teachings, such as "all knowledge leads to self-knowledge" are very similar in thought to the teachings of the Gnostic Christians, who were another group that developed from the apostles of Christ but were eradicated by the Holy Roman Empire during the first millennium. It was absolutely fascinating to read about some of these alternative teachings attributed to Jesus, many of which echoed the words of Bruce Lee.

John Little: The Gnostic gospels that you mentioned are *very* interesting as they not only share many similarities with Bruce's thought but, predating Bruce, they also share many similar positions as the Buddhists and the Hindus -- which speaks to the "there is but one family" human "root" that Bruce was so interested in seeking.

It's also interesting that these gospels had as much validity of any of the ones from rival Christian sects that were later canonized, but, owing to political -- rather than spiritual -- influence, the politically expedient doctrines were adopted and the rival opinions banished and destroyed (or so they thought), with the result that one belief became orthodox and the other heretical. Alan Watts and Joseph Campbell (who sites the book of Thomas from the Nag-Hammadi find quite frequently) make mention of these writings. Campbell, in particular, makes an interesting observation when he points out:

"...those Coptic papers talk about the brotherhood of all -- which is a Gnostic tradition. And there's that wonderful last answer in the Thomas Gospel when the disciples ask Jesus, "When will the kingdom come?" Now, the orthodox tradition has it that the kingdom will come historically. But the answer given in the Gnostic Gospel is that the kingdom comes psychologically, and not by expectation. This is a change in the point of view: it's a change of perspective. You can look on the other person as an "It," or you can look on the other person as your brother or sister, and consequently, the whole world changes."

This, of course, parallels Bruce's thinking, spiritually-speaking, in that "under the sky, under the heavens, there is but one family. It just so happens that people are different."

Similarly, there is one brotherhood -- one "divine" (if you will) source of energy from which all life comes. Call it "God," call it "Tao," call it the "living Void," call it what you will. And each one of us -- and everything else, for that matter -- is this energy expressing itself in various forms (ala Yin-yang). The Gospel of Thomas passage cited by Campbell is at the very end of the gospel, passage 113:

> "His followers said to him, 'When will the kingdom come?' 'It will not come by watching for it. It will not be said, 'Look, here it is,' or 'Look, there it is.' Rather, the father's kingdom is spread out upon the earth, and people do not see it.'"[26]

This viewpoint, that the "kingdom" is a metaphorical one that one needs to "wake up to" (bodhi), is essentially the Buddhist position that you must open your eyes to what is here and now and experience the fact that you are connected to this vast, eternal (cosmic) process. Alan Watts has written brilliantly on this point in his book *Myth and Religion* (Charles E. Tuttle Company).

James Bishop: You are well-informed of the Gnostic tradition! It's funny; I used to think how peculiar it was that Bruce's life, in many ways, mirrored that of Jesus. He died in his early thirties; he had a handful of students who continued his schools of thought; eventually, some of these students and their approaches grew away from each other. And then I come across the Gnostic tradition and find that the similarities become even more striking. I say similarities in an anthropological sense and how human belief systems develop, of course. It goes to show the parallelism of human development.

---

[26] Source: Page 65, *The Gospel According to Thomas*, translated by Marvin Meyer (c) 1992, Harper Collins, New York.

John Little: *I think there are actually more people who could benefit from his motivational and inspirational philosophy than would benefit from a learning how to execute the leg obstruction or hand-immobilization attack.* I must say that Martin O'Neill's work in Ireland is causing me to look at this very seriously; I must emphasize how impressed I am by his "knowing is not enough" approach. That impressed me more than just about anything else I've heard about in the Bruce Lee world and reveals a deeper understanding of what it's all about than most instructors of the art would be able to comprehend.

James Bishop: It's interesting, the effect that Bruce Lee can have on people. For example, I interviewed for an internship last year. It was for a technical writing position. They were so interested in my experience with the Bruce Lee thing (more so than the possible job in question) that it became less an interview than a philosophical class for the two supervisors who "interviewed" me. A simple 15 minute job interview turned into a 2 1/2 hour question and answer session on the philosophy of Bruce Lee, it's impact on me, and how it can be applied to life. At one point, one of the supervisors broke down and confided in me that she was going through a tough emotional time because she was just diagnosed with a lupus-like illness. I found myself becoming a confidant to this complete stranger, through no intention of my own. Most unusual, but I think the discussion had a profound effect on her, as well as on the other supervisor. Regardless of whether I got the position or not (I did), it felt good to know that I had impacted two individuals in a positive way.

I think one of our most daunting tasks is getting the academic philosophical circles to accept him. Obviously, they proceed from some of their preconceived notions of him. For instance, in my last year of undergraduate school I took a test on Ayer's *Language Truth and Logic*. I had to write an essay on his verification principle, including giving my opinions on it. I was able to throw in some Bruce Lee-influenced "partial segments of a totality"-type statements in the part where I questioned the positivistic versus metaphysic polarity, without mentioning his name. My teacher was impressed with my line of thinking, and when I told him that Bruce Lee was the genesis of that line of my thought, he was rather surprised. I feel that he might have been less accepting of the statements had he known that they were Bruce Lee-influenced in the first place. Instead, he was able to contemplate them without bringing in his prejudices of Bruce Lee first, and he found that the ideas were sound ideas.

I've had the opportunity to bring Bruce Lee's philosophical side to the attention of some rather surprised academics. When I spoke with Dr. Elaine Pagels (Harrington Spear Paine Professor of Religion at Princeton University and the author of *The Gnostic Gospels*) for my article on Bruce Lee and Gnostic Christianity, she was quite intrigued by the depth of Bruce's philosophy. Of course, like most, she only knew of Bruce as the action film star.

I caught the following comment from a French fan on an Internet Bruce Lee newsgroup. His English is not very good, but he said something I thought you might find interesting:

"We have to not forget that Bruce studied philosophy at a university. I have even seen one of his sentences in a seminary of the university La Sorbonne, in Paris. (You know, the sentence about becoming like water, form and non-form, strong and soft...)"

The Sorbonne, no less! It made me feel good.

John Little: Thanks for the sleuth work. I, too, am impressed that Bruce's water simile made it to the annals of the University of Sorbonne -- that's wonderful! I would like to find out who this professor was -- he would be a perfect candidate to write a preface to my forthcoming book in the Bruce Lee Library Series about Bruce's philosophy.[27]

James Bishop: You did an interview for radio station WBUR in Boston about Bruce Lee's philosophy in 1998. Do you remember what the name of the program was and on what date it aired?

John Little: The radio show was "The Connection", hosted by Christopher Lydon. It was a NPR show based in Boston. They have a web site, and I think you can order back copies of the show from them. I appeared on November 27, 1998 (on what would have been Bruce's 58th birthday). We really only touched on Bruce's philosophy as it was, more or less, an overview of Bruce Lee as something more than a fighter. I recall that it took

---

[27] Though I made some inquiries with some of my professional contacts in France, we never determined what professor had used the quote. The book that John Little is referring to is *Artist of Life*, from the Bruce Lee Library Series.

Lydon a while to thaw his existing perspective on Bruce Lee as simply a Van-Damme-esque character who commanded a "cultish" following, and to warm to the idea of Bruce Lee as a paragon of intellectual achievement and philosophic merit -- but, I'm pleased to say that he finally did come around, which was nice because Lydon, I believe, is a student of philosophy himself.

James Bishop: I received my copy of the Chris Lydon interview in the mail yesterday. I have to say how impressed I am again with your ability to talk about Bruce and convey the important points about him. I think Lydon best represented the ignorant viewpoint that so many people out there have about Bruce Lee. He already put me in a place I didn't want to be when he prefaced the interview by stating that Bruce had died in his mistress' bed. But you, of course, corrected him on that, and a great many other things as well. Also, the stories of the callers were very inspirational, and some mirrored my own in a sometimes uncanny sense. I think more interviews like this could go a long way toward spreading the word on Bruce Lee and his philosophy.

Even students of Bruce's martial art seem to have a problem accepting Bruce Lee as a philosopher. Your statement in the latest issue of *Knowing Is Not Enough*[28] that Bruce is the true root of Jeet Kune Do is drawing some criticism on some of the Internet forums. I think it was a valid point but apparently some people are still clinging to the old paradigm of Wing Chun as the "root" of Jeet Kune Do. I agree that the focus should be shifted from the base physical art Bruce evolved from to the "evolver" himself. After all, the genesis of JKD really took place in the mind of Bruce Lee.

John Little: I'm not surprised that some people with a partiality towards Wing Chun would disagree with my position. However, it seems to me irrefutable that there would not have been a Jeet Kune Do without Bruce Lee and, as you say, it was the mind of Bruce Lee that led him to study martial art in the first place, to question, to evolve, to research, to hypothesize, to create, to evolve, to grow, etc., etc.

James Bishop: I find that too many people are only interested in following the physical trail of his learning without acknowledging that it was his philosophical and analytical mind that was the true

---

[28] The official newsletter of the Bruce Lee Educational Foundation.

source of his genius. Paraphrasing Bruce, "It is unlikely that, when the root is neglected, what grows from it will be well-ordered."

Yet, many of them just don't get that. I have followed these Internet discussion threads (I learned fairly quickly after discovering such groups that it is really useless to participate in such discussions) and the latest one, for instance, begins: "Philosophy aside, Jeet Kune Do is the physical......," and goes on to argue their point about physical aspects of it. Their argument is self-defeating, however, because you cannot set the "philosophy aside". That's clinging to one partial segment of a totality!

In the argument about your statement that Bruce Lee is the true root of Jeet Kune Do, one forum poster said this: "I think what he [John Little] was saying was this thing is about Bruce and not a system. But it doesn't change the fact that Bruce took a lot of good stuff from Wing Chun and I don't think that was what John Little meant. There is a movement to make Bruce some kind of spiritual guru or even like Plato."

Obviously, there is resistance to the idea of Bruce Lee as a philosopher, as anything other than a martial artist. When it comes down to it, I think it is a combination of fear on the part of the practitioner about the complex philosophies and the prejudicial view of Bruce Lee that is the unfortunate by-product of his movie legacy.

John Little: The passage you site of Bruce's is one of my favorites as "root" (in terms of plumbing the depths of ultimate truth and seeking a common denominator) is a touchstone of Bruce's thought that keeps resurfacing in all of the many "branches" of his thought, such as martial art, film, philosophy, etc.

James Bishop: What, in your opinion, is the ultimate philosophical question? I believe it is the question of what lies after death. In fact, I think that that question (or fear of death) is the primary basis for all philosophy. We question existence because our own is so finite. That's my take on it. What's yours?

John Little: Your question is an interesting one. I think Pilates' question "What is truth?" is, perhaps, the "ultimate" philosophical, as--until that is answered--i.e., until we can know what is true, and have standards for determining what is true, no other answer can hold any meaning. I even think the question "What is death?" precedes "What lies after death?" as, again, until we know what we mean by a given term, what "lies after it" is meaningless. There...my hat has now been thrown into the "ultimate philosophical question" ring!

James Bishop: I understand you point. However, I feel that the fear of death is what causes us to question in the first place. It is, as Shakespeare put it, the "undiscovered country, from whose borne no traveler returns." Sounds like the ultimate chicken or the egg argument. Hey, maybe that's the ultimate philosophical question!

John Little: It's funny, with Bruce you read about his life story, his views, and how he dealt with adversity, and you realize that anything is possible. I would have never, in a million years, guessed that I would be supporting myself and my family from doing something that I love, which is telling people about the significance of Bruce Lee. I never would have guessed that that would have been a possibility. And yet, now there is a Bruce Lee Educational Foundation that has been established and there are twelve volumes of the Bruce Lee Library Series in total that will be released. I was able to do a film in which Bruce was given a platform to speak for himself about his life, his art, and his career."

What's nice about the *Bruce Lee Library Series* is that whenever you want to visit with Bruce he's between the pages of his books. If you want an answer to a question about Bruce you don't have to rely on an interpreter or some other martial art instructor who might be trying to sell you real estate.

James Bishop: I'm eager to move on to the next essay I will write on Bruce's philosophy of self-actualization. I really think this can be an answer to a great deal of society's problems. Further on down the line I would like to even build on the concept of self-actualization and maybe do a self-help book on just that. Do you know of any books or authors that influenced Bruce in this area? Besides Hugh Prather, whose excerpts I found very interesting (and enjoyable) in the latest "Knowing".

John Little: Books that influenced Bruce in the self-help arena -- God! Where would I start? Carl Rogers, Fritz Perls (*heavy* *influence*, in fact, almost all of the "psychology" section of *Artist of Life*[29] are verbatim jottings of Bruce's from reading the works of Perls. These would resurface later in Bruce's own essays on "Self Actualization and Self-Image Actualization in the art of acting" and other writings). Krishnamurti, Lao Tzu, Chuang Tzu, Watts, Hesse, Buddha's admonition to be "a refuge unto yourself" (among other were also undoubtedly contributors to Bruce's conclusions in this regard). With regard to self-help, there is a vast array of authors and titles such as Napoleon Hill, W. Clement Stone, Vernon Howard, Robert Powell, to name but a few.

James Bishop: I think I speak for the majority of Bruce Lee fans when I say we are extremely grateful to you for disseminating the work and teachings of Bruce Lee. Speaking for myself, you continue to be an inspiration and role model to me as a Bruce Lee fan, a friend, and a writer.

John Little: I'm of very little worth as a role model or inspiration. I'm simply trying my best to allow Bruce Lee to have a say in how his life, legacy, art and philosophy are presented. I think he has suffered over the years from being "interpreted" by just about everybody. With so much material available -- written in his own hand -- there exists no need for any "representatives" to speak for him (hence, the premise behind "In His Own Words").

What I like, and what I think is why I feel so strongly about it, is that it is so important to let him speak for himself, not to get it second-hand or to rely on someone's faded memory of what he said or how he believed because, by and large, everyone who has claimed to be his representative has been wrong. His words reveal that. That's okay for them; they are allowed to grow and develop and do whatever it is they feel they must to get through life. But when they start bringing Bruce Lee into it as the reason that they are doing it, and trying to mangle quotes or misquote him, that I take offense to. I guess it would be because somebody has to protect the purity of what he said so people will know what he said. Otherwise, it will be lost. I think that's the best job as an editor, to keep your thumbprint off of stuff. That's how I edit the Bruce Lee Library books. I don't want my thumbprint on it

---

[29] The title of the book, *Artist of Life*, comes from a statement that Bruce Lee made in which he said he considered himself an artist of life. Lee took this phrase from Eugen Herrigel's book, *Zen in the Art of Archery*, in the preface by D.T. Suzuki, where Suzuki writes: "When a man reaches this stage of 'spiritual' development, he is a Zen artist of life."

anywhere because then how credible would it be? It's got to be from Bruce, and it's got to be *pure* Bruce; otherwise, it's not worth any of it. In fact, you would be masking his voice instead of giving him a megaphone through which to broadcast it.

THE IRISH VISIT

Acknowledgement should be made to Paul Crossey and Martin O'Neill, who contributed a wee bit to the text of the following chapter. Slainte!

Perhaps my most meaningful work on behalf of Bruce Lee's philosophy involved our visit to Northern Ireland. We journeyed to Ireland at the behest of Martin O'Neill, a senior social worker and Jeet Kune Do instructor, who (as I mentioned in detail in a previous chapter) was having great success in uniting Protestants and Catholics using Bruce Lee's celebrity and inclusive philosophy. I, along with John Little and Andy Kimura, Taky Kimura's son, shared Lee's philosophy with the people of Ireland, giving them insights into his life and how his philosophy could be applied to their own.

Martin O'Neill explained the reasons behind the visit, saying, "I wanted to give Bruce Lee's philosophy an opportunity to reach out to my students and also non-martial artists in Ireland. Everyone has heard of Bruce Lee; his striking cinematic stardom has made him known the world over. However, during the past few years, the publicity of his writings has been able to illustrate that Bruce Lee was much more than a martial artist."

Martin O'Neill says that the visit came at an important time in Irish history. "The cease-fires in 1994 brought a new sense of hope in Northern Ireland," notes O'Neill. "When the Loyalist and Republican paramilitaries declared cease-fires, it lifted a terrible pressure from the community (1.5 million people), which had endured and coped with the relentless violence of the conflict since the mid-1960s. There have been 4,000 deaths, 40,000 injured and billions of pounds in damage to the economy. Unfortunately, the cease-fires were too late for many people, those dead, injured, bereaved and traumatized. For the first time, it became possible to examine the depth of bereavement, loss, and pain felt across the country because of the deep division between the two main traditions, Loyalist (allegiance to Britain) and Nationalist (allegiance to Ireland). Those who have been injured or bereaved have been mainly civilians unconnected to the paramilitaries or security forces. These individuals have often been randomly targeted in a brutal campaign of terror."

In Northern Ireland everyone has been affected in some way by the conflict. "No one has a monopoly on suffering or the moral high ground although many try to claim this," O'Neill noted. "If Ireland is to have a peaceful future, we must be willing to acknowledge the deep hurt and mistrust there has arisen over decades of injustice and hatred. If we are to have a future as a civilized society we must work to comfort those bereaved and hurt and also those physically and psychologically injured. We must listen to each other, not with hard hearts but with compassion. We need to value real peace if we can achieve it and not forget how precious it is."

It was against this backdrop that Little, Kimura, and I visited Ireland to give a lecture tour. The purpose of the lecture tour was to share Bruce Lee's authentic legacy with people in Ireland, give people an insight into his philosophy, and demonstrate how Bruce Lee's ideas can help people overcome obstacles and barriers and reach their goals in life. The lectures also celebrated Bruce Lee as a human being, a man who stood against racism and sectarianism and once said, "Under the stars, under the heavens there is but one family." The Jun Fan/Jeet Kune Do Association Ireland also wished to use Bruce Lee as a role model for people in Ireland who stood against hatred and bigotry.

On Monday evening, September 25th, we visited the Clann Eireann Youth Club. This club is based in a deprived Nationalist area and is the location of Martin O'Neill's Jun Fan/Jeet Kune Do club. There was an informal discussion and certificates were presented to students of the year Paul Crossey and Andre Farrell.

I was very impressed with the character of Martin O'Neill's students. There was a real feeling of honest enthusiasm evident in the club that night. Their sincere inquiries into Bruce Lee's philosophies (and our work) were an absolute delight.

On Tuesday, September 26th, the day began with an interview on BBC radio's *Talkback* program, which focuses on current affairs. Despite being a short interview, John Little managed to an excellent job of summarizing the key elements of Bruce Lee's philosophy.

In the evening, we gave a lecture on Bruce Lee's philosophy at Queen's University in Belfast, Northern Ireland. I chose the opportunity to explore Bruce Lee's interest in humanistic psychology, teaching the students about self-actualization and reclaiming their locus of evaluation. The lecture gave me an opportunity to introduce them to the works of Carl Rogers and Abraham Maslow via Bruce Lee.

Irishman Keith Coffey found the concepts of self-actualization particularly interesting, saying, "The lecture put what I had read into perspective. James Bishop went very deep into the concept of self-actualization, and it was a bit hard to understand, but given the time-limit of one lecture he managed to fit in a lot of information."

The lecture succeeded in introducing fans to a new side of Bruce Lee. Said Tony McAtamney, a Belfast resident: "It helped us understand Bruce Lee's mind. When I had trained before I had not known this deep, philosophical side of Bruce Lee, and now I can apply his philosophy to my own training." It is safe to say that most people left the lecture hall with at least a slightly different outlook on life and possibly gained a wider and more positive perspective on the world.

On Wednesday, September 27th, we visited the Ashton Centre and Star Youth Club in the New Lodge area of Belfast. This area has been the brunt of much violence and tension and is situated on the peace line between loyalist and nationalist communities. Little, Kimura, and I spoke to Ashton Centre representative Jim Deery and his colleagues about their efforts to promote peace and community development in the area.[30]

"I was very impressed by the fact that the social workers in Ireland were bringing people together using elements of Bruce Lee's philosophy," said John Little. "Tenets such as self-empowerment, self-actualization and the eroding of sectarianism -- all touchstones in the philosophy of Bruce Lee -- were being applied to positive effect in Ireland. In facing these facts, and recognizing that the Irish people cannot afford to waste time on inert ideas or vague speculations, lest people die -- one can no longer say that Bruce Lee's realm is solely within the circle of martial arts enthusiasts.

"Linda Lee Cadwell once observed that 'Bruce viewed himself as a citizen of the world with a mission.' This was certainly proven true in Ireland. Walking the "Peace Line" with Jim Deery, and talking to Jim, Martin O'Neill, and other social workers who likewise saw value in Bruce Lee's approach to civil issues further underscored the growing belief that Lee's appeal and greatest

---

[30] We were all thoroughly impressed with Jim Deery and his work at the Ashton Centre. In the summer of 2001, the Ashton Centre was the victim of a sniper attack by a Loyalist hit squad. Fortunately, no one was injured in the attack.

contribution may well be in the more 'human' sciences, such as sociology, civil rights and, of course, philosophy."

Later that day we ate dinner at the home of Martin O'Neill. On our way there we witnessed a group of young boys mercilessly beating and kicking another boy in the street. They were run off by O'Neill, but I got a strong sense that it was a common sight.

On Thursday, September 28th, we traveled to Dublin in the Republic of Ireland. That evening, Little, Kimura and I gave a lecture at Dublin's Trinity College, the home to such historic luminaries as James Joyce, George Bernard Shaw, Oscar Wilde, and Bram Stoker. John Little's lecture focused on Bruce Lee's philosophy of goal setting. Andy Kimura spoke about his father's friendship with Bruce Lee and how his father became Bruce Lee's highest ranked student. There was a great atmosphere at the lecture and the audience asked many questions. I spoke on Bruce Lee's efforts to erode racial and nationalistic boundaries and the effect that he has had on the way others perceive people different from them.

"It was quite a feeling being at Trinity College," said Andy Kimura. "It was a very impressive location for Bruce Lee's thought to be laid out. I believe that this is the kind of place that Bruce's thought should be presented in, the hallowed halls of Trinity and places like that, which are deserving of hearing his thought."

John Blessing, a Dublin resident, was quite impressed with the lectures. "The lectures the Bruce Lee Educational Foundation gave were extremely meaningful to me and my friends. We all learned quite a bit about Bruce Lee's teaching and how to live a better life. When you study such a great man's life, one can't help but learn from it and apply it to your own."

"I think the lectures were a great success," said Martin O'Neill. "People enjoyed them and those who came to the lectures were not necessarily just martial artists. I think there was a good mix of people. There were men and women there from all walks of life, people who were interested in Bruce and had heard about Bruce in a host of different ways and weren't necessarily interested in the martial arts side. They were interested in the deeper meanings of what Bruce was about and had to say, and what he had to say is still relevant. I believe it speaks out in Ireland and particularly Northern Ireland. We have had a lot of problems, and Bruce Lee himself acts as a rallying point for people, and I think that is tremendous. Obviously, we need all the help we can get in Northern Ireland, and I think having Bruce Lee's art brought to the people here is just excellent."

To me, it was tremendously gratifying, the opportunity we had to travel to Ireland and use Bruce Lee's philosophy and his notoriety to make a difference in the lives of its people. I believe the work we have done there is going to have positive repercussions. It was a great honor to launch our philosophy symposiums in such prestigious places and make a little bit of history.

For John Little, the trip was especially meaningful. The day before we left, he told me, "I think this week represents the culmination of a personal dream for me, which was to see Bruce Lee's philosophy and thought accepted and taught at the highest possible academic level: Trinity College, with its rich history and tradition, and Queen's University before that. Trinity, in particular, because it was home to the likes of James Joyce and Bram Stoker, was a particularly meaningful environment to present Bruce's thought because it put Bruce Lee's thought on a par with all of the other great philosophers and thinkers that were taught there, and it's no secret that I think that Bruce's true legacy lies in his thought."

We had great hopes as a result of the trip. The three of us returned with a commitment to continue the path we had begun. At the next meeting of the Bruce Lee Educational Foundation's board of directors, Andy Kimura and John Little, both members of the board, informed them of our work in Ireland. Some on the board reiterated their aversion to the idea of Bruce Lee's philosophy, but they could not argue about the value that it was beginning to represent. They agreed to Little's idea to spin off a special division of the foundation to concentrate entirely on the philosophy of Bruce Lee and a plan to establish a book publishing division through the foundation.

The first book published was to be a book about Bruce Lee's effect on the people of Ireland, which would include our lectures and talks. Little, Kimura and I agreed to forgo any compensation and allow all the proceeds to go to the social programs run by Jim Deery and Martin O'Neill. In addition, I filmed the entire visit, and we planned to edit the footage into a documentary to sell through the foundation, generating yet more money for the social programs in Ireland. My only stipulation, of course, was that none of the money went into the martial art seminars and training programs of the board members.

Our dreams never materialized, however. Shortly thereafter, Bruce Lee's daughter Shannon assumed the role of executor of the Estate of Bruce Lee, and there was a marked shift in focus, leading to the resignation of John Little from the board of directors of the Bruce Lee Educational Foundation and his involvement with the Estate of Bruce Lee. It was a disturbing turn of events, and one that left so much promise unfulfilled.

The Bridge
That Bruce Lee Built

This chapter was a lecture I gave at Trinity College in Dublin, Ireland on September 28, 2000. It was both an indirect appeal for peace in Ireland and a recognition of the cosmopolitan worldview of Bruce Lee fans in every part of the globe.

As much as Bruce Lee rejected "styles" of martial arts, he also rejected "styles" of human beings. Many fans and devotees of Lee have recognized this philosophy in the way that he lived and expressed himself. Indeed, his recognition of the unity of mankind and his determination to eliminate those boundaries was at the heart of his success and appeal, creating a "bridge" between people and cultures. Just as his legacy continues to spread throughout the world, the bridge that Bruce Lee built continues to grow as well.

Bruce Lee's own cultural makeup and early experiences may have played a large part in the formulation of his unified worldview. It has been said that other students of Sifu Yip Man discriminated against Lee (who was 1/8th German) because they objected to Yip Man's teaching of someone who was not "completely" Chinese. This was, in itself, a response to the long history of discrimination and persecution that the Chinese had suffered at the hands of other races, most notably the Japanese and the British. Regardless of his mixed ancestry, Bruce Lee was as impacted by British discrimination as any other Chinese person living in Hong Kong at the time.

Bruce Lee's education in racial prejudice continued in the United States, where his arrival coincided with the beginning of the civil rights era. Lee bore witness to the struggles of black Americans, as well as experiencing prejudice against Asians and immigrants himself.

Taky Kimura, one of Bruce Lee's senior students and a Japanese-American, remembers the impact that Bruce Lee had on him. "All the time we were growing up my mother and dad always said: 'Look, we're nothing but second-class citizens, so don't ever put yourself in the mainstream of life because you are going to get hurt.' We argued with them because the educational system told us that we were equal under the constitution. But then (when World War II came along) all of a sudden things changed, and we were put in the internment camps, even though we were citizens. The Selective Service put us in the 4Y category, which was an alien classification, and they told us that there were rumors that they were going to take us and ship us off to some island as soon as they could get rid of us."

Kimura spent five years in a United States internment camp and suffered difficulty in getting a decent job afterward, under the shadow of post-war anti-Japanese sentiment. "I came out and I was just a broken man because of this humiliation that occurred within myself. And then in 1959 I had the wonderful honor of being in the right place at the right time to meet Bruce.

"He was eighteen, a typical teenager with all this boundless energy, telling dirty jokes and all that, and I was thirty-six and just mentally devastated. I couldn't relate to that, but he understood.

"Bruce came along and helped me out. He used to say, 'Jesus Christ, Kimura! Look at these clothes you're wearing! You look like an old man!' He told me to wear different clothes and all this kind of stuff. It was all a part of making me realize that I am a human being, no better or worse than anyone else. He told that repeatedly to me, and (by teaching you the fundamentals of physicalness within yourself) obviously, you start feeling better about yourself when you know that you can do something. I think that that is one of the great things. Unfortunately, we all have to go through this process to understand what our capabilities are."

It is remarkable, given his experiences, that even at the age of 18, Bruce Lee had developed a perception of people that was not divided across lines of race, gender, nationality, or socio-economic background. "To me," said Lee, "this kind of racial barrier does not exist. If I say I believe that 'everyone under the sun' is a member of a universal family, you may think that I am bluffing and being idealistic. But if anyone still believes in racial differences, I think he is too backward and narrow. Perhaps he still does not understand man's equality and love."[31]

---

[31] Source: page 119 of the book *Words of the Dragon*, edited by John Little, Published by the Charles E. Tuttle Publishing Company, Boston, copyright 1997 Linda Lee Cadwell.

"Bruce's first group of students were from a variety of races," says Jesse Glover, an African-American and Bruce Lee's first student. "He was certainly proud of being Chinese, but he never thought less of his students for not being Chinese." From the time that Bruce Lee started teaching the martial arts, he broke tradition by teaching people, regardless of their ethnicity, a fact that eventually brought him into direct conflict with the immigrant Chinese community in America.

In late 1964 Wong Jack Man, a newly arrived member of the Chinese-American community in San Francisco, challenged Bruce Lee on behalf of the Chinese elders of the community, who were upset that Lee was teaching gung fu to the *gwei lo*, or "foreign devils". Lee took up the challenge and won, asserting his right to teach whomever he chose. This event is considered a turning point in the evolution of Lee's martial art of Jeet Kune Do, but it is also important because it showed how resolute Lee was in defending and advancing his belief of racial unity.

As a developing actor in Hollywood, Bruce Lee found that his race had become an obstacle to his success. Producers were resistant to his portrayal of Kato in the *Green Hornet* and, aware that he was fast becoming more popular than the star of the show, actively tried to restrain him. After the cancellation of the *Green Hornet* series, Lee found it almost impossible to make a living as an actor. Parts in Hollywood for Asians were few and far between, and the roles that were available were invariably demeaning. Lee insisted that he would not reinforce Chinese stereotypes. "It's always the pigtail and bouncing around going 'chop-chop'. I have already made up my mind that in the United States, something about the Oriental, I mean the *true* Oriental, should be shown."[32]

"Bruce was quite aware that skin color mattered in the United States and, for that matter, most places in the world," says Jesse Glover. "He knew that it would be very difficult for him to break into the movies over here."

The culmination of Hollywood's mistreatment of Bruce Lee occurred with the launch of the television series *Kung Fu*, a concept that Lee created and intended to star in. The producers, citing Bruce Lee as being too Chinese, chose Caucasian actor David Carradine to play the role of the Asian immigrant.

---

[32] Source: Bruce Lee quoted on page 16 of the book *Bruce Lee: Words From a Master*, edited by John Little, Published by Contemporary Books, Chicago, copyright 1999 John R. Little and Robert Wolff.

Despite the mounting prejudice that Bruce Lee faced in Hollywood, he was determined to succeed. Following the Taoist belief that, "when two opposing forces collide, the victory will go to the one that knows how to yield," he took an opportunity to make films in Hong Kong. If Lee could not yet conquer Hollywood, he would conquer the rest of the world.

Perhaps through these experiences Bruce Lee observed that humanity has many commonalities, including the capacity to discriminate and hate. "Human traits are the same everywhere," said Lee.[33] It is clear that he began to realize that divisions of race, religion, and nationality were illusory boundaries that men imposed on themselves. "I, Bruce Lee, am a man who never follows those fearful formulas. So, no matter if your color is black, white, red or blue, I can still make friends with you without any barrier."[34]

Discovering the "Root" of Man

"When you understand the root," said Bruce Lee, "you understand all of its blossoming." Lee was concerned with finding out what it really means to be human, in all its various facets. As individuals come to understand what "humanity" really is, they can then begin to truly accept and embrace the diversity of cultures and ideas. No longer are they influenced by xenophobia; they see these differences in people as a natural progression of the "root" as it continues to grow outward - splitting into different branches of the same "family" that take on their own distinct appearance. Yet the common "root" between the branches of man remains an important and vital link. To ignore that common link is to invite inevitable destruction. No tree can ignore its roots - it is that upon which its continued survival is based. Or in Bruce Lee's own words: "It cannot be when the root is neglected, that what should spring from it will be well ordered."[35]

By recognizing the root, the individual is able to discard notions of separativeness and look at the world and the people in it with a liberated mind. "To understand," said Bruce Lee, "there

---

[33] Source: page 5 of the book *Words of the Dragon*, edited by John Little, Published by the Charles E. Tuttle Publishing Company, Boston, copyright 1997 Linda Lee Cadwell.

[34] Source: page 119 of the book *Words of the Dragon*, edited by John Little, Published by the Charles E. Tuttle Publishing Company, Boston, copyright 1997 Linda Lee Cadwell.

[35] Source: Bruce Lee quoted on page 36 of the book *Letters of the Dragon*, edited by John Little, Published by the Charles E. Tuttle Publishing Company, Boston, copyright 1998 Linda Lee Cadwell.

must be a state of choiceless awareness in which there is no sense of comparison or condemnation, no waiting for a further development of the thing we are talking about in order to agree or disagree - don't start from a conclusion above all."[36]

Racism and the need for unity were underlying themes in all of Bruce Lee's films. In Fist of Fury Lee invigorated the Chinese sense of pride with his heroic portrayal of a man who stands up to imperial Japan, proving that the "Chinese are no longer the sick men of Asia". In *Way of the Dragon*, Lee confronted Western prejudice. The concluding fight between Lee and Chuck Norris was not a fight between a Western and a Chinese, but a battle between gladiators who saw each other in terms of ability, not race.

Bruce Lee succeeded on two fronts: in a sense, he knocked down the "Great Wall of China", revealing the beauty of a culture and society to the Western world in a way that no one else could do. For the Chinese themselves, Lee became a symbol that they could be proud of. They knew that, through Bruce Lee, the rest of the world would recognize the value and strength of the Chinese people.

"Although I never met him, Bruce has been a positive role model in my life and has impressed me deeply," says Jeff Chinn, a Bruce Lee memorabilia collector from Daly City, California. Chinn has one of the most extensive Bruce Lee memorabilia collections in the world. "He was the first person I've ever heard say that he was proud to be Chinese. Bruce, more than anyone else, showed me how a Chinese could be just as good as anyone else. In fact, some of my favorite scenes from his movies are the ones in which Bruce fought racism."

"My very first exposure to Bruce Lee was watching him as Kato on the ABC TV series *The Green Hornet* in 1966," continues Chinn. Since I was only five years old at the time, I only knew him as Kato and not as Bruce Lee. I remember that my entire family watched this TV show every Friday night, and it was very special to all of us. Chinese were practically invisible on TV in those days (even now), and we always noticed whenever a Chinese appeared on the screen. But it was even more special watching Kato because he was not the usual stereotypical weak 'Ahh So' Chinese that were so common back then. For once we felt good after watching 'one of us' on TV."

---

[36] Source: page 357 of the book *Jeet Kune Do: Commentaries On the Martial Way*, edited by John Little, Published by the Charles E. Tuttle Publishing Company, Boston, copyright 1998 Linda Lee Cadwell.

"In the entertainment field and sports, American martial arts expert Bruce Lee captivated the movie audiences of this nation, while destroying the stereotype of the passive, quiet Asian male," said the Honorable Eni F. H. Faleomavaega, a United States congressman.

Ripples in the Pond

Bruce Lee has continued to inspire people along this path long after his passing. There are new generations of people who embrace the tenets of his philosophy of racial unity. It is one of the primary lessons that his many fans worldwide absorb from his movies, writings, and martial art.

"I was just a kid when I first saw *Enter the Dragon*," says Marcos Ocaña, a teacher from Madrid, Spain. "My father rented it when I was around 6 years old. I had never seen other cultures (meaning that I was not aware of any other cultures but mine). In Spain there weren't many people from other races, no black people or Asians. I watched *Enter the Dragon* at night when my parents were sleeping, and I discovered a whole new world with plenty of beautiful things and that 'strange' philosophy that I had never heard before (and, of course, I didn't understand very well). That created a desire in me to learn more and more about this incredible man."

Ocaña says that he developed a fascination with other cultures through Bruce Lee. "I felt captivated by the oriental atmosphere, and I started reading books about the subject. I discovered the samurais, the Japanese culture, and many other things. Of course, I wanted to be like Bruce Lee and all those things, and each time I did see an Oriental person I started asking myself how it would be in their country.

"Oriental culture took me to other cultures, and I discovered the Indian cultures. I own a lot of books about cultures and things related to them: tales, legends, stories, poetry, and biographies."

As a child growing up, Ocaña began to recognize the way in which people separate themselves. "I was in a class with plenty of children who enjoyed insulting each other because they didn't wear certain kinds of clothes or because they had physical defects. Sometimes it was my turn to hear people calling me 'poor man' or things like that because my pants weren't "Levi's" or nonsense like that. I saw many people emotionally broken, tired of always hearing the other children against them. Some chose to quit school, others (like the girls) developed problems such as anorexia. It was also very common to be insulted by other people when you did something better than them. The truth is, after several years like this, either you developed a strong personality or you ended up being stepped on by the rest. I personally did not have much trouble. I always 'flowed' with these things quite well, but it made me trust very few other people."

Ocaña's fascination with Bruce Lee spotlighted some of the discrimination and misconceptions that Lee was trying to expose. "My father always referred to the martial arts (that included Bruce Lee) as nonsense. When I was a child, he didn't want to buy me books about Bruce Lee and I developed a kind of self-shame when I talked about martial arts. I only felt comfortable when I talked to someone who shared my interest in the arts. Only now that I've earned my second degree black belt and published a Bruce Lee book does he (my father) see that it's something quite serious and seems to accept it (although he'll never let me know it)."

Through Bruce Lee, Marcos Ocaña learned to look past the appearance of a person and appreciate what is inside them. "I tended to be one of those who think that after talking ten minutes with a person, I can have a very accurate view of him. Studying Bruce Lee's life, how he learned from so many different sources, I realized I should never reject people because of 'first impressions'. You never know what good things a person can offer you."

Marcos Ocaña gives expression to the lessons he learned from Bruce Lee through his job as a teacher at the School Gredos San Diego in Madrid. "I've always used Bruce Lee's lessons in the schools where I have worked. I'm a teacher, and I try to make people understand that there are not differences among people. We are diverse yet similar at the same time. In the school where I now work I have pupils from many different nationalities. It's so big, the amount of exponents from different cultures, that it's like a good 'rock' to work with, chiseling all those 'imperfections' that make some children want to prove that they're better than the rest. Bruce Lee's way of seeing things is really helping me to give them examples of how things can be done through cooperation, learning from different cultures and taking what they can for their own self-improvement. That way, we can honestly express ourselves in life. I think that I'm succeeding in teaching my pupils at school this way."[37]

Bruce Lee's example as a person who respected all people taught Dean Routledge, a Bruce Lee fan from Cardiff, Wales, to look past the prejudices of other people and to evaluate his own as well. "I'd like to say I was never prejudiced, but that's just not true. We all tend to prejudge to a certain extent. I think the main thing I have learned from reading Bruce's work and philosophy is to see every person of every nation as the same as I am. It doesn't matter what color, shape or size a person is. We are all the same. We have the same traits, fears, goals and disappointments as we go through our lives. I know that when I get up in the morning to go to work, in Calcutta another guy is doing exactly the same. Just because someone is a different color or speaks a different language doesn't mean that essentially, as a human being, they are any better or worse than I am. To say that they are is, in my opinion, very narrow-minded, and to propagate such a belief is very cruel.

"Through reading Bruce Lee's work, I feel that I myself have learned an appreciation, a tolerance, and a caring for my fellow man. I've learned to be open-minded and embrace other cultures. It's something I believe, and it's the way I try to live my life and the way I will try to raise my sons. Bruce has made me aware of myself as a human being and has helped me discover my own process. I am honestly expressing myself and I have him to thank."

Macario Rivas, also of Spain, thinks that Bruce Lee's impact on world culture has been profound. "I think that Bruce changed a great deal of people of my generation in my country and in all the world's people. All cultures respect Bruce Lee."

Bruce Lee believed that racism was an extension of the racist individual's inner fears, a convenient outlet for their own angst. "Any idea that is constantly held in the mind and emotionalized begins at once to clothe itself in the most convenient and appropriate physical form that is available."[38] Man fears losing what he works for and instead of reflecting internally on the logic

---

[37] In the years since I met Marcos Ocaña, we have come to be great friends. Ocaña is the recognized leading historian on Bruce Lee in the Spanish-language world, and, in 2003, T&B Editores, one of Spain's premier publishers of books on cinema, released Ocaña's *Bruce Lee: El Hombre Detrás de la Leyenda*, one of the most comprehensive biographies ever written on the subject of Bruce Lee.

[38] Source: page 369 of the book *Jeet Kune Do: Commentaries On the Martial Way,* edited by John Little, Published by the Charles E. Tuttle Publishing Company, Boston, copyright 1998 Linda Lee Cadwell.

of that fear, he justifies his paranoia by identifying those different from him as the "source" of his frustrations, when the true "source" is within him.

"Suffice to say, racism is everywhere. Having lived in the United Kingdom for over 20 years, I've seen and experienced it," says Hong Kong resident Simon Leung, who spent his childhood growing up in Scotland. "It's not a pretty picture, but then racism - as it's often been described - can have quite an ugly face to it.

"Since growing up there from the age of seven, I've gotten into many, many fights over it. It's ranged from the petty school yard taunts to grown drunken men attacking me for no other reason than the fact that they perceived me as belonging to the Triads and that I should be going back to my own country. I've seen my parents' house and shop windows smashed countless times, and my uncle was even stabbed in the stomach by a brother of a girl he was dating (yes, she was white). The list goes on and on, and it's not uniquely the experience of me, my family, or the Chinese here, but that of most, if not all, immigrants and other ethnic minorities."

"As I said, racism is pretty ugly when you see it up close. But, thankfully, it's not always there. It happens, and when it does it's pretty bad, but there is appreciation and acceptance as well. Many, many times, my friends have told me that they don't even see me as Chinese and that race isn't even an issue at all."

Leung says that, while prejudice still exists, Bruce Lee has made a definite impact on the way the West views the Chinese. "Of course, there are those who still do see the Chinese in me, but that's cool because when they ask me sincerely whether I know kung fu or Bruce Lee, or ask me what Hong Kong is like, or ask me if I know what a certain Chinese food is called, it shows an appreciation and respect of me and my culture that is the total antithesis of what it otherwise could be. This makes me hopeful and proud."

Many of today's generation are benefiting from the path that Bruce Lee tread in the sixties and seventies, such as Alwen Laguatan of California. "As for the prejudice thing, I've been pretty lucky in that point. I've never encountered it at all. I guess I owe that to all those that came before me. I've done research on how bad it was just 30-40 years ago here (the San Francisco Bay Area). Today, Filipinos (in general) have it pretty good here. Those that grew up here have it even better, including me. With the fact that we are so culturally diverse here in California, there is no choice but to tolerate every nationality, or we cannot function in society as a whole.

"I also believe that Bruce Lee, beyond the martial arts, was a man of tolerance. I think that was his biggest influence on me, and also the belief that it doesn't matter who you are--you can do and be whatever you want to be."

The "Totality" of Men

When asked whether he considered himself Chinese or American, Bruce Lee responded: "You know how I like to think of myself? As a human being. Under the stars, under the heavens, there is but one family."[39] This statement is a continuation of his premise that "there is no such thing as an effective segment of a totality". It is an idea that echoes the words of many noted advocates of racial unity, including Abraham Lincoln and Martin Luther King, Jr. Peace and progress come only when we recognize the human race as a whole. "Completeness is an absence of the conscious mind striving to divide that which is indivisible," said Lee. "For once the completeness of things is taken apart, it is no longer complete."[40]

One of the most profound examples of Bruce Lee's impact on cultural relations is in Belfast, Northern Ireland, where Martin O'Neill, a Jeet Kune Do instructor and senior social worker, is using Bruce Lee's philosophy to bridge the gulf between Protestants and Catholics.

"In Northern Ireland people live separate lives and a separate existence," says O'Neill. "It's hard for Americans to understand that. Many Protestants and Catholics live in separate areas, which is very sad. But I think that Bruce's art gives us an opportunity to bring people together because his art transcends color or creed. It gives people an opportunity to come together and train and build friendships. That's what's important, I think. Here in my school they come together and, through the example of Bruce Lee, discover that they have much more in common than they have in differences."

Wrote Bruce Lee: "When the elder generation says "no" to something, they strongly disapprove of it. If they say that

---

[39] Source: Bruce Lee quoted on page 20 of the book *Bruce Lee: Words From a Master*, edited by John Little, Published by Contemporary Books, Chicago, copyright 1999 John R. Little and Robert Wolff.

[40] Source: page 40 of the book *Artist of Life,* edited by John Little, Published by the Charles E. Tuttle Publishing Company, Boston, copyright 1999 Linda Lee Cadwell.

something is wrong, they also believe that it is wrong. They seldom use their minds to find out the truth and seldom express sincerely their real feeling. In fact, tradition is nothing but a formula laid down by experience. As we progress and time changes, it is necessary to reform this formula. For example, some people fight against each other because they believe in different religions. Actually, if they think a bit more, they will not fight for such a foolish cause."

In Martin O'Neill's Jun Fan/Jeet Kune Do school Catholics and Protestants train side by side and are immersed in the principles of Bruce Lee's personal philosophy. They learn to understand the deeper meaning of Bruce Lee's words and soon realize that they are a part of a greater whole called humanity, and not simply an isolated sub-group which can afford to ignore the rest of society. They begin to see people in terms of the bigger picture, something that 800 years of fighting and politicizing has failed to accomplish.

"We, as a planet, have so much to offer one another, yet we can't see to cross the great cultural divide," says Dean Routledge. "As we find it easier to travel to foreign parts, it is becoming easier to access foreign cultures and traditions. I think that Bruce Lee helped to push the notion that we are all the same beings, just with different languages and colors of skin. I am very much aware of my own culture, but that doesn't mean I will exclude others. It's almost a yin/yang type situation. In order to be total in my own culture, I have to understand others."

This is a key component of Bruce Lee's philosophy, encapsulated in his statement that "to be is to be related". Man cannot exist without his fellow man. Or, as the poet and philosopher John Donne said so eloquently, "No man is an island, entire of himself; every man is a piece of the continent."

The importance of this idea is in the relationships between human beings. "Man is living in a relationship, and in relationships we grow."[41] Bruce Lee recognized that human existence requires relating to other human beings. Problems arise when people try to ignore this fact and reject their fellow man. Wrote Lee, "How on earth can we truthfully understand and feel relationship if we

[41] Source: page 29 of the book *Jeet Kune Do: Commentaries On the Martial Way*, edited by John Little, Published by the Charles E. Tuttle Publishing Company, Boston, copyright 1998 Linda Lee Cadwell.

merely follow the one straight line - here we have merely isolation in an enclosed idea of a straight line."[42]

Marcos Ocaña believes it is important to see the full picture of Bruce Lee's legacy. "Many people appreciate Bruce Lee with the mouth, but not with the facts. Many say they are not racist and that they like Oriental culture, but they are racist with other people and races. I know of people who talk bad of black people and Oriental people, but they liked Bruce Lee a lot (for what he did and got).

"I think that Bruce was like that finger pointing the way to the moon. We must look at what he's pointing to and see the good things (what is positive for us after researching our own experiences). Open-minded people will look further, and they'll discover the real Bruce Lee, and through him, other cultures. These are the people I have the greatest empathy for. There are many others who only look at his kicks and punches, and I think most of those are missing all that heavenly glory."

Ultimately, understanding the commonalties between human beings is key to understanding ourselves. "Yes, we possess a pair of eyes, the function of which is to observe, to discover, and so forth" said Bruce Lee. "Yet many of us simply do not really 'see' in the true sense of the word. I must say that when the eyes are used externally to observe the inevitable faults of other beings, most of us are rather quick with ready-made condemnation. For it is easy to criticize and break down the spirit of others, but to know yourself takes maybe a lifetime."[43]

---

[42] Source: page 57 of the book *Jeet Kune Do: Commentaries On the Martial Way*, edited by John Little, Published by the Charles E. Tuttle Publishing Company, Boston, copyright 1998 Linda Lee Cadwell.
[43] Source: page 230 of the book *Artist of Life*, edited by John Little, Published by the Charles E. Tuttle Publishing Company, Boston, copyright 1999 Linda Lee Cadwell.

BRUCE LEE AND SELF-ACTUALIZATION

One of author Davis Miller's chief complaints about Bruce Lee centers around Lee's intense dedication to the concept of self-actualization. Miller rails against self-actualization simply because Bruce Lee advocated it, and the truth is that Miller doesn't have a clear understanding of self-actualization, a concept that predated Bruce Lee's advocacy of it by many years.

On that point, Abraham Maslow, the psychologist who developed the concept, described a pyramid-style hierarchy of human needs that led ultimately to self-actualization. Maslow said that all people have an inherent drive toward this eventual goal, though few achieve it. At the bottom of the pyramid are deficit needs. The first is physiological needs, the need for air, water, and food. The next is safety needs, shelter and safety. Then you start moving into what Maslow called "being needs", which includes the need for belonging, group association, a sense of community. Then comes self-esteem needs, the need to be recognized and appreciated. Finally, when all those needs are met, you leave all that behind and enter a phase of self-actualization, where you are trying to develop your human potential to its maximum.

As Miller's book *Tao of Bruce Lee* shows, Miller himself was moving along this path. With the loss of a parent and the difficulties of growing up in a single parent household, he was in the safety needs phase. When he was friendless, hanging out with the African-Americans and trying desperately to be like them because he felt "black", it was the need for the belonging phase. Then his ultimate and miraculous "development" into his bulked-up, fighter-guy image was clearly the phase of self-esteem needs, a need to create an image of himself that he could accept and project to others. This also ties back (somewhat) into safety needs, because it is an underlying fear that made him want to give the appearance of not being a viable target, hence all the manly, chest-pounding, cock-of-the-walk projecting. It is almost a textbook case for self-actualization. Any student or professional in humanistic psychology would identify these points immediately. So, as you can see, I find it tremendously amusing when he criticizes self-actualization without even knowing what it is.

Bruce Lee's interest in self-actualization was a simple realization of a truth in organismic development. Said Professor Nicholas Rescher: "Some element of reflexive self-orientation (self-realization, self-formation, self-perpetuation, and the like) is inherent in virtually every physical process, seeing that throughout nature everything tries to realize itself, to constitute itself as that which its inner impetus dictates its destiny to be. The basic drive or nisus of the world's furnishing is not so much (as with Spinoza) one of self-preservation *(conatus se preservandi)* as one of self-realization, of bringing itself to its own fullest actualization *(conatus se realizandi)*. Creative self-determination rules: everywhere there are processes at work bringing heretofore nonexistent beings and modes of being to realization."[44]

---

[44] Source: page 85 of the book *Process Metaphysics*, by Nicholas Rescher, copyright 1996 State University of New York Press, New York.

Bruce Lee was introduced to the concept of self-actualization through the work of Abraham Maslow's contemporary and colleague, Carl Rogers. Rogers, one of the preeminent psychotherapists of the twentieth century, shared Maslow's vision of the human being as a positively developing organism. Their humanistic psychology came to be known as the "Third Force" in psychology, with Freudianism being the first force and the Behaviorism of B.F. Skinner being the second. Humanistic psychology drew upon the works of existential philosophy, Krishnamurti, and included the Gestalt Therapy of Fritz Perls, all of which influenced Bruce Lee as well.

I immediately recognized the need for the concepts of self-actualization and a person-centered approach in Northern Ireland. I used Bruce Lee's interest in the subjects as a platform to teach the concepts to his fans during my lecture trip there in 2000. It was only after I had returned that I learned that Carl Rogers, coincidentally, had giving seminars in Belfast in the 1980s on these very subjects. So, in essence, I was not only promoting Bruce Lee's philosophy; I was continuing the work of Carl Rogers there. As a student of Carl Rogers' teachings and a member of the Association for Humanist Psychology, I was extremely gratified to learn this.

The following chapter is a lecture I gave on this subject at Queen's University in Belfast, Northern Ireland, on September 26, 2000. An abbreviated (and poorly misprinted) version also appeared in the July 2000 issue of *Bruce Lee Magazine*.

In the first draft of his essay titled "In My Own Process", Bruce Lee wrote: "Ever since I was a kid, I have possessed within myself this instinctive urge for growth and daily expansion of my potential. It has been some time now since I acquired and really understood the distinction between self-actualization and this illusion of self-image actualization. Through my own observations, I am convinced that an absolutely honest and direct inquiry into oneself will lead to understanding."

Of everything in his martial art, philosophy, and teachings, Bruce Lee's message of self-actualization has had the most profound effect on me.

Individualism is the fundamental issue. Human beings have an inherent need for individuality but are essentially mimetic animals, meaning we tend to imitate rather than originate. It is the most primary way that we start to develop our identities, by assuming aspects of the identities of others. The problem arises when we fail to grow out of this pattern of mimetic behavior and into a process of self-actualization where we should be defining our own identities based on our developing sense of self.

At the Third Annual Jun Fan Jeet Kune Do seminar in Seattle last year, I saw a lot of people in the training classes who were trying to "be Bruce Lee". They were imitating everything he did in the movies, such as the little hand he made in his movies with his pinkie finger and thumb out, the head movements and facial expressions, even the vocal noises, doing imitations that would have put an Elvis impersonator to shame. These people were trying to be Bruce Lee (or what they thought was Bruce from watching his movies) instead of trying to be themselves and see what Bruce left as a legacy that could be of value to them in their own personal growth as martial artists and as people. They were concentrating too much on the "finger", as it were, and not the moon.

There were plenty of people who were there without pretension, who came to get the knowledge and weren't "Bruce Lee wannabes". I got the distinct impression from observing these people that they were "getting it" before the wannabes were.

It's great if you are a Bruce Lee fan, but if your life is not complete outside of Bruce Lee then you are missing the point: the idea is to complete and define yourself on your own terms, not through your association with something or someone.

We imitate what we see in society in order to affirm our identity: we have to have the right clothes, the right car, money, the right friends, and be in the right social class. We "act" like the person we wish to emulate, whose success we think we can achieve by copying their path.

The problem is that it is only an act. We, as human beings, are not designed to "act" continuously, so eventually we will slip if we try to keep it up too long. The longer a person plays this game the more schizoid they become. They don't realize that they have neglected the root while trying to nurture the outside. They have a sense of emptiness that they can't define, so they blindly try things in an attempt to fill that void. They sample drugs; it doesn't bring them any fulfillment. They have affairs, thinking that the emptiness comes from an unfulfilled marriage. In the worst cases, they act out against society, blaming others for their internal problems. The realization that the medicine for their own suffering is inside them escapes them. They fail to see that the secret to being a fully-actualized human being is in self-exploration and cultivation, not self-image, that "face" that so many of us try to wear. The saddest part is that it is a "face" that not only masks our identity from others, but from ourselves as well.

Yet society seems to thwart our efforts at individualism at every level. In modern life there is no encouragement for self-mastery. We have a culture that obstructs higher functions, but also obstructs the formation of will.

Our education system further reinforces this sense of non-individualism with its factory-like process of educating students. A single curriculum is established that is supposed to promote intellectual growth in all students, regardless of their individual natures, aptitudes, or inclinations. Students are taught to define their intellectual self-worth through this systemized evaluation system and in relationship to how their fellow classmates perform in the same system. They are not taught to seek out their own potential or to think for themselves, only to accept the dogma of their educators, which is mainly their own experiences and opinions fragmented, obscured, and partialized by their own personal worldviews and presented as unassailable fact. The result is that the educational system, which should be a source of liberation for the student, becomes a cage in which the students unknowingly find themselves.

On the social side of education, the students feel the compelling need to belong to groups or fraternities--activities and associations give them a sense of identity. I found it funny to watch students pledging to get into sororities and fraternities at my college, the University of North Texas, because they were so desperate to be identified by these labels that they would humiliate themselves, following the most demeaning, dehumanizing and obnoxious directives. All of this is done in an effort to "get into" an organization. Such complete subordination to any group or institution is directly opposed to the idea of self-actualization because a self-actualized person does not feel the need to be so closely identified with anything. It is not even a clan mentality for these people; it's not a desire to be a part of an extended family, but rather an intense need to be identified with a label. Labels only mask the real identity of the individual.

We all feel the need to follow something or someone else in our lives because following is so much easier than honestly looking into ourselves and asking, "Who am I?" When you eliminate labels, many of you will find that you can't really say who you are because you yourself do not know.

If I ask you who you are, what would you say?

"Well, I'm a stockbroker."

That's what you do for a living, but that's not who you are.

"Okay, I'm a husband and a father."

Those are social functions. You still haven't answered my question.

"I'm a fighter. A student of Jun Fan Jeet Kune Do."

Good for you, but being tough and being complete are two different things. If I ask you why you are studying Bruce Lee's art, what would you say?

"I want to be a great fighter."

That's self-image actualization. Rather than want to be a great fighter, I would much rather be able to fight great.

Too often I see practitioners of Bruce Lee's art only concerned with the idea of being a super fighter, as if the world will in turn regard them with absolute awe and respect. As Lee said himself, "As he matures, a martial artist will realize that his kick or punch is really not so much a tool to conquer his opponent, but a tool to explode through his consciousness, his ego, and all mental obstacles." Yet many people ignore the deeper aspects of the art, concerned only with perfecting that punch that they believe will make all the difference in their lives.

That is why I feel fortunate to have studied Jun Fan Jeet Kune Do under Sifus Willie Wilson and James Roberts of the Jeet Kune Do Institute of Dallas. They are concerned with perfecting people as well as punches. Sifu Wilson, for example, a prison guard, has the perspective of seeing many people caught in the trap of self-image actualization, people who felt driven to commit crimes to fulfill their own external needs. It's a perspective and lesson he brings to his students. Not only does he teach them to master their techniques, he also teaches them that what matters most about a man is not the clothes he wears or the car he drives, but who he is inside.

Before I discovered the idea of self-actualization from Bruce Lee, I was, like many people, so concerned about self-image actualization instead of self-actualization. My personal relationships were very unsuccessful. I desperately strived for a healthy relationship, yet I couldn't sustain one. In time I came to understand that I had developed a need to be completed by a partner such that, to me, my sense of self was incomplete without a girlfriend in my life. The women I dated picked up on this "neediness" and withdrew from me. Only when I came to realize that being a complete and fully realized person meant cultivating the self, independent of others, did I find a steady, healthy and lasting relationship. Now I realize I am complete with or without someone else.

Bruce Lee championed the idea of self-actualization, but he did not create it. The idea has existed in various forms throughout history. The psychologist Dr. Abraham Maslow first coined the term self-actualization. Dr. Maslow believed that only two percent of the world's population was self-actualized.

Dr. Maslow recognized several characteristics of a self-actualized person. The self-actualized has a more efficient perception of reality. They have superior reason, are logical, and unafraid of the unknown. They see problems as challenges rather than immobilizing obstacles. Self-actualizers are self-accepting: they make no apologies for the way they are and recognize that they are a functioning part of the natural world. They value their privacy. They do not bow to social pressure, are unhampered by convention and rely on their own experience and judgments. They embrace ethnic diversity and personal individuality and share the quality called *Gemeinschaftsgefühl* -- social interest, compassion, and humanity. They prefer intimate personal relationships with a select group of friends and family members, rather than many shallow associations. They feel that the journey is often more important than the destination.

Sound like anyone we know?

For many people, self-actualization is the answer for dealing with the inner demons that beset them. These people have been so unsuccessful in their search for some kind of meaning or sense of value in their life that they allow these psychological stresses to control them. They become a stew of psychoses. This sometimes results in violent outbursts from seemingly harmless people.

Recently, in the city next to mine, a man was compelled by his inner demons to walk into a church full of worshipping children and take seven lives, not counting his own suicide.

As information has begun accumulating about the killer, it is developing into an all-too-familiar picture. He was a loner, rejected, despondent over his inability to hold down a job and depressed over the death of his elderly father, who remained the killer's caretaker and provider up until little over a month ago. Investigators searching the killer's home found the house itself physically brutalized: holes knocked in walls, furniture broken, family photographs torn up, all significant signs of the pain and rage churning inside him. Letters left behind further expressed his growing frustration with life.

Said sociologist Eric Hoffer, quoted by Bruce Lee from the book *A Passionate State of Mind:* "A fateful process is set in motion when the individual is released 'to the freedom of his own impotence' and left to justify his existence by his own efforts. The autonomous individual, when he can neither realize himself nor justify his existence by his own efforts, is a breeding of frustration, and the seed of the convulsions that shake our world to its foundations. The individual on his own is stable only so long as he is possessed of self-esteem. The maintenance of self-esteem is a continuous task that taxes all of the individual's power and inner resources. We have to prove our worth and justify our existence anew each day. When, for whatever reason, self-esteem is unattainable, the autonomous individual becomes a highly explosive entity. All social disturbances and upheavals have their roots in a crisis of individual self-esteem, and the great endeavors in which the masses most readily unite is basically a search for pride."[45]

Hoffer's words have an eerie immediacy to them, in light of the actions of the killer. Like the student killers of Columbine High School, the killer of Wedgwood Baptist Church had difficulty assimilating into regular society. Incapable of attaining the respect and appreciation of his peers, which so many people find absolutely essential to their own sense of self-worth, he exploded in anger and defiance at the world's perceived rejection of him. As reported by the teenagers that were present during the massacre, he became more enraged when, after announcing his presence and his "mission", the crowd of kids refused to take him seriously. "I am for real!" he told them repeatedly, as if demanding, just once, that he be taken seriously. His need for validation, for recognition, was at the heart of his emotional troubles.

In the book *The Art of Happiness* the Dalai Lama states, "There are some people who, right from the beginning, have suffered much and have lacked other's affection--so that later in life it seems almost as if they have no human feeling, no capacity for compassion and affection, those who are hardened and brutal.

"Such people suffer from a kind of nagging sense of insecurity and fear. Even when they are sleeping, I think that sense of fear remains...All that might be very difficult to understand, but one thing you could say is that these people lack something that you can find in a more compassionate person--a sense of freedom, a sense of abandonment, so that when you sleep, you can relax and go. Ruthless people never have that experience. Something is always gripping them; there is some kind of hold on them, and

---

[45] Source: passage 29 of the book *A Passionate State of Mind*, by Eric Hoffer, copyright 1954 Harper Collins, New York. This was one of many passages incorrectly attributed to Bruce Lee.

they aren't able to experience that feeling of letting go, that sense of freedom."[46]

Is this, then, the answer to this conundrum of our existence, or is there no answer--such as in the Hegelian view that it is all the uncontrollable passion of the *Weltegeist* (world spirit), consuming itself as it progresses toward its evolution of consciousness of freedom? I choose to believe in the individual's ability to make a difference through self-actualization, a stronger sense of community, and self-acceptance that is not predicated on emotional validation or the perceptions of others.

In Taoism the idea of self-acceptance is apparent in the concept of *Te*. A person centered in the Tao does not predicate their self-worth on the opinions of others. A Taoist does not feel the need to prove himself and is free to express his individuality in its fullest measure. He is unconcerned with the pretentious activities of fitting in to society and of trying desperately to be "part of the pack". As Diane Dreher wrote in her book *The Tao of Inner Peace*, "In nature everything is valuable, everything has its place. Each form has its own expression. Only human beings suffer from low self-esteem."[47]

United Kingdom Bruce Lee fan Dean Routledge is a prime example of the liberating effect that Bruce's message of self-actualization can have on people who are pressured to conform to a standard that is often impossible to attain. "As a young man I was very overweight, terrible skin, and badly groomed," says Routledge. "Altogether, I suppose, it's a common story: the neurotic teenager who thinks the world is against him. High school was very difficult. If you are on the plump side, you know that sometime during everyday someone is going to call you 'fat'. The worst thing is that it is usually the good-looking girls in their little groups who will have a giggle as you go by. It does wear you down, and some days you don't want to get out of bed. I wasn't naturally athletic; I suffered from asthma, which meant I couldn't really take part in sport, and I often felt as though I didn't fit in. Looking back though, even then, I knew that I would be doing myself no favors by 'running' with the rest of the crowd, dressing in the latest fashion, having my hair the way every other kid did. I knew it wasn't me, so even at that stage in my life I was aware

---

[46] Source: page 122 of the book *The Art of Happiness* by the Dalai Lama and Howard C. Cutler, M.D.
[47] Source: Page 269 of the book *The Tao of Inner Peace* by Diane Dreher, HarperPerennial, New York, New York, 1991.

that a person needs their own identity and their own sense of self-actualization, as opposed to self-image actualization."

Today Dean feels that it was Bruce's example that enabled him to liberate himself from the bondage of that cycle of self-abuse. "I'm a lot lighter now in comparison. My asthma cleared up when I came out of my teens, so I could begin to exercise a bit more vigorously, and I still try to stay in some form of shape even though I'm creaking at the age of 30. One thing I always try to remember is how it felt when someone was insulting to me. I remember the despair that I felt at that age, the feeling of utter rejection by my peers. Looking back, I realize that this was a time that truly defined me. I feel that we only really get a sense of our own worth when things are terrible. It's then that we find out just what we are truly made of. At the time I hated it, but now I look back and think that without it, without those experiences as a young man, I wouldn't be who I am today."

We are taught this pattern of conformist behavior from birth. As a child, we are trained to be like everyone else, placed in a constant state of comparison. There is a certain way to think, to fit in. Our notions of identity are directly linked to models and archetypes that are homogenized by design. Everything that is an ill of our society, from racism and xenophobia to class struggle to alienation, is a product of this phenomenon. Yet, we allow ourselves to either jump in line with this parade of self-ignorance or become trampled under its feet when we have the choice to simply step outside the crowd and "march to the beat of our own drum".

Look at society's heroes. Everyone who has made a lasting impact in a positive way on society has been someone who has stepped out on his or her own and established something new and different or fought a cause that couldn't be fought, sometimes at great personal cost. They are remembered today for their achievements because they cast off the restriction of conventionalism and defined themselves in their own unique way.

To be self-actualized means to hear that silent flute, that call of the soul within us. Too many people are deaf to the call of their own flutes, never realizing the music that is within them.

Said Bruce Lee: "My personal message to people is that I hope that they will go toward self-actualization rather than self-image actualization. I hope that they will search within themselves for honest self-expression."

BRUCE LEE: GNOSTIC CHRISTIAN?

Throughout my work with Bruce Lee and his philosophy, I have tried to use it as an opportunity to educate people on other areas of vital human interest and knowledge. In the previous chapter, I used Bruce Lee to introduce people to humanistic psychology. In the following chapter, I use Bruce Lee to introduce people to Gnostic Christianity, a long-dead sect of Christianity that was eradicated in the fourth century, anno domini.

This article is distinctive because it marks the first time that his philosophy has been discussed and recognized by the scholarly establishment, among them Princeton University's Dr. Elaine Pagels, a world-recognized expert on the Gnostic scriptures.

This article was also somewhat scandalous at the time of its publication. It was a bold move on my part to make such a comparison. Fans of Bruce Lee had already been accused of deifying him. What I did in this article was seen by some as the ultimate deification: making a direct comparison between Bruce Lee and Jesus Christ. However, those critics missed the entire point of the article, which clearly stated that Bruce Lee, by his own definition, was no saint. The real point of the article was to introduce his fans to some new ideas and to show them that there are other sources of knowledge arriving at similar conclusions. Part of my work in philosophy, psychology, and theology has been to show the commonalties that exist between different belief systems. My position has always been, and continues to be, that the clearest vision of what is can be gleaned from the consensus that develops from unrelated fields.

For example, quantum physics teaches us of the principle of the "Big Bang", the primal atom from which all things developed. Taoism teaches us that all things derive from a single source called the *Tao,* or the "Grand Terminus". And Judeo-Christian theology teaches that all things came from a single, primal source, which they identify as God. The fact that these different groups, in many ways in direct opposition to each other, would find themselves at a crossroads together is very telling.

Likewise, I found it fascinating that Bruce Lee came to share so many similar ideas with a long dead religion that he never had an opportunity to know about. It seemed, to me, another example of that consensus of truth.

Perhaps for many fans and students, the most difficult aspect of embracing Bruce Lee's philosophy comes from the seeming inability to reconcile his revolutionary ideas with what is often a Christian perspective. Much of what Lee spoke and advocated seems to be in direct opposition to Christian theology. That is, until now.

Gnosticism

With recent discoveries in the world of theological archeology, a new image of Christianity is developing that bears an almost uncanny resemblance to Bruce Lee's own philosophical school of thought.

These discoveries, perhaps the most profound development in Christianity since the Reformation, have re-ignited a long-dead school of Christianity known as *Gnosticism.* The Gnostic school of Christian worship was developed out of the apostolistic teachings, concurrently with Orthodox Christianity, but by 180 AD the Catholic Church had declared Gnosticism to be heresy, ordering the executions of its advocates and the destruction of its gospels and religious texts. Backed by the strength of the Roman Empire, the Catholic Church was enormously successful in its efforts to eradicate Gnosticism, and by the end of the fourth century the Gnostic movement was virtually dead. All that remained was fragmentary evidence of its prior existence, mostly from the writings of the Catholic clergy who condemned it.

All that changed in December 1945, when an Arab peasant named Muhammad Ali al-Samman discovered a clay jar in the fields of Nag Hammadi in Upper Egypt. What he found inside was nothing short of a miracle: thirteen papyrus codices containing fifty-two sacred texts of the Gnostic tradition, gospels with a claim to legitimacy that challenged the standard Christian Bible – all preserved through the ages.

What is Gnostic Christianity, and how does it relate to Bruce Lee? The Gnostic tradition actually had its beginnings several centuries before the birth of Jesus Christ. The term Gnostic is derived from the Greek *gnosis*, which means "knowledge" or the "act of knowing". Most importantly, *gnosis* means knowledge of an internal nature, as opposed to knowledge acquired from the outside world through science.

Contrary to popular belief, Catholicism was just one of many Christian sects to develop out of the teachings of Jesus Christ's apostles. It wasn't until the end of the second century that Christianity finally settled into its Catholic (literally, "Universal") form. Prior to that, there were many different groups of Christians, each as legitimate as the next, among them Pauline Christianity, Jewish Christianity, and Gnostic Christianity. Just as there were many different groups, there were also many different gospels, written by the apostles and their students, and they varied in their approach to Christ's message.

Revelatory Gnosis

To Gnostic Christians, the path to salvation was not external adherence to church doctrine but rather an internal journey that leads to enlightenment and salvation. Internal reflection would reveal the spark of God that is within each of us, the knowledge that we are all, in a sense, a part of God.

If this sounds like an all too familiar theme to the students of Bruce Lee's philosophy, it should. Like Bruce Lee, Gnostic Christians were concerned with finding the "cause of their own ignorance". Like Lee, they believed that "all knowledge leads to self-knowledge". "It's an intriguing parallel that had never occurred to me," says Dr. Elaine Pagels, Harrington Spear Paine Professor of Religion at Princeton University and the author of *The Gnostic Gospels,* the authoritative examination of the Nag Hammadi discoveries. "But then I knew little about Bruce Lee except his public image."

It is equally interesting to note that the Nag Hammadi discoveries were not available to the public until the late 1970's, years after Bruce Lee had died. Lee never had the opportunity to study them, which makes the parallels between his philosophy and Gnostic Christianity all the more compelling.

One of the most complete and telling documents from the recovered "Gnostic Gospels" is the codex *Gospel of Saint Thomas*, which begins with the words: "These are the secret words which the living Jesus spoke, and which the twin, Judas Thomas, wrote down." In this codex, Jesus states:

> If you bring forth what is within you, what you bring forth will save you. If you do not bring forth what is within you, what you do not bring forth will destroy you.[48]

This passage echoes the words of Bruce Lee, who said:

> The process of maturing does not mean to become a captive of conceptualization. It is to come to the realization of what lies in our innermost selves.[49]

---

[48] Source: verse 70 of the book *The Gospel of Thomas: The Hidden Sayings of Jesus*, translated by Marvin Meyer, copyright 1992 Harper Collins, New York.

[49] Source: Bruce Lee quoted on page 197 of the book *Artist of Life,* edited by John Little, Published by the Charles E. Tuttle Publishing Company, Boston, copyright 1999 Linda Lee Cadwell.

The supreme goal of Gnostic Christians was direct, personal, and absolute knowledge of the authentic truths of existence, which they believed were accessible to the individual who sought them in internal reflection. Unlike Orthodox Jews and Christians, who believed that God and man were separate, the Gnostics taught that self-knowledge is knowledge of God. When writing about the Coptic *Gospel of Thomas* in his book *The Secret Sayings of Jesus,* Robert Grant notes that, "The kingdom of God is almost entirely inward, unrelated to time or history. Self-knowledge is all important."[50] This piercing insight into the state of being is similar to the Buddhist concept of enlightenment. It is known that the early Christians were in contact with Buddhists in South India, and modern scholars believe that the Buddhist movement did have an impact on the early formations of Christianity. There are even some ancient Buddhist texts written around the time of Christ that identify a visitor from the West eerily similar to Jesus' description, fueling many theories that Jesus traveled to India and studied Buddhism during his unrecorded years.

"There are a good many factors that would provide a partial explanation or the correlation of Bruce Lee's philosophy to that of Gnosticism, and I'm not sure that any one thing would explain it completely," says Dr. George James, Professor of Religion and Philosophy at The University of North Texas. "Buddhism began in the northeast of India. By the First century, AD, it had spread west into what is today Pakistan. There it met the culture of Greece that had spread that far under Alexander the Great. There is some evidence that there was a Buddhist community in Alexandria in Egypt around the first century AD. The form of Buddhism that was prevalent in this region was called Mahayana. It is a form of Buddhism that was influenced and supported by Taoist ideas prevalent in the Southern part of China. The contact between Taoism and Buddhism (as Buddhism spread into Southern China) is sometimes seen as a decisive factor in the development of what came to be called Zen Buddhism. The trade routes that took Buddhism into China also took Chinese ideas back along the same routes into the Middle East and India. Clearly it was a time of great intellectual ferment. In light of these developing cross currents, we should not be surprised to find ideas that are characteristic of Buddhism and Taoism and persons

---

[50] Source: Robert Grant quoted from page 208 of the book *The New Testament and Early Christianity* by Joseph B. Tyson, Published by Macmillan Publishing Company, New York, copyright 1984 Macmillan Publishing Company.

influenced by these traditions in forms of Christianity that prevailed in the second century."

For Gnostic Christians, self-revelation was at the heart of their spiritual salvation. Said Jesus in *The Book of Thomas the Contender*.

> Now, since it has been said that you are my twin and true companion, examine yourself, and learn who you are, in what way you exist, and how you will come to be. Since you will be called my brother, it is not fitting that you be ignorant of yourself. And I know that you have understood because you had already understood that I am the knowledge of the truth. So, while you accompany me, although you are uncomprehending, you have (in fact) already come to know, and you will be called "the one who knows himself". For he who has not known himself has known nothing, but he who has known himself has at the same time already achieved knowledge about the depth of the all. So then, you, my brother Thomas, have beheld what is obscure to men, that is, what they ignorantly stumble against.[51]

Gnostic Christians are monists, in that they believe that we are all fragments of God that have drifted away from the greater whole. This idea of the unity of all things is shared with Chinese Taoism, by which Bruce Lee was heavily influenced.

Said Bruce Lee:

> Taoism is a philosophy of the essential unity of the universe (monism)...the return of all to the primeval one, the divine intelligence, the source of all things.
>
> From this philosophy naturally arise the absence of desire for strife and contention and fighting for advantage. Thus the teachings of humility and meekness of the Christian Sermon on the Mount find rational basis, and a peaceable temper is bred in man.[52]

Here Bruce Lee makes the connection between the teachings of Jesus and the Taoist concepts of harmony and yielding. Of the connection between Lee's Taoist influences and Gnosticism, Dr. Pagels is quick to point out that, "Taoism developed at the same time as this Gnostic tradition, historically speaking."

---

[51] Source: Verse three of The Book of Thomas the Contender from *The Nag Hammadi Library*, Harper Collins, San Francisco, copyright 1990.

[52] Source: Bruce Lee quoted on page 116 of the book *The Tao of Gung Fu*, edited by John Little, Published by the Charles E. Tuttle Publishing Company, Boston, copyright 1997 Linda Lee Cadwell.

In describing the concept for his philosophical story "The Silent Flute", Bruce Lee said, "Basically, this is a story of one man's quest for his liberation, the returning to the original sense of freedom."[53] In that, he described the goal of Gnosticism perfectly.

"The Gospel Truth"

Unlike the Catholic Church, which insisted that redemption was available only through the dictates of the physical church, Gnostic teachings expressed an idea of salvation that came from the internal self-discovery of the true nature of the "self" and its relationship to God. To Gnostics, the "self" is a spark or seed of the Ultimate Being imprisoned in human form and awaiting its re-awakening. Those who fail to achieve this awakening must go through the process again in another life. This is very comparable to the Buddhist Dharma, which teaches that the individual must continue to reincarnate on the physical plane until it achieves enlightenment, at which point it will ascend to nirvana. To the Gnostics, nirvana meant reuniting with the Ultimate.

For John Little, the former director of the Bruce Lee Educational Foundation, the similarities between the Gnostic tradition and Bruce Lee's philosophy speak to the universality of his thought. "The Gnostic gospels are very interesting as they not only share many similarities with Bruce Lee's thought, but, predating Bruce, they also share many similar positions as the Buddhists and the Hindus—which speaks to the 'there is but one family' human 'root' that Bruce was so interested in seeking."

Both Gnostics and Bruce Lee rebelled against the idea of organized doctrine. The primary cause of the Catholic Church's attack on Gnosticism was that it spoke out against the "oppressive ecclesiastical forms" of the orthodox Christianity.

Bruce Lee himself may have experienced some of these "oppressive ecclesiastical forms" when he was educated under the Catholic system at LaSalle College in Hong Kong. He may have been frustrated by the rigidity of the doctrine and the inability of Catholics to question its dogma. Father Donald W. Hendricks of the Archdiocese of New York writes: "What a Catholic believes

---

[53] Source: Bruce Lee quoted on page 203 of the book *Artist of Life,* edited by John Little, Published by the Charles E. Tuttle Publishing Company, Boston, copyright 1999 Linda Lee Cadwell.

by faith, he believes absolutely. He is ready to take the Church's word on what constitutes a danger to his faith."[54]

When later writing on the subject of Saint Thomas Aquinas, a staple of Catholic education, Lee reflected on his experience in the Catholic school, saying: "What is disturbing about those arguments (despite the fact that my early schooling in Hong Kong was directed along these lines by Roman Catholic priests) is the overwhelming fact that I can either accept them or reject them, regardless of their validity."[55] It is highly probable that Lee's own experience with Catholicism may have influenced his decision to reject the concept of "styles" and rigid organization. The words of Bruce Lee in the book *Artist of Life* parallel the opinions of the Gnostic tradition:

> By an error repeated throughout the ages, truth, becoming a law or faith, places obstacles in the way of knowledge. Method, which is at its very substance ignorance, encloses "truth" within a vicious circle. We should break such circles, not by seeking knowledge, but by discovering the cause of ignorance.[56]

From the *Gospel of Phillip:*

> Names are given to the worldly are very deceptive, for they divert our thoughts from what is correct to what is incorrect. Thus one who hears the word "God" does not perceive what is correct, but perceives what is incorrect. So also with "the Father" and "the Son" and "the Holy Spirit" and "life" and "light" and "resurrection" and "the Church (Ekklesia)" and all the rest—people do not perceive what is correct but they perceive what is incorrect, unless they have come to know what is correct. The names which are heard in the world deceive.[57]

In the Gnostic view, organized religious dogma is a trap that blinds the believer into thinking that they have found salvation while their "true self" remains unawakened. This is an argument that Bruce Lee applied to the martial arts, specifically, and to life in general:

---

[54] Source: page 51 of the book *Religions of America*, edited by Leo Rosten, published by Simon and Schuster, New York, copyright 1975 Cowles Communications, Inc.

[55] Source: Bruce Lee quoted on page 67 of the book *Artist of Life*, edited by John Little, Published by the Charles E. Tuttle Publishing Company, Boston, copyright 1999 Linda Lee Cadwell.

[56] Source: Bruce Lee quoted on page 208 of the book *Artist of Life,* edited by John Little, Published by the Charles E. Tuttle Publishing Company, Boston, copyright 1999 Linda Lee Cadwell.

[57] Source: *The Gospel of Phillip,* translation by Wesley W. Isenberg. Gnostic Society Library. http://www.webcom.com/~gnosis/library.html.

The founder of a style may be exposed to some partial truth, but as time passes by, especially after the founder has passed away, "His" postulates, "His" inclination, "His" concluding formula—we constantly learn, we never conclude—become a sect, a law, or--worse still--a prejudicial faith. Creeds are invented, solemn, reinforcing ceremonies are prescribed, separative philosophies are formulated, and, finally, the institutions are erected, so what might have started off as some sort of fluidity of its founder is now solidified, fixed knowledge—organized and classified response presented in logical order—a preserved cure-all for mass conditioning. In so doing, the well-meaning followers have made this knowledge not only a holy shrine, but a tomb in which the founder's wisdom is buried.[58]

The Catholic Church could not overcome the inherent problems in its own organization, and even with the threat of heretical "Gnosticism" destroyed, the inevitable fracturing of the universal church finally came to pass with Martin Luther and the Reformation of the Middle Ages. From this movement blossomed many different sects of Christianity, each with its own religious doctrine, reflecting its own views and society. "All versions of Christ are interpretations," says Dr. Joe Barnhart, a Christian scholar and the author of *Religion and the Challenge of Philosophy.* "Christ represents the identity of God in man." Thus, what was one became many again, with Christianity finding itself in a self-defeating cycle of dogmatic conflict. This, in Bruce Lee's opinion, was the logical end to any system that becomes too rigid and organized, lacking fluidity. "Many more 'different' approaches would spring up, probably as a direct reaction to 'the other's truth'. Pretty soon these approaches, too, would become large organizations with each claiming to possess the 'truth' to the exclusion of all else."[59]

"Teachers"

Both Bruce Lee and Jesus were concerned with leading their students to freedom, whether it was the freedom of religious

[58] Source: Bruce Lee quoted on pages 123/156 of the book *Artist of Life,* edited by John Little, Published by the Charles E. Tuttle Publishing Company, Boston, copyright 1999 Linda Lee Cadwell.

[59] Source: Bruce Lee quoted on page 176 of the book *Artist of Life,* edited by John Little, Published by the Charles E. Tuttle Publishing Company, Boston, copyright 1999 Linda Lee Cadwell.

salvation or the freedom to express themselves in their totality. Like Bruce Lee, Jesus saw himself as a guide for the seeker—that through him one could find the seeds of his own transcendency. As Lee said: "A teacher, a really good teacher, is never a giver of truth; he is a guide, a pointer to the truth."[60]

"Bruce Lee made me aware of the need to look into myself for direction, rather than depend on the outside," says Bruce Lee's friend Leo Fong, a Methodist minister. "Some of the things that he talked about I felt was closely related to my own faith journey in studying the life and teachings of Jesus Christ."

There was another characteristic that Bruce Lee shared with Jesus. Says Joe Hyams, a student of Lee's and the author of *Zen in the Martial Arts*: "He often spoke in parables." Both Bruce Lee and Jesus were inclined to use parables as a method of indirectly teaching a certain point that they wanted to get across. Very often, like Jesus' teachings, it was left up to Lee's students to find the meaning in the story.

One argument that the Catholic Church had with the Gnostic tradition is that the Gnostics claimed that they were privy to secret teachings of Jesus that he shared with a select few. This was directly opposed to the Catholic Church's position that all of Jesus' teachings were freely given and shared with all of his followers. To the Gnostics, Jesus was more selective. Said Jesus in the *Gospel of Thomas*: "I disclose my mysteries to those who are worthy of my mysteries. Do not let your left hand know what your right hand is doing".[61] It is known that Bruce Lee did withhold information at times, and some he shared with only a select few of his students. "Jeet Kune Do is not for everyone," said Lee. "I have taught many pupils, but very few become my disciples. Many of the students do not show their capability of understanding, nor the application of it in the right way."[62]

It has often been argued that Bruce Lee has been deified, turned into some sort of revered religious figure in his own right. A recent post by a Bruce Lee fan on an Internet discussion forum suggested that, "It is not inconceivable that Bruce Lee was, in fact,

---

[60] Source: Bruce Lee quoted on page 141 of the book *Artist of Life*, edited by John Little, Published by the Charles E. Tuttle Publishing Company, Boston, copyright 1999 Linda Lee Cadwell.

[61] Source: verse 62 of "The Gospel of Thomas" in the book *The Complete Gospels*, edited by Robert J. Miller, Published by Harper Collins Publishing Company, San Francisco, copyright 1994 Polebridge Press.

[62] Source: Bruce Lee quoted on page 167 of the book *Artist of Life*, edited by John Little, Published by the Charles E. Tuttle Publishing Company, Boston, copyright 1999 Linda Lee Cadwell.

the second Messiah; his message was so powerful." "'Messiah' is simply anyone with a message, and Bruce Lee's message is one worth listening to," says Doctor George Braddock, a civil servant in the United Kingdom. "He was radical. He was unique. And eventually his teachings may become a religion, although that may not necessarily be a good thing." For some fans, the division between reverence and "worship" has become blurred. Lee himself made no such claims, arguing that he was just a man with a vision. "Well, let me put it this way," he told British broadcaster Ted Thomas. "To be honest and all that, I'm not as bad as some of them, but I definitely am not saying that I am a saint, okay?"[63]

It should be noted, however, that Gnostic Christians recognize that Jesus was not the only revealer of the truth, and that others will also speak of these things in the course of human history. They do, for instance, recognize the insights of Buddha, Mohammed and Lao-Tzu. For that matter, the Catholic Church itself is no longer the rigid institution that it used to be. The historic second Vatican council of 1962-1965 developed major advances in Catholic thought and doctrine. Under Pope John XXIII, the Catholic Church issued a declaration addressing religions and philosophies such as Buddhism and Taoism, acknowledging that "the Catholic Church rejects nothing which is true and holy in these religions...which often reflect a ray of that Truth which enlightens all men."[64]

More recently, Pope John Paul II made a trip to New Delhi, India, where he met with many religious leaders of Asian belief systems. His trip was intended to promote peace among the differing religious groups. "No state, no group has the right to control either directly or indirectly a person's religious convictions," the Pope told the religious leaders during his Apostolic Exhortation.[65] Later, he paid homage to the late Mahatma Gandhi at a memorial where, before leaving, Pope John Paul II wrote in a visitors' book, quoting from Gandhi, "A culture cannot survive if it attempts to be exclusive."[66]

---

[63] Source: Bruce Lee quoted on page 4 of "Bruce Lee in Conversation with Ted Thomas", *Knowing is Not Enough* Volume 3, Number 2.

[64] Source: paper entitled "Declaration on the Relationship of the Church to Non-Christian Religions" from the collection *The Documents of Vatican II*, edited by Walter M. Abbot, S.J., translated from Latin by Msgr. Joseph Gallagher, Published by Geoffrey Chapman Publishers, London, copyright 1966 Geoffrey Chapman Publishers.

[65] Source: "Pope Says Religion Conversion is Human Right." *The Irish Times,* November 7, 1999, sec. 1.

[66] Source: "Pope Encourages Spreading of Christian Message in Asia." *The Dallas Morning News,* November 7, 1999, sec. A.

Bruce Lee himself was, at best, an agnostic. In an interview with writer Alex Ben Block conducted in the summer of 1972, Block asked Lee if he believed in God. He replied: "To be perfectly frank, I really do not."[67] Though this statement seems emphatic, it is possible that he simply had not been convinced of the existence of a god, because he made several references to a god or godhead over the years that suggested he was at least open to the possibility. But, being the critical individual he was, he refused to accept the existence of a Supreme Being on the basis of faith alone. At the same time, he had a great deal of respect for people of faith. "I cannot and will not 'scoff' at faith when reason seems to be such a barren thing," he said.[68] Bruce Lee did feel driven by something, though, and he sometimes wondered about the source of this drive.

"Bruce believed in a higher force," insists his friend, Leo Fong. "He might not have believed in God in a traditional way by going to church. Bruce believed in himself, and he was very spiritual. Religion can get you in trouble. I'm not religious myself, and I am a minister. I'm a spiritual person. You can call it chi, ki, God, Jehovah or whatever you want; it's just this creative force that is within us and around us."

In a letter to his friend Pearl Tso, Bruce Lee wrote: "Whether it is the God-head or not, I feel this great force, this untapped power, this dynamic something within me. The feeling defies description, and [there is] no experience with which this feeling may be compared. It is something like a strong emotion mixed with faith, but a lot stronger."[69]

Today, Gnostic Christianity has been resurrected, phoenix-like, from the discoveries at Nag Hammadi. New churches have been established, including the Ecclesia Gnostica of the United States and the Eglise Gnostique Catholique Apostolique of France. Their numbers are growing. Likewise, the philosophies of Bruce Lee have enjoyed a recent growing base of support, which in time will increase as more people are drawn to his

---

[67] Source: Bruce Lee quoted on page 63 of the book *Bruce Lee: Words From a Master*, edited by John Little, Published by Contemporary Books, Chicago, copyright 1999 John R. Little and Robert Wolff.
[68] Source: Bruce Lee quoted on page 68 of the book *Artist of Life*, edited by John Little, Published by The Charles E. Tuttle Publishing Company, Boston, copyright 1999 Linda Lee Cadwell.
[69] Source: Bruce Lee quoted on page 31 of the book *Letters of the Dragon*, edited by John Little, Published by the Charles E. Tuttle Publishing Company, Boston, copyright 1998 Linda Lee Cadwell.

message of self-actualization and personal exploration. As Lee stated: "Not conviction, not method, but perception is the way of truth."[70]

> *I wish neither to possess,*
> *Nor to be possessed.*
> *I no longer covet paradise,*
> *More important, I no longer fear hell.*
> *The medicine for my suffering*
> *I had within me from the very beginning,*
> *But I did not take it.*
> *My ailment came from within myself,*
> *But I did not observe it*
> *Until this moment.*
> *Now I see that I will never find the light*
> *Unless, like the candle, I am my own fuel,*
> *Consuming myself.*[71]

---

[70] Source: Bruce Lee quoted on page 356 of the book *Jeet Kune Do: Commentaries On the Martial Way,* edited by John Little, Published by the Charles E. Tuttle Publishing Company, Boston, copyright 1998 Linda Lee Cadwell.
[71] Source: Bruce Lee quoted on page 113 of the book *Artist of Life,* edited by John Little, Published by the Charles E. Tuttle Publishing Company, Boston, copyright 1999 Linda Lee Cadwell.

DIALOGUE WITH DAVIS MILLER

Bruce Lee fans are divided on the subject of Davis Miller's book, *The Tao of Bruce Lee*. Some love it, hailing it as the first independent look at the Bruce Lee legacy. Others claim it is a monumental disappointment, a factually inaccurate book that is more about Miller than about Bruce Lee.

I will not go into my own opinion of the matter here, except to say that I find Davis Miller to be an exceptional writer whose own story included in *The Tao of Bruce Lee* is worth the price of the book. It is a continuation of the story he began in his first book, *The Tao of Muhammad Ali*, which was lauded by critics when it was released. However, Miller and I have markedly different points of view when it comes to Bruce Lee.

The following is compiled from a dialogue that occurred in the fall of 2000 on my old Internet discussion forum, *Everything About Bruce Lee*. Fans that participated and viewed the dialogue may be shocked that I chose to include it, as Davis Miller and I disagree on a great many points. However, I am in the professional philosophical and educational community, and I am used to dealing with argument and disagreement. One of my colleagues, Dr. Joe Barnhart of the University of North Texas' philosophy department, once told me a story. He said he took his daughter along to a philosophical conference where he was presenting a paper and argument on Karl Popper. Some of the other scholars who were present took great exception to his position, and strenuously attacked it. After the conference, his daughter was surprised that her father seemed undisturbed over the way that they had attacked his argument, and she asked him why he was not upset. He told her that it was not a personal attack, that they were attacking his idea, and that allowing his idea to contrast with their own would only help him to make it stronger.

Therefore, it clearly does not bother me that Davis Miller takes the position that he takes, nor should it bother others. If the fans and students of Bruce Lee are so insecure or fragile with regard to their own opinions on the matter, then they deserve to be shocked and rattled. Beyond that, in the best Socratic style, I respect that Miller has an opinion and that it is his.

Out of further respect to Davis Miller, this dialogue has been edited to reduce it to the most salient points, and the more rancorous exchanges that ensued have not been included.

Davis Miller: One of the basic reasons I wrote *The Tao of Bruce Lee* is as a commentary on the ways that religions are created. Bruce Lee himself, largely through reading Jiddu Krishnamurti, was quite suspicious of the very nature of religion and other mythologies. Indeed, he regarded them as impediments to truth.

117

Yet, in death, Lee has taken on a nearly religious significance to many of his fans -- as well as to others who aren't fans. He has become regarded, in effect, as the twentieth-century god of martial art. How did this happen?

As a human being, as one of us, there are many things about Bruce Lee that I find less than admirable. I wish it weren't so, but the more I've dug, the more people I've spoken with, the less likable he's become. And that's okay. But it's the basic reason I had to write about him in the ways that I have.

My concern is with the nearly religious nature of the way Lee is regarded, which I find minimizes him as a person. Bruce Lee was not a punching and kicking machine; he was a flesh and blood human being. Period. Maybe that's obvious, but in some ways we don't come to him that way. Like just about everyone I've spoken with about Lee over the past twenty-seven years, I originally came to Bruce Lee, not as a real live human being, but as something of a punching and kicking vehicle who whups up on all of his oppressors (which, by extension, and not necessarily consciously, we regard as *our own* oppressors). In effect, people idolize him, not so much for who he was, but because of what he could do.

Finally, I don't think that reductive way of being with Bruce Lee is fair to him. And I don't think it is fair to us.

James Bishop: However, you look at what Bruce Lee read, and it was all about growth and positive empowerment. That says something about the man. It is through Lee that so many people have discovered the works of Alan Watts, Fritz Perls, Jiddu Krishnamurti, Hugh Prather, Carl Rogers, etc.; people who would not otherwise have studied their works.

People should research some of Bruce Lee's sources of inspiration and find their own as well. In fact, I have found great success in getting people to look at some of these minds through their influence on Bruce Lee.

Davis Miller: Over the past almost thirty years, Linda Lee (and more recently Linda Lee Cadwell) pursued and/or authorized the publication of numerous volumes of Bruce Lee's handwritten notes, almost all of which are not original but which are copied more or less verbatim from the writings of Eric Hoffer, Alan Watts,

Napoleon Hill, and particularly the work of anti-mystic Jiddu Krishnamurti, himself a very remarkable man. Would these notes have been published if Lee had lived? Certainly not. None of them. Period. Did he claim these words as his own? Not as far as I can tell.

I feel that they should attribute these (not just a few quotes) to Krishnamurti, Watts, Hoffer, and others.

James Bishop: As for other people's thoughts, I agree that there should be attribution, if such a case exists. I think any writer would expect that of their work. Perhaps a disclaimer at the beginning of each book would have been in order. As a scholar I would like to give credit where credit is due.

You take the Tuttle series to task, but the fact is it is the most direct resource we have for the life of Bruce, the way he thought. These are Bruce Lee's writings and notes, beliefs that he had. Whether or not they were originally his does not take away from the fact that he believed in them. They are not the reports of people who knew him. They are not filtered or skewed through the second-hand stories of anyone, especially Linda Lee Cadwell or John Little.

Part of my philosophical studies in college had been in early Christian philosophy, and I can tell you that scholars rely on the earliest most authentic writings of the gospels for their research, codices of the gospels that are the least suspect in terms of replicative revision, much like the Tuttle series is the clearest picture we can have of Bruce Lee, as opposed to the testimony of dubious "friends" of Bruce Lee, whose positions in his life take on a suddenly greater importance post-mortem.

Davis Miller: In addition, after Lee's death, his mostly well-intentioned former students, who, in 1972 he'd told not to teach his martial art because, Lee said, "none of you are capable of doing so," continued to teach and, at times, have incorrectly been regarded as heirs to Bruce Lee. In the interest of making reputations for themselves and, of course, money from something they care about, as well as to attempt to honestly perpetuate some of Lee's teachings, these folks, along with the former Linda Lee, have become the "official" caretakers of the Bruce Lee legacy. And this is another place where things start getting a bit funky, where the Bruce Lee statue becomes more important than the actual, breathing, sleeping, dreaming, farting, snoring, bleeding, hurting, laughing, crying human being who lived and who died.

James Bishop: I agree that many of Bruce Lee's original students, passing friends, and family have, since his death, "expanded" upon their relationships and experience with him. Clearly, the adoration that the fans bestow on them is a powerful narcotic. Since they are the "closest" connection to Bruce Lee in the fans' minds, they are drawn to them like moths to flames.[72] Sadly, I do feel that the privilege of having known Bruce Lee is something that is often abused.

On a tangent, as for lack of originality, few of those people mentioned originated their own ideas. Bruce Lee took self-actualization from Carl Rogers, who in turn took it from Abraham Maslow. Krishnamurti was accused of simply repeating what the Buddhists have been saying all along. As for the Alan Watts connection, Watts' son Mark said himself that his father did not come up with the ideas he wrote about, that it was nothing new. I could go on, but suffice it to say, taking the works of others, and progressing them, is a standard in the areas of science, philosophy, and psychology.

It is fair to point out that Bruce Lee would not have claimed these other people's words as his own. What is important is that he recognized truths in their words, truths that do not belong to any one person and do not originate from people but are sometimes expressed through them. That someone would simply take Bruce Lee's words and not research his influences would be myopic and

---

[72] What follows is an example of the powerful adoration that these individuals receive because of their association with Bruce Lee's memory. It is the recollections of Terence Del Rosario, a fan who attended the Bruce Lee Educational Foundation's annual convention in Las Vegas in April 2000. "While I waited in line to check in, a familiar face appeared. I wasn't sure who he was, but I knew he was one of Bruce's students (Steve Golden). Since I was both shy and unsure, I didn't do anything. Fortunately and unfortunately, this happened several times. I saw Dan Lee waiting to go up on an elevator. Jesse Glover went down on the same elevator as I did. I passed by Taky and Andy Kimura outside of the hotel. I saw Richard Bustillo and Joey Orbillo at the Burger Palace and Linda and Shannon Lee dining at the Ming Terrace. Unfortunately, I still found myself shy and silent most of the time. When I first met Shannon Lee, I told her 'I don't know what to say,' and she smiled and said, 'That's okay!' Attending the Expo was my very first 'real' Bruce Lee experience. It was the closest I could every get to his family, his friends, his students, his art, and his life."

lazy, and would cheat the individual of all the extra knowledge and experience that Lee drew upon that is not reflected in his notes, and, in fact, much that he might not have been exposed to.

Davis Miller: You're right. And, once again, I have no problem to speak of with Bruce Lee. My thesis is about how he is perceived, some of the factors that have contributed to this perception (a good topic for discussion would be to explore additional factors other than those I'll mention in this series of posts), and how this perception, this chimera, differs from the actual human being.

Bruce Lee was one heckuva scholar when it came to things he liked. And the fact that some folks would get offended by me saying this makes me refer again to what I'll call the Bruce Lee orthodoxy, the notion that he is the primary source for all/most things martial. The obvious irony is that this is just the kind of stuff that Bruce Lee himself (sometimes noisily) protested against.

And how can anyone claim to know what the truth is when he looks the other way from those things that make him uncomfortable, that make him question what he's believed -- translation: what he's invested so much of himself in. I've found that there's considerable benefit in looking at Lee as roundly and completely as possible, in the beauty of his scars and seeming limitations, as well as his talents and the (sometimes money driven) pseudo-religious propaganda of literal-loyalists. And that's why little of that is in *Tao of Bruce Lee*, not because I didn't do my research. Ten years ago and twenty years ago I believed the "official" Bruce Lee stuff, too. And then I finally got kicked around enough in my life to sort of grow up -- which required me to force myself to look at Bruce Lee in fresh-eyed ways.

Sorry if any of this sounds preachy. I don't want it to be.

On this forum, I've seen several people touch on something that I feel is very important: none of this fighting stuff is important. Yet, probably ninety percent (or more) of the posts on this site are about people striking and kicking, clawing and grabbing, etcetera, about people physically hurting, or pretending to hurt, other human beings whose lives are every bit as full, large, round, and interesting as their own. In this way, and others, fighting can be seen as anti-important. It gets in the way of coming to one another as gentle, roundly developed human beings.

121

Another way to say some of what I mean is this: The posts about Jiddu Krishnamurti and Alan Watts, have inspired basically no responses, heated or otherwise. So many of you guys would rather quibble about punching and kicking one another. Does anything seem a bit out of balance here? To me, it's also interesting that no one seems much interested in Bruce Lee as a person: Who was he? What mattered to him? How does that relate to who we are? Ninety-five percent of posts on this site, and I bet others about Lee, are what I'll call "thing" related, a groping for plain (dull) surface facts. There are much larger, more interesting worlds out there, I assure you.

James Bishop: That has been my point all along. If you look at my writing on the subject, I have been using Bruce Lee as a starting point to discuss social problems, to introduce people to new ideas that they would not otherwise be exposed to, and to inspire people to try to achieve their own dreams. Yes, when this forum started out, my hope was that it would be more philosophical in nature, but it has leaned toward "surface facts", an apropos choice of words because, as you say, it rarely reaches below the surface. Still, by and large, we have a large group of engaging people on this forum and some quality stuff does result. Along the way I try to slip in something in the way of an educational experience and suggestions for self-growth. In the end, spending so much time studying one individual is pointless unless there is something productive you can learn from the individual's life and experiences. And as I have said before, you can learn as much from a person's faults and failures as you can from their successes.

Davis Miller: Yeah, all of that strikes me as real and true. As I've written and re-written here, my problems, if I have any, and I'm not sure I do, mostly aren't with Bruce Lee -- they are with our perceptions of him. And I honestly, fully believe/feel that Bruce Lee's life and death say something important about the distinctly American religious product of self-actualization, and how as a world culture, we seem to be "youth-anizing" ourselves. As far as I can tell, what killed Bruce Lee was his own obsessive, myopic ambition. And finally, for me, that's one of the most powerful, and certainly most "meaningful", things about his story.

But that's not what fans come here to read now, is it? And that's why I'm regarded as a bit of a problem by some of the faithful. We all need to inflate a few balloons at times in our lives. Some of us also grow up enough to be willing to pop them when and where it's appropriate to do so.

And Bruce Lee popped a few balloons himself, now didn't he? Not exactly a pious fellow, young Mr. Lee. So how and why did all this piety fester up around him?

Although this puzzles me, I find myself regularly referring to what seems to be obvious: Bruce Lee's tale being something of a Jesus story. I bet those old (even when they were young) Jesus disciple coots -- not to mention the disciples of the disciples -- might've felt personally threatened, too, if and when someone offered to share a take on their man that didn't fit into their Son of God rigor. Is anything wrong with any of this? Of course not. It seems to be in and of the nature of being human to need to make gods that look an awful lot like ourselves.

James Bishop: The point you make about comparing it to the Jesus story is one I had come to as well. Without giving a sense of deifying Bruce, but in a strictly anthropological sense, there are several parallels that are worth noting, and the way both their legacies developed out of their students is interesting, in regards to the motivations of their students in perpetuating that legacy.

Davis Miller: I don't mean to sound self-important here, or ambiguous for the sake of avoidance, or cynical (I'm not a cynic), or mean in any way; I simply think it's healthiest and best for you to make your own discoveries, which I'm sure will happen if you keep spending time with Bruce Lee and his (in some ways Jesusy) legacy."

The Gospel According to Bruce Lee. There's a danger in literalism -- and in the twin gods of celebrity and hero worship. Surely this is not something that Lee himself would have said he wanted, though I bet he knew it was likely to happen.

Is any of this wrong? Right and wrong seems a small-smart way of looking at the world. It's simply what is. But all of this does say something about the way religions and other major and minor mythologies are born.

Conclusion

I agree with Davis Miller on one important point: there is a danger in "jesusfying" Bruce Lee. I have seen some references from fans stating that he was the second coming of Christ, or hyperbolic statements in the same vein, such as: "When the wind blew, a *savior* emerged." Yet, in one laughable instance, I received an email from one fan with a decidedly *anti*-Christ take on it. "Bruce Lee," the fan informed me, "said himself, 'be formless like water' and if I am not mistaken the devil was said to be formless. Also, Bruce Lee was born on the exact hour of the Dragon on the Chinese calendar, which, as you know, is the Biblical Beast."

Make of that what you will.

TAKY KIMURA

Bruce Lee is best remembered by those who knew him, not as a martial artist or movie star, but as a teacher and friend.

When Bruce first arrived in Seattle, he began to develop a reputation for teaching gung fu. Soon Bruce had many people wanting to study under him. One of those people was a thirty-eight year old Japanese-American named Taky Kimura. Kimura had spent five years in a United States internment camp during World War II and suffered difficulty in getting a decent job afterward, under the shadow of post-war anti-Japanese sentiment. Demoralized, Kimura was seeking something to give him back his self-confidence. He found that in the young Bruce Lee, who became his mentor, spiritual guide, and best friend.

Of all the people associated with Bruce Lee, Taky Kimura is the finest. That, I believe, is why Bruce Lee referred to Kimura as his senior-most student and made it clear to others, such as the man seen by some as Lee's protégé, Dan Inosanto, that Kimura was always to be respected by them. Was Kimura the best martial artist? No, but he was the best friend of Bruce Lee and a man of sterling character. I believe it was Kimura's *moral core*, not his martial art skill, that Lee recognized, and which he felt was so important to his art. Kimura has never accepted compensation for his work in Bruce Lee's name, and has quietly been the caretaker of Bruce Lee's grave for almost 30 years. He is a man who is universally respected in the Bruce Lee community, and a shining example of the positive impact that Bruce Lee's philosophy has had on people.

James Bishop: Taky, tell me about your experiences in the United States internment camps during World War II.

Taky Kimura: All the time we were growing up, my mother and dad always said: "Look, we're nothing but second-class citizens, so don't ever put yourself in the mainstream of life because you are going to get hurt." We argued with them because the educational system told us that we were equal under the constitution. But then (when the war came along) all of a sudden things changed and we were put in the internment camps, even though we were citizens. The Selective Service put us in the 4Y category, which was an alien classification, and they told us that there were rumors that they were going to take us and ship us off to some island as soon as they could get rid of us. Anyhow, they put us in camps.

I came out and I was just a broken man because of this humiliation that occurred within myself. And then in 1959 I had the wonderful honor of being in the right place at the right time to meet Bruce.

James Bishop: What was it like meeting Lee?

Taky Kimura: He was eighteen, a typical teenager with all this boundless energy, telling dirty jokes and all that, and I was thirty-six and just mentally devastated. I couldn't relate to that, but he understood.

James Bishop: What did Lee do for you?

Taky Kimura: Bruce came along and helped me out. He used to say, "Jesus Christ Kimura! Look at these clothes you're wearing! You look like an old man!" And I would say, "I'm clean aren't I?" But you know, he told me to wear different clothes and all this kind of stuff, and it was all a part of making me realize that I am a human being, no better or worse than anyone else. He told that repeatedly to me, and (by teaching you the fundamentals of the physicalness within yourself) obviously you start feeling better about yourself when you know that you can do something. I think that that is one of the great things. Unfortunately, we all have to go through this process to understand what our capabilities are. But if you don't progress any further than that, then you're not going to get anywhere.

James Bishop: What do you think Bruce Lee would have been like today, had he lived?

Taky Kimura: My whole contention is - people have asked me this numerous times, you know, Bruce was a guy that had that overbearing confidence and didn't want to lose. What do you think would happen to him today? I say, "Look, I knew Bruce Lee pretty damned well. He was a guy that had himself together in a lot of ways. From the letters he had written me, there was no question in my mind as to what he'd be doing today. My answer is he would have made that transition from the early stage of the power structure of his life. He'd be about 60 years old now. Even at 60, at this point (if he were still alive), with all of his attributes and doing all the things and climbing all the mountains that people would like to in their lifetime, he would still have been a tremendous force to be reckoned with. The other thing: if Bruce were alive today, he would be getting more into the philosophical plateau of life and doing and creating all these sort of aphorisms that great men do.

James Bishop: On my forum, one of Davis Miller's arguments was that this whole philosophical angle relating to Bruce Lee is, as Miller describes it, "John Little's fantasy". He also called it the "reductive, fortune-cookie wisdom" of Bruce Lee.

Taky Kimura: You know, I'm just so distressed and feel so badly that when I met Davis Miller and he came up here to interview us for the "Curse of the Dragon" documentary, he spoke so highly of Bruce and was so positive in his conversation with me. It just really hurts me to hear him saying something like that. You know what I mean? I don't know where he is getting all of this stuff from. He's certainly getting it from some [*chuckles*] source I can't conceive of.

You know, Bruce was a normal human being. You have to put that in perspective. I mean, in one of the last interviews he did, he said, "I've yet to control my anger." The interviewer said, "Well, you've matured." And Bruce Lee said, "No, not matured because when you mature, you are in the pine box. Let's put it that I am maturing still yet." But he recognized his flaws like anybody else does. There's not a man on the face of the Earth that has not some things that he wished he could have done better. When they put that lid on your coffin, then you can't go any further. Life is a constant struggle for getting better, and, my God, we're all human, you know! You've got to be God if nothing is wrong with you.

James Bishop: My perspective has always been that you can learn a lot from what Bruce Lee accomplished, but you can also learn from his human flaws, as you can from anybody's. It just depends on how you look at the situation, whether you try to learn something positive from it, or whether it serves as fuel for your negative leanings.

Taky Kimura: Well, I'm just a frail old man, Jim, and I have had a lot of people say a lot of positive things about me, and, that being the case, a large part of that is because of what Bruce Lee did for me. So, this really just irks me that someone would take advantage of someone that isn't here anymore. If you have to succumb to that negativeness to try to write a book or get some kind of notoriety for yourself, you have to pity that person, you know?

[At this point Taky shifts the subject to the philosophy lectures we recently completed in Ireland at Trinity College in Dublin and Queen's University in Belfast, which included myself, John Little and Andy Kimura, Taky's son and my friend.]

I certainly appreciate you putting up with Andy. I know that he really respects you and John and some of the other people he met over there. He certainly has learned a lot from it, you know, even about himself.

James Bishop: We really had a great time and were able to accomplish something really positive and meaningful. Andy and I were both profoundly affected by the experience, going through those slums in Northern Ireland, seeing what was going on in that society, the violence and abject poverty, talking to the social workers there and asking them how we could help their progress; talking to the Irish fans of Bruce Lee who told us how Bruce Lee's philosophy helped them look past the sectarian hatred and embrace their enemies. We saw the way in which we can make a positive impact.

Taky Kimura: That is why I strongly feel that if you don't find yourself in the upper plateau of life (which is beyond the physicalness of yourself) you haven't lived. I really do believe that we are all on this earth to leave a legacy behind us and Bruce has. Certainly, for me, it is not going to be a big circle of people like Bruce has inspired, but every one of us has friends that, someday after we are gone, are going to be saying, "Hey! That guy was really a great guy!" And that is what we are here for.

James Bishop: I completely agree.

Taky Kimura: You know, Jim, I go up to the cemetery at least once a month and sometimes five or six times a day depending on who comes in from some far away place to check in with me. I usually take them up to the cemetery, and maybe I'll take them out to lunch when it's over with. But, there are a lot of people like that,

that I bump into when I'm up there, and I usually speak to the people and say, "Gee, where are you from, and what brought you up here?" And there are so many people who come up there looking for something positive through Bruce Lee to try to help them find themselves. They are not even martial artists! That's what really blows my mind. I'll ask them, and they will say, "No, I'm not a martial artist. I'm from England. I just had to come to visit his grave because he has done so many wonderful things." He stands out to be such a person. And you know, that's not happening very much in current affairs. People are becoming more selfish. They want everything handed to them on a silver platter, and they could give a damn whether something good happens to you as long as something good happens to them. And it's all because there are no role models out there anymore.

James Bishop: Precisely. I was 23 years old when I discovered Bruce and the kind of man he was, and he was a tremendous role model. It was the way he lived his life and his philosophy that encouraged me to go back to school and finish my education, to study the philosophical disciplines, to become a writer, now a teacher; and to achieve everything I have achieved. His example did that.

Taky Kimura: But we are all human, you know, Jim? There's not a one of us who can stand up before God and say he never made a mistake. If you say that, it's because you're not doing anything.

James Bishop: Right.

Taky Kimura: I'm a guy that's low-key. But there's a higher level of perspective that I believe in.

Bruce Lee, if he were alive today, would be at the level of the great philosophers. At the beginning stages, when he came here, he emulated and spoke the words of the philosophers. Then he became the philosopher. Then from the letter he had written me when he was down and out and just never gave up, he was always back on the trail, dreaming up something more, planning something more positive. These are things that he told me constantly and for that reason.[73]

---

[73] It is my belief that Bruce Lee had his life divided into three parts. The first was dedicated to the physical, the development of his fighting skills and his body. I believe that the second third of his life was to be committed to some sort of political activism. This belief is

reinforced by a statement made by Chuck Norris, his friend and student, who said Bruce Lee told him that he planned on retiring around 1975-1976, spend ten years enjoying his family, then reemerge into the public arena to serve in some philanthropic capacity. I believe that Bruce Lee saw the autumn of his life, the last third, dedicated to his spiritual development. Again, a statement Bruce Lee made just prior to his death seems to concur with that assessment. He told his brother that he intended to live to be a hundred years old, and envisioned himself as an old Taoist priest. If we then divide a life of a hundred years into thirds, we will arrive at roughly the same age at which Bruce Lee died, having completed only the physical third of his development.

KNOWING IS NOT ENOUGH. WE MUST KNOW WHERE IT CAME FROM

This chapter grew from my own studies in philosophy, literature, and psychology. I found that many of the statements and writings that had been credited to Bruce Lee were not his own. It has been a source of venom from many critics of Bruce Lee, most of whom get their information second-hand, not having the acumen or background to have made such discoveries themselves.

I, too, have found it disturbing that Bruce Lee was miscredited, perhaps more legitimately so, for I have quoted him on a few occasions in articles and lectures only to find out the words were not his. As a scholar, it is a distressing experience, but as a *learner*, as a *seeker*, it afforded me the opportunity to learn of other great minds whose posterity could be yet another guide to me. Without these misattributions, I would never have come to know the works of Carl Rogers, Eric Hoffer or Krishnamurti.

Yet, instead of seeing it as productive opportunity, most critics have used it to fuel their own agendas. In this article, I attempt to head off the critics by not only voicing an *apologia* for Bruce Lee and his biographers, but also pointing out many new discoveries I have made of words being wrongly attributed to Bruce Lee.

I do feel that, to some degree, there has been a conscious effort on the part of those in control of Bruce Lee's memory to discourage the discovery of such examples of misattribution, through the reluctance to release information about his source material, such as an inventory of his personal library. I don't feel that it serves them or Bruce Lee in any manner to do so.

One of Bruce Lee's most popular aphorisms is: "Knowing is not enough; we must apply...willing is not enough; we must do." It's a mantra that has been repeated by thousands of Bruce Lee fans throughout the world. It is a valid piece of advice to live by. However, it's not the words of Bruce Lee-it's the words and idea of Johann Von Goethe, a German poet/novelist.

Is the issue of authorship even an important one? Said a Bruce Lee fan in a recent Internet forum message: "It amazes me how caught up in nonsensical BS so many people seem to find themselves. All these 'questions' as to whom Bruce's quotes were 'really' attributable is neurotic babble. Who gives a shit? It's just information, and if I got it from Bruce then why would I worry about who said it?"

This precisely illustrates the problems inherent in such misattribution. Quotes like the one by Goethe merely scratch the surface of the wisdom and experience of the actual author.[74] When fans look no further than Bruce Lee, they are missing the entire body of work of the real author, which likely will contain more equally significant statements that Bruce Lee neglected to mention or perhaps never even read. To put it in martial art terms, it is comparable to researching Wing Chun to better understand Jeet Kune Do. Wing Chun was Bruce Lee's martial foundation, and many original students of Bruce Lee's, such as Patrick Strong, have found the answers to many unresolved questions by examining Wing Chun.

An easy example of this is in the works of Jiddu Krishnamurti. Since Bruce Lee's "borrowing" of Krishnamurti's words came to light, many Bruce Lee fans have discovered an engaging philosophy that yields many valuable pearls of wisdom. Likewise, the works of Carl Rogers, Eric Hoffer, Alan Watts, Napoleon Hill[75], and Hugh Prather are likewise examples of Bruce Lee's sources which, when researched further, are fountains of wisdom.

Beyond the obvious point, that it is important to give credit where credit is due, misattributed quotes such as these have created a political circus in the Bruce Lee community. On the one hand, you have "Bruce Lee Deconstructionists" who seize these quotes as fodder for their campaigns to tear down Bruce Lee.[76] On the other hand, there are Bruce Lee zealots who have a

---

[74] Nevermind that it is, at best, misleading, and , at worst, a form of second-hand plagiarism. The Bruce Lee Estate is currently selling a poster through the Century Martial Arts supply company that features Goethe's "Knowing is Not Enough" quote and gives credit to Bruce Lee for the statement. Marketing these statements for profit is tantamount to stealing from the real author and in the same token defrauding those who buy it, believing it to be the words of Bruce Lee.

[75] Napoleon Hill's book, *Think and Grow Rich,* was a very big inspiration to Bruce Lee, and was the reason he began writing daily affirmations and the genesis of the idea for his "Definite Chief Aim" declaration, where he put to paper his belief that within a few years he would be the top Chinese movie star in the world.

[76] Ayn Rand, in her essay, *The Age of Envy,* does an excellent job of examining such "deconstructionists". Rather than aspiring to elevate humanity, the deconstructionist seeks to keep it down. "This is particularly clear in the more virulent forms of hatred, masked as envy, for those who possess personal values or virtues: hatred for a man because he is beautiful or intelligent or successful or honest or happy. In these cases, the creature has no desire and makes no effort to improve its appearance, to develop or use its intelligence, to struggle for success, to practice honesty, to be happy (nothing can make it happy). It knows that the disfigurement or the mental collapse or the failure or the immorality or the misery of its victim would not endow it with his or her value. *It does not desire the value: it desires the value's destruction.*"

strange need to get their wisdom from Bruce Lee and Bruce Lee alone and will rationalize any questionable truths to maintain their psychological paradigms.

"Bruce Lee, judging by the size of his library, spent a lot of time reading a wide variety of things, which is something *all* of us should engage in," says David Williams, a California Wing Chun instructor. "Read the source material, and don't just assume it all sprang from the godhead version of Bruce Lee."

Bruce Lee's genius was not in originality so much as it was in taking the old and making it new again, in taking many disparate ideas and philosophies and finding the commonality in them. It is something that many philosophers did, especially Alan Watts, whose own son Mark said that his father did just exactly what Bruce Lee is being criticized for, which is to simply reinterpret old beliefs for a new audience. Watts' entire body of work was predicated on that. Was Bruce Lee on a level with Watts? Certainly not, but perhaps he might have achieved that status in time. Keep in mind that Alan Watts had many more years to learn, grow and write. Watts was a more august student of the philosophies, and would be higher up the ladder of the hierarchy, if one were to exist in philosophy. But the value of Bruce Lee's philosophy is up to the individual alone to decide.

Many of the Bruce Lee Deconstructionists have used such misattributions to criticize both the Bruce Lee Educational Foundation and its former director, John Little. Said Tom Bleecker, the second husband of Bruce Lee's widow and the author of the book *Unsettled Matters,* "I'm interested in people's thoughts concerning the most recent John Little plagiarism. For those who don't know the particulars, it began years ago when Linda Lee auctioned off what she claimed to be the authentic writing of Bruce -- an original essay called *The Passionate State of Mind.* This eight-page essay exchanged hands a few times, and John Little published the essay in one of his books on Lee. Then someone was smart enough and perceptive enough to suspect that this could not be Bruce Lee's writing. A simple search engine resulted in what has become a major headache and embarrassment of Lee historian Little. It turns out that this 'essay' was not Bruce's essay at all, but instead the work of renowned philosopher Eric Hoffer, recipient of the Presidential Medal of Freedom."[77]

---

[77] Bleecker's criticism is ironic considering he was the silent author on Linda Lee's book *The Bruce Lee Story,* which also wrongly attributed passages to Lee.

It is apparent that (for such people) the motive is not edification or proper attribution; instead, it is a desire to generate a negative image of someone that they are trying to deconstruct. *Passionate State of Mind* is just the vehicle the individual believes will help to achieve his end. If it weren't that, it would just be something else. The argument that "Passionate" was miscredited is legitimate; the critic's motivations for bringing it up are not. More than this, the critic's primary hope is not to tear down Bruce Lee so much as it is to tear down the personal respect that people have for him. The target is not Bruce Lee, but his fans.

While it is easy for such people to criticize, the truth is much more complicated. Let's break it down for everybody. The writings of Bruce Lee amounted to several thousand pages of material. I have seen a bit of this myself, first-hand. Bruce Lee had over 2,500 books in his library. [78] It would require reading every one of those books to check every single word that Bruce Lee wrote down. It also requires you to have imprinted in your memory every single phrase that Bruce Lee has written, so that you can recognize the work when you come across it. The act of correlating every single word, and trying to find if it had its origins elsewhere, would be a tremendous undertaking in itself. I should point out that Little was definitely under pressure, from both the publisher and the Bruce Lee Estate, to get these books out in a timely fashion. Reading every book in Bruce Lee's library first was not an option. Beyond that, there is the issue that much of it may not be from the library of books that he had, but instead from other sources, such as public libraries, audio recordings, and lectures.

I can say with certainty that John Little had no intention of giving Bruce Lee improper credit for other people's words. In fact, he welcomed the opportunity for eagle-eyed scholars to help him find such instances where they may have taken place, so that proper crediting could be made in future editions. John told me he received hateful mail pointing such things out, and on the other hand very positive mail from people who were far more helpful and understood that taking on such a project is comparable to the mapping of the human genome in terms of difficulty. For the record, it was John Little who recently discovered the Goethe

---

[78] The Bruce Lee Estate is said to have over 2,500 books in Bruce Lee's personal library. It is also known that Lee possessed other books that are no longer in that collection. Just going by the figure in the current estate archives, and proceeding from 1959 (when Lee first arrived in America) to 1973 (when he died), Bruce Lee would have had to have read three and a half books every week for those fourteen years just to cover the 2,500 books. I don't believe he could have possibly accomplished that, and I believe many of the books in his collection went unread.

quote while researching his current philosophical project. Though no longer involved with the Bruce Lee world, he asked me to make sure that people were aware of its proper source.

The point to the last statement is that no matter how well read you are, there is always something you haven't read. That is why the naysayers didn't take into account, didn't even consider, all the things that John Little did find in Bruce Lee's notes which he was able to recognize as not being original prior to publication, and either noted it as such or did not include it whatsoever.

A few months ago, Canadian Doug Klinger, a private Jeet Kune Do student under Ted Wong, found another example of misattribution when he discovered that the poems "Who Am I?" and "Which Are You?" (which are often attributed to Bruce Lee) are the work of Harry and Joan Mier in their 1968 book *You Too Can Work Wonders*.

A few that I have come across in recent months include: "If I said I could beat Patterson, you'd think I was bragging. If I said I couldn't, I'd be lying." This is a statement by Rocky Marciano to a group of high school kids about then champ Floyd Patterson. It is obviously Bruce Lee's inspiration for his statement: "Well, if I tell you I'm good, probably you will say that I'm boasting. But if I tell you I'm not good, then you'll know I'm lying." (Source: Ted Thomas interview).

This is from Carl Rogers' 1951 book *Client-Centered Therapy:* "We cannot teach another person directly; we can only facilitate his learning." You will immediately recognize this as incredibly similar to Bruce Lee's: "I cannot teach you, only help you to explore yourself." Carl Rogers' impact on Bruce Lee was profound. Much of Lee's personal philosophy (particularly on self-actualization) was taken directly from Rogers.[79] It seems clear to me that this is yet another example of a quote that Bruce Lee borrowed and adapted for his own use.

Here is another quote by Amos Bronson Alcott, so close to Bruce Lee's statement that it needs no explanation: "The true teacher defends his pupils against his own personal influence."

The following is attributed to Bruce Lee on the Bruce Lee Educational Foundation's website: "If you love life, don't waste time, for time is what life is made up of." It is actually Ben Franklin, who wrote: "Dost thou love life? Then waste not time, for time is the stuff that life is made of."

---

[79] According to former Bruce Lee Educational Foundation director John Little, in Bruce Lee's copy of Rogers' *On Becoming a Person* there were over 1,000 lines of text highlighted by Lee and numerous annotations throughout the book.

The following is attributed to Bruce Lee in the book *Striking Thoughts:* "The ego boundary is the differentiation between the self and the otherness." It is actually the words of Dr. Fritz Perls in his 1966 book *Gestalt Therapy.*

I have spent considerable time tracking down Bruce Lee's research material to find instances where quotes attributed to him were not original. Though I found many, I was unable to find any instances where Bruce Lee, himself, consciously plagiarized. That was until I read Alan Watts' book, *This Is It,* first published in 1960. I was disturbed to discover that Bruce Lee had borrowed liberally from it for a college English paper.

The essay, titled "A Moment of Understanding", recounted a series of epiphanies that Bruce Lee supposedly had as a student of Wing Chun gung fu under Professor Yip Man. In it Lee recounted reaching an impasse in his training in gung fu. Wrote Bruce Lee: "When I said I must relax, the demand for effort in 'must' was already inconsistent with the effortlessness in 'relax.'"[80]

I was deeply disturbed to find that Bruce Lee had taken this from Alan Watts' book. "Need it be said," wrote Watts, "that the demand for effort in 'must' is inconsistent with the demand for effortlessness in 'relax'?"[81]

Bruce Lee's story continued. "When my acute self-consciousness grew to what the psychologists called double-blind type, my instructor would again approach me and say, 'Loong, preserve yourself by following the natural bends of things and don't interfere. Remember never to assert yourself against nature: never be in frontal opposition to any problem, but control it by swinging with it.'"[82]

This shocked me even further. Not only did Bruce Lee take from Watts yet again, he had placed Watts' judo metaphor in the mouth of Yip Man, for as Watts wrote, "To maintain control we have to learn new reactions, just as in the art of *judo* one must learn not to resist a fall or an attack but to control it by swinging with it. Now *judo* is a direct application to wrestling of the Zen and Taoist philosophy of *wu-wei,* or *not asserting* oneself against nature, of not being in frontal opposition to the direction of things."[83]

---

[80] Source: Page 37 of the book *The Bruce Lee Story* by Linda Lee. Ohara Publications, Inc. Santa Clarita, California, 1989.
[81] Source: Page 63 of the book *This Is It* by Alan Watts. Vintage Books edition, 1973. First published in 1960.
[82] Source: Page 37 of *The Bruce Lee Story.*
[83] Source: Page 67 of *This Is It.*

Perhaps most disturbing was yet to come. Bruce Lee continued his story, telling of his growing frustration and his decision to take a boat out onto the water to find some meditative solitude. In frustration he struck at the water and had an epiphany. The water was soft and adaptable. He realized he must be like water. "Suddenly a bird flew past and cast a reflection on the water. Right then, as I was absorbing myself, another mystic sense of hidden meaning started upon me. Shouldn't it be the same then that the thoughts and emotions I had in front of an opponent passed like the reflection of the bird over the water? This was exactly what Professor Yip Man meant by being detached - not being without emotion or feeling, but being one in whom feeling was not sticky or blocked. Therefore, in order to control myself I must accept myself by going with, and not against, my nature. I lay on the boat and felt that I had untied with *Tao*; I had become one with nature. I just lay there and let the boat drift freely and irresistibly according to its own will. For at that moment I had achieved a state of inner feeling in which opposition had become mutually cooperative instead of mutually exclusive, in which there was no longer any conflict of mind. The whole world to me was unitary."[84]

This was the most shocking discovery of all. Not only was text borrowed verbatim from Watts, but the entire bird incident was taken from Watts and *passed off as Bruce Lee's own personal experience.* Wrote Watts: "This is what Zen means by being detached - not being without emotion or feeling, but being one in whom feeling is not sticky or blocked, and through whom the experiences of the world pass like the reflections of birds flying over water...their goal is a state of inner feeling in which oppositions have become mutually co-operative instead of mutually exclusive, in which there is no longer any conflict between the individual man and nature...their view of the world is unitary."[85]

At the very least, this confirms that the bird part of the story and Yip Man's comments to Bruce Lee are a fraud. At the most, it calls into question the veracity of the entire account. If Yip Man never said what he said, if the whole boat trip served as a set up for the use of Watts' bird-over-the-water analogy, then it is likely that the "be like water" portion of it was equally unlikely or, worse yet, another example of plagiarism (it did not appear in Watts'

---

[84] Source: Page 39 of *The Bruce Lee Story*.

[85] Source: Pages 68 and 48 of *This Is It*.

book). Therefore, one of the pillars of Bruce Lee's martial art philosophy, his water epiphany, is shattered, putting the whole structure in jeopardy.

In Bruce Lee's defense, there is no indication that he tried to defraud anybody with this tale other than his college English teacher.[86] The story never appeared in anything that he published during his lifetime, nor did he refer to it in any interviews. It is no less disturbing, however, to have discovered it.

It is not the only such discovery I have made. Aware of the possibility of Bruce Lee borrowing from Alan Watts in his Seattle era work, I searched further. I discovered that Lee had also borrowed from Watts' book, *The Way of Zen*. In the essay title "On Wu-Hsin" (obviously another school paper) published in the book, *The Tao of Gung Fu,* there were several instances where Bruce Lee either paraphrased or directly copied the writing of Alan Watts. One of the most humorous examples was at the very beginning, preceding a passage which he identifies as Alan Watts, when Bruce Lee writes, "The phenomenon of wu-hsin, or 'no-mindedness,' is not a blank mind that shuts out all thoughts and emotions; nor is it simply calmness and quietness of mind. Although quietude and calmness are necessary, it is the 'non-graspingness' of thoughts that mainly constitute the principle of no mind. A gung fu man employs his mind as a mirror - it grasps nothing and refuses nothing; it receives but does not keep."[87]

Lee took this from *The Way of Zen,* when Watts writes: "It is not simply calmness of mind, but 'non-graspingness' of mind. In Chuang Tzu's words, 'The perfect man employs his mind as a mirror. It grasps nothing; it refuses nothing. It receives but does not keep."[88] Bruce Lee also re-uses Watts' "sticky or blocked" passage from *This Is It* in the same essay.

Likewise, in the essay titled "On Wu-Wei" that follows the Bruce Lee essay on wu-hsin in *Tao of Gung Fu*, the introductory sentence is taken from the same book by Alan Watts. "Wu means 'not' or 'non' and wei means 'action,' 'doing,' 'striving,' 'straining,' or 'busyness.'"[89]

---

[86] The late Ed Hart, a former gung fu student of Bruce Lee's during his time in Seattle, admitted to writing some of Lee's college essays for him. That being the case, the *Bruce Lee Library Series* may very well be the *Ed Hart Library Series* as well.

[87] Source: Bruce Lee's essay titled "On Wu-Hsin" on page 127 of the book, *Bruce Lee: Tao of Gung Fu*, Charles E. Tuttle Publishing Company, 1997.

[88] Source: pages 19 and 20 of the book, *The Way of Zen,* by Alan Watts. My copy is the 1989 Vintage Books edition, although it was originally released in 1959 by Pantheon Books.

[89] Source: page 19 of the book, *The Way of Zen,* by Alan Watts.

Perhaps even more disturbing are the misattributions in Bruce Lee's only self-published book, *Chinese Gung Fu: The Philosophical Art of Self-Defense.* In it Lee takes liberally from Tsai Lung-Yun's Chinese language book, *Fundamental Training on Martial Arts*, copying text, exercises, and drawings. Ironically, the only change Lee makes to the drawings is to place the figures in more classical gung fu uniforms instead of the non-classical attire in which they are drawn in Tsai Lung-Yun's book.[90] Lee actually has the audacity to indicate (in the table of contents) that "All drawings by author".

While I defend Bruce Lee on misattributions of which he had no control, these conscious examples are clearly a human failing on his part. As a professional in the philosophical and educational community, it is of great concern to me when Bruce Lee is given credit for another writer's work. To do so is not fair to the writers who originated the passages nor to the readers who are misled by them. Clearly, a better job could have been done to compile the notes of Bruce Lee and verify their originality. Certainly, an abundance of the blame must fall to *Bruce Lee Library Series* editor John Little. Yet, the responsibility rests with more than just John Little, as many of these examples predate his involvement with the Bruce Lee world.

Linda Lee Cadwell also has a responsibility with respect to the material. It is questionable that Linda Lee Cadwell could retain Lee's personal library for the past thirty years and not stumble upon the fact that many of the writings were not his own. It seems to indicate, at the very least, that she had no inclination to read the books in her house. Surprising, considering she herself was a teacher at one point. It also gives the appearance that the former Linda Lee did not pay enough attention during her marriage to Bruce Lee to realize that he was occupying a lot of his time taking notes, not writing original works. From that one could come to the conclusion that she knew little of what Bruce Lee was doing.

Some of the blame must also fall to the fans. Much of this material has been around since Bruce Lee's death. Given the amount of energy that many fans have put into dissecting the life of Bruce Lee, it is equally disappointing that, with a few exceptions, they have not made these discoveries already. It's indicative of what I have come to expect from many Bruce Lee fans: a myopic concentration on Bruce Lee that leaves no room

---

[90] This particular example I cannot claim credit for. It was published in a 1977 collector's book from Hong Kong titled *Bruce Lee: His Unknowns in Martial Arts Learning*; Published by the Bruce Lee Jeet Kune Do Club of Hong Kong.

for anything else, such as a fully-rounded self-education. Although they are fond of reciting Bruce Lee's "don't concentrate on the finger pointing to the moon" analogy (which Bruce Lee himself took from Zen), they are doing just that.

Finally, Bruce Lee must accept some of the blame as well. Not only did he consciously plagiarize in his only self-published book and university papers, Lee's shockingly poor record-keeping of where he obtained his quotes indicates, at the very least, that he had poor scholarship skills, and, at most, that he may have consciously intended to use them without attribution to their original sources. While Bruce Lee may never had intended them to see print, according to the recollections of many of his friends and students (many of whom still quote him erroneously believing Lee the source of the material), he was quite unabashed in verbally sharing these nuggets of wisdom and allowing the credit to fall to him.

Most importantly, Bruce Lee misquoted in books is one thing; Bruce Lee erroneously quoted on licensed merchandise (such as posters and t-shirts) is quite another. A new series of Bruce Lee posters from the Century Martial Arts Supply Company feature both the "knowing is not enough" quote as well as another: "Life is a journey, not a destination." The former I have already identified as Goethe; the latter is by author Ben Sweetland. These posters are licensed by Concord Moon, the new licensing arm of the Bruce Lee Estate. While I believe the estate is not aware that these are not really Bruce Lee quotes, such examples are much harder to defend for their misattributions than books, as their sole purpose is to generate profit, not education.

I understand that no one person is omniscient and rather than criticize I would prefer to edify. As Lao Tzu said: "The wise seek solutions; the ignorant only cast blame." I would like you to see these examples of misattributions as new opportunities to gather knowledge from different sources. Bruce Lee merely took a cup of water from the wells of these geniuses. It's now time for you to go to the wells yourself and drink liberally. In time, my hope is that we can identify any other such misattributions that have not yet been identified. A person should approach what Bruce Lee left behind, particularly his philosophy, with a critical eye but not reject it simply because it may not be original to him. The words have value, not because Bruce Lee said it, ergo it must be true, but because you feel it to be true yourself. I invite the readers to ultimately make up their own minds.

THE
BRUCE LEE EDUCATIONAL FOUNDATION

I feel I would be remiss if I did not devote just a little space to the Jun Fan Jeet Kune Do Nucleus, the Bruce Lee Educational Foundation, and the Bruce Lee Estate. As the groups chiefly responsible for perpetuating Bruce Lee's martial, philosophical, and historical legacy, they bear noting. I feel that most fans, thus far, have only received a partial picture of the Nucleus and the Estate from their official publications and member interviews. While I hope the following chapters are illuminating for the fans of Bruce Lee, I have chosen not to write about some darker occurrences while refraining from giving too many specific details about others.

In 1996, a group of people associated with Bruce Lee met in Seattle to discuss the future of Bruce Lee's martial art. This group consisted of family, friends, and students of Bruce Lee, as well as a few second-generation instructors in his art and the Bruce Lee Estate's historian. Concerned that the memory of Bruce Lee's martial art was degrading, they decided to form an organization to preserve Lee's art and history and to act as a resource for others. They called the organization *Jun Fan Jeet Kune Do*, after Lee's Chinese name, "Jun Fan", and the name of his martial art, "Jeet Kune Do". Jun Fan Jeet Kune Do was established as a non-profit foundation under federal guidelines. The founders would function as the core of this organization, or its "Nucleus", and would open it up to general membership for fans of Bruce Lee and students of his art. In addition, the Jun Fan Jeet Kune Do Nucleus would host annual seminars that would allow general members to gather, meet, and train with the members of the Nucleus.

Said Linda Lee Cadwell: "We all know why we're here. We're here for Bruce, and so that the philosophy that Bruce was practicing and studying in his lifetime can continue to benefit people all over the world."

One of the first people to join as a general member was Doug Klinger. Klinger is a private student of Nucleus member Ted Wong. "The Jun Fan Jeet Kune Do Nucleus seminars were the first time a majority of Bruce's Students *(either in the Nucleus or outside...ala Jesse Glover)* had gathered to perpetuate Bruce Lee," says Klinger. "The Jun Fan Jeet Kune Do organization also provided a means of contacting the students of Bruce Lee. Some have even met their current instructors through the Nucleus."

Klinger recalls a time without the Nucleus. "You have to remember that, when I started training martial arts, Jeet Kune Do was nothing more than Dan Inosanto and a book by James DeMile on the 1 and 3-inch punch (my first exposure) to most of us. No one outside certain circles knew who the original students were or where they were. As average students, we had no exposure to these people."

The inability to retain one of the prime spokesmen for Bruce Lee's martial art, Dan Inosanto, was an initial failing on the part of the Nucleus that remained a sticking point throughout its existence. Inosanto, considered by many to be the primary torchbearer for Bruce Lee's martial art and the man that Linda Lee Cadwell had herself chosen to train Lee's son Brandon in his father's art, chose to remove himself from the Nucleus after their very first meeting. Speculation has abounded since Inosanto's split with the group. Certainly Inosanto's concern that the Nucleus was trying to solidify and stylize Bruce Lee's art of "no style" was a contributing factor. However, it is also likely that his personal disagreements with some of the Nucleus members, including reported rifts between himself, Steve Golden, Jerry Poteet and Daniel Lee, were additional factors in his decision to disassociate himself with the group. At any rate, this decision created a division in the ranks of Bruce Lee's martial art, dividing them by original Jeet Kune Do advocates (those who favored the Nucleus and strict adherence to what Bruce Lee taught in his lifetime) and the Concepts group (those who favored Inosanto's organization and a continual development of the art).[91] Without the unity of both groups, this became a contentious division not dissimilar to the division between the Republican and Democratic political groups. In addition, Joe Lewis, the kickboxing champion who was the only person to ever prove the efficacy of Lee's art in the ring, chose not to accept an invitation to be a consultant for the Nucleus because of his dislike for John Little, who refused to retract a statement he made in an article for *Black Belt Magazine* in which he recounted a confrontation between Joe Lewis and

---

[91] A letter Linda Lee Cadwell sent to Dan Inosanto, in response to his resignation, harshly critical of Inosanto and admonishing him not to use Bruce or Brandon Lee's name to promote his own efforts, further exacerbated the rift between the two camps.

Bruce Lee which Lewis claims never happened.[92] As a result, the Nucleus was never truly complete and many potential supporters stayed away.

The Nucleus sought to curb the rampant abuse of Bruce Lee's martial art of Jeet Kune Do. Many people who never trained in Bruce Lee's art were promoting themselves as instructors, defrauding people with instruction and curriculum that bore little resemblance to what Bruce Lee actually developed. Little could be done about it as the name "Jeet Kune Do" had become so widely used that it had fallen into public domain. The Nucleus decided to amend the name of Bruce Lee's martial art from "Jeet Kune Do" to "Jun Fan Jeet Kune Do". In this way they could trademark the name and restrict its use. Although drawn from an understandable concern, I believe it was a bad decision; "Jeet Kune Do" was hard enough to remember; adding the "Jun Fan" to it only made it harder. Some outside instructors were already using Jun Fan/Jeet Kune Do, and discovered that, by keeping the slash in the middle, they could continue to use it without violating the Nucleus' trademark. So it was a rather futile effort on the part of the Nucleus.

The Bruce Lee Estate's decision to sell the licensing rights for Bruce Lee merchandising to Universal Pictures in the early 1990s placed a heavy restriction on the Nucleus, handicapping them from the start. Though Universal gave the Nucleus permission to produce some products with Bruce Lee's name and likeness, it heavily restricted what those items could be and stated that the items could only be sold to members of the Jun Fan Jeet Kune Do organization and only advertised within organizational materials. This meant that a vital source of revenue for the Nucleus' projects was not available to them.

A questionable aspect of membership in the Bruce Lee Educational Foundation is a section in their "code of ethics" that forbids public dissension among its members. It forbids any negative comments about the members of the Nucleus, and was recently used to terminate the membership of Lamar Davis, an instructor in Lee's art, when he criticized Nucleus members Cass

---

[92] The incident, familiar to many Bruce Lee fans, involves an angry Joe Lewis confronting Bruce Lee at Lee's home about an alleged sexual advance that Lewis' then girlfriend claimed Bruce Lee made toward her. Little, for his part, claims that Joe Lewis admitted to the incident in an audiotaped interview Little conducted with him (one which he reminded Lewis he still retained when Lewis demanded that he retract his story). Little also claimed to have corroborated the story directly from Linda Lee Cadwell (who was present at the incident) and Bob Wall, a friend and associate of both Joe Lewis and Bruce Lee whom Little claims told him the same story as related to Wall by Joe Lewis.

Magda and Chris Kent. "We all were witness to a recent event that occurred that resulted in a certified instructor being de-listed from the Nucleus and distanced altogether due to comments that occurred on a forum (a closed one at that)," said Matt Wallace, a general member of the Bruce Lee Educational Foundation. "Our rights as Americans, yes, are protected, but our duties as [foundation] members and instructors in Bruce Lee's art are to be ethical and show respect for our sihings, sifus, and anyone associated with Bruce Lee. Conjecturing about Nucleus members, including the Lee family, is not where we want to be as individuals or as Jeet Kune Do practitioners."

I can certainly say I am not surprised by the Nucleus' decision, as Davis is known to be a rebel and prone to inappropriate slips of the tongue. However, I am bothered by their desire to quell dissent. For an organization predicated on the philosophy of a man who believed in the freedom to criticize the status quo openly and publicly, it disturbs me that they expect no criticism of themselves. To only allow public praise from its members is one-sided and promotes blind sycophancy. At any rate, many fans saw this as too restrictive and stayed away.

One of the most important products for the promotion and expression of the Jun Fan Jeet Kune Do Nucleus was the publication of the *Bruce Lee Magazine: The Official Voice of the Jun Fan Jeet Kune Do Nucleus*. This was intended to be their platform from which to speak. Published by CFW Enterprises, the publishers of *Inside Kung Fu* magazine, this was a mass-market publication that held a lot of promise. While it did have its high points, the magazine suffered from lack of contributions by members of the Nucleus, the very people it was being published for. Nucleus member Tim Tackett lamented to me toward the end of its publication that the only people who seemed to be contributing to the magazine were Tackett, John Little, and myself. Little, who served as the editor of the magazine, also expressed his frustration to me that he was having difficulty motivating the rest of the Nucleus members to contribute to the magazine. What resulted was a lot of philosophy articles by John Little and me with Tackett bearing the burden of the majority of technique-related articles. The rest tended to be reprints of existing articles and filler material.[93]

---

[93] On the written contributions of the Nucleus members, an examination of the nine issues of the now-defunct *Bruce Lee Magazine* reveals the following (in order of most credited): John Little (53 articles), Chris Kent (14 articles), Tim Tackett (eight articles), Linda Lee Cadwell (seven articles), Tommy Gong (five articles), Steve Golden (five articles), Ted

The inability of the Nucleus to come to a consensus on a curriculum for Bruce Lee's art was also a point of contention for general members. The Nucleus members were supposed to be the spokespeople for Bruce Lee's original art, yet they could not decide on what that was. The subject of recognizing authentic instructors in "Jun Fan Jeet Kune Do" was also a topic that the Nucleus dragged their proverbial feet on. Then they did a disappointing about-face and declared that they would not recognize instructors at all; they would leave that for Nucleus members to do on an individual basis.

"Although I am sure the majority of Nucleus members are capable of judging one's character, shouldn't it be more of a group decision rather than one person's decision?" asks Paul Bax, an amateur Bruce Lee historian. Bax's groundbreaking article, "The Return of Bruce Lee's Jeet Kune Do" was the catalyst for the formation of the Nucleus. "The Nucleus members all seem like independent Jeet Kune Do contractors now as opposed to a solid organization representing Jeet Kune Do. Before the Nucleus there wasn't any real owner of Jeet Kune Do. Now there are 17 owners and all the 'subcontractors' giving out certificates in Jeet Kune Do, too."

Instead of the clarification of Bruce Lee's martial art as he called for in his historic article, Bax says that the problem has become worse, with what he describes as now three variations on Bruce Lee's Jeet Kune Do: Original, Concepts, and (in his words) "Quick-trip Jeet Kune Do". "I would just like to see a little more quality control over who is getting certified out there. Is it necessary to give out full certification to people with the authority to do their own seminars and certify other people when they have met and trained with a legitimate instructor very little? It seems that there are no standards and no rules as to when and who can do what. If the Nucleus members don't enforce a little more quality control, I think their seminar certified guys are going to start churning out half-baked people representing Bruce Lee's art. I know being certified in Jeet Kune Do by an original student of Bruce Lee means a lot to some people. However, when it becomes too easy I don't think the credentials will mean too much to anyone anymore, and Jeet Kune Do will only suffer from it. It

---

Wong (four articles), Bob Bremer (three articles), Pete Jacobs (three articles), Richard Bustillo (two articles), Andy Kimura (two articles), Cass Magda (two articles), Jerry Poteet (one article), Herb Jackson (one article), Taky Kimura (no articles), Daniel Lee (no articles), Allen Joe (no articles), George Lee (no articles), Greglon Lee (no articles), and Shannon Lee (no articles). Forty-five articles were written by non-Nucleus writers, including five by me in four of the last five issues.

just seems to me that as careful as Bruce Lee was about giving out certification, the individual members of the Nucleus should be the same way."

Non sequitors abounded as well. Linda Lee Cadwell, addressing the Jun Fan Jeet Kune Do/Jeet Kune Do Concepts debate at the 1999 Seattle seminar, referred to the two approaches to Bruce Lee's art as "two sides of the same coin". When the idea of the two schools of Jeet Kune Do being two side of the same coin was put to Nucleus member Steve Golden, his reply was: "*Concepts and Jun Fan Jeet Kune Do are two sides of the same coin?* No way. At best I'd say that they are both money but from different countries. Sometimes each country may accept the other's currency, but not always."

The Jun Fan Jeet Kune Do Nucleus' third annual seminar in Seattle in 1999 was a spectacular affair. The location of the seminar was rich with Bruce Lee history and drew many of his original students. The seminar included a tour of Bruce Lee spots in Seattle where Lee lived, worked and taught martial arts, as well as a solemn visit to his grave.

In an address to the seminar attendees at the evening banquet, Linda Lee Cadwell called on them to continue to create a positive impact on the world and spread Bruce Lee's legacy further. "I think we are making an impact in a positive way," said Cadwell, "so we need all of you to join with us as you have been. We need to continue this and bring more people in. Bruce benefited so many people in this world. I've received letters from all over the world all the time; the stories of such great inspiration he has provided for people, how people's lives have been changed because of Bruce. We need to see that this continues and multiplies, because it's so much help to people."

Following Linda Lee Cadwell's speech, John Little announced the establishment of the Bruce Lee Educational Foundation, a separate but parallel foundation set up to concentrate more on Lee's philosophical legacy rather than his martial art. "I think you'll be very pleased by some of the new information that is coming out about Bruce over the next year, because you are going to have to make room to meet Bruce Lee the philosopher, the poet, the psychologist, the artist, the physical fitness aficionado, the scientist, the sociologist--*all of these*. What we want to do is to actually have courses which will be available through the Foundation, which will help to broaden your understanding and appreciation of Bruce Lee's art, life and philosophy."

Non-martial art fans enthusiastically embraced the announcement. However, some Nucleus and general members met the formation of the Bruce Lee Educational Foundation division of the Nucleus with resistance. Many of the hardcore martial art devotees saw it as watering down the martial art. "Some people who didn't care about philosophy may have thought it was more than enough for them," notes Marcos Ocaña, Spain's leading Bruce Lee historian. "Just different tastes, opinions, interests... different people." Marcos is correct in pointing out that not everyone had an interest in the philosophical side of Bruce Lee. In truth, some members who were there strictly for the martial art aspect canceled their memberships in the false belief that the martial art was going to become subordinate to the intellectual pursuits of the foundation.

In many ways the fans' expectations of the Jun Fan Jeet Kune Do Nucleus and the Bruce Lee Educational Foundation were simply unrealistic. An example of this was evident in a message Nucleus member Tim Tackett posted on his training group's Internet forum. "The other day I received an e-mail from some fan who complained about the Bruce Lee Educational Foundation," wrote Tackett. "He said that there was a crack in Bruce's star on the Hollywood Walk of Fame and that the Bruce Lee Foundation should take care of it. We really have nothing to do with maintaining the star. We can't repair it. The only one who can is the Hollywood Chamber of Commerce. This person was upset with the Bruce Lee Educational Foundation but left no way to respond to him."

Confusion over the purpose and the authority of the Nucleus was a constant since its inception. The Nucleus was a body of students dedicated to preserving Bruce Lee's art, however, most fans seemed to believe that they controlled all aspects of Bruce Lee's legacy, including the rights to his name and likeness, films, and licensing of products; all of which was under the control of the Estate of Bruce Lee - not the Nucleus. Fans often gave the Nucleus credit for everything produced under the Bruce Lee banner. Neither the Jun Fan Jeet Kune Do Nucleus nor the Bruce Lee Educational Foundation had anything to do with the publication of the *Bruce Lee Library Series*, which was a joint effort of John Little and the Estate of Bruce Lee, unrelated to their work for the foundation. Contrary to the general fans' beliefs, the Nucleus had nothing to do with any publications or products that were released during its existence (other than its members-only products, magazine and newsletter); Nucleus members' first involvement in the *Bruce Lee Library* material (with the exception of a few members writing some brief prefatory comments in a couple of the titles) was buying it at the bookstore like the rest of us. All the authority, decision-making, and project development related to the name and image of Bruce Lee has always rested with the Estate of Bruce Lee alone; the Nucleus had absolutely no voice in such matters. The only authority the Nucleus controlled was in the use of the trademarked names Jun Fan Jeet Kune Do and Bruce Lee Educational Foundation.

In 2000, the Jun Fan Jeet Kune Do Nucleus decided to merge the Bruce Lee Educational Foundation and Jun Fan Jeet Kune Do into one organization after recognizing that the name "Bruce Lee Educational Foundation" was much more accessible to the general public than the esoteric "Jun Fan Jeet Kune Do". Additionally, from a logistic standpoint, having two separate foundations was overcomplicating their efforts.

The fourth Annual Jun Fan Jeet Kune Do Annual Seminar, held in April 2000, was less than stellar for fans. While the previous seminars had all been held in places of historical significance to Bruce Lee, the Nucleus chose to hold the 2000 seminar in Las Vegas. The official reason for this was to provide members of the foundation who were unable to travel to the West Coast an opportunity to attend an event closer to their homes, although some fans suspected that the Nucleus was using the seminar as their own personal vacation package. Regardless, fans were less than enthusiastic about the seminar. Their reasons were numerous: they were unable to travel to sites were Bruce Lee once lived and taught, as in previous seminars; Las Vegas was just too busy; there were too many people, too much going on; friends and fans could not find each other amid all the chaos; parents were disturbed to have brought their families to a hotel the outside of which was littered with pornography flyers and ads for Sin City's red light district; and fans were not allowed to use video cameras as they had previously been able to do. Martial art students who had attended the previous seminars began to complain that the training was always basic and no attention was being paid to those with established experience. In addition, many fans felt that the seminar's staff was not only unappreciative of their presence, but also downright rude and condescending. Add to that a few public disagreements between first-generation students of Bruce Lee witnessed by fans[94], and the result was a seminar that paled in comparison to the seminars that preceded it.

In 2001, John Little chose to resign from both his work for the Bruce Lee Estate and as director of the Bruce Lee Educational Foundation. Not long after John Little's departure, Chris Kent, one of the most well regarded member of the Nucleus, resigned as well. His reasons were various, but the resignation of John Little, whom he considered a friend, reportedly played a role in his decision. Not coincidentally, both John Little's and Chris Kent's resignations were cited in the foundation's next newsletter. While the report stated that the Nucleus tried to convince Kent to remain on the board, it was extremely noticeable that the write-up on Little's resignation did not mention such an effort.

Infighting between members of the Nucleus further complicated matters for the Bruce Lee Educational Foundation. A rift reportedly developed between members Ted Wong and Jerry Poteet over competing seminar schedules. Likewise, Poteet caused another uproar on the board of directors when he suggested that only members of the board who actually trained with Bruce Lee should be involved in decisions, a suggestion that was not acceptable to second-generation instructors.

As a result, very little productive work was being done in the name of the Bruce Lee Educational Foundation. The donations and contributions to the foundation were reportedly to go to the following projects:

- The establishment and maintenance of the future Bruce Lee Center (Seattle).
- The establishment and maintenance of regional and international satellite office of the Bruce Lee Educational Foundation.
- The production and distribution of Bruce Lee Educational materials such as books, audio courses, instructional videos and our on-going world-wide internet programs.
- Staffing and administration of the Bruce Lee Educational Foundation.[95]

---

[94] Including one very public argument between Nucleus member Steve Golden and Seattle-era Bruce Lee students Patrick Strong and Jesse Glover, in which Jesse Glover allegedly referred to Golden's Jeet Kune Do techniques as "pitty pat".

[95] Source: Bruce Lee Educational Foundation website: www.bruceleefoundation.com. The website no longer exists, although the domain was signed over to Shannon Lee, who launched a sparse website for a new "Bruce Lee Foundation".

Yet, with the exception of a single secretary as the sole staff member of the foundation and one website that was rarely updated (it is still spotlighting 1999 issues of the foundation's magazine as current), by the end of 2001 no discernible progress had been made toward any of these goals.

Ironically enough, it was next to impossible to get the Bruce Lee Educational Foundation to respond to queries. Questions sent to the foundation via mail or email (more often than not) went unanswered. Worse still, people sending in their memberships or simply renewing existing ones would sometimes have to wait months for it to be processed. Many members simply did not renew after unsuccessful attempts to do so.

Fulfilling membership obligations became an increasing problem as well. Part of the membership package included a quarterly newsletter. The only regularity related to the newsletter was its irregularity; it simply did not come when it was supposed to. This further alienated members, who felt that they were not getting their money's worth.

To add insult to injury, the Bruce Lee Educational Foundation announced that it was raising membership fees and reducing the newsletter to semi-annually.[96] It was promised to be an extra large edition to compensate for the reduced schedule. The first "giant-sized" edition was amateurish and full of obvious filler. In one of the most blatant examples of filler material, several of the pages consisted solely of single-sentence snippets of Bruce Lee quotations, centered within the page. These quotes occupied less than ten percent of the pages and the rest was blank. Giant-sized issue? Yes. What good is that, however, when the vast majority of the added space is blank paper? "I don't know if you have seen it," wrote one fan to me about that issue of the newsletter, "but it is terrible. My friend cancelled his membership, as did several of the people we know. What an insult...I'm sure others will jump as well."

"I am not a member of the Bruce Lee Educational Foundation any longer," said Marco Hernandez, a Jeet Kune Do instructor. "I wasn't going to pay $50 a year for two issues of a magazine without John's [John Little] input in them. I agree that it is a terrible shame that he is no longer associated with the Bruce Lee Educational Foundation."

---

[96] Where the Nucleus got the idea that increasing the membership charge while reducing membership perks would be an act of prudent logic is beyond me.

What's more, the magazine included a full-page appeal for donations for secretary Tammy Ledda's son, who was injured in an accident. While most fans can sympathize with what the Ledda family is going through, it seems to be a clear conflict of interest, for not only is it questionable whether a non-profit foundation can solicit donations among its members specifically for an employee (and not for the purposes of the foundation), but also because Ledda served as the editor and layout person on that issue of the newsletter.

As a result of the various problems, public opinion of the Nucleus began to turn in 2001. "In my opinion most of the Nucleus members are the same," said one fan on an Internet chatroom. "They all want Bruce to get them somewhere. Bruce Lee is a great, if not, the ultimate advertisement for them and their martial arts.[97] If they were teaching Shotokan karate that they learned from Gichin Funakoshi [the founder of the Shotokan style], would they still be as well known? I think not."[98]

That shifting perspective of the Bruce Lee fans had a definite effect on the Bruce Lee Educational Foundation's general membership. Foundation tax records obtained under federal guidelines reveal a remarkable drop in membership in the year 2000. Membership fees received by the Bruce Lee Educational Foundation in 1999 were reported at $63,511; the next year the revenue from membership fees was reported to be $24,903. If we assume that the amount represents members who paid the minimum membership fee amount of $35 (a generous assessment, representing the most members possible), that represents roughly 712 people for the year 2000 compared to 1,815 for the year 1999. That's a staggering decrease of almost 61% in one year's time! Continuing the hemorrhaging, by 2001 the Bruce Lee Educational Foundation's general membership had dropped to below 200 members. Membership dues for the foundation for 2001 were reported on its 2001 tax return as

---

[97] Though the members of the Jun Fan Jeet Kune Do Nucleus often pointed out that they don't get paid for their foundation work, it is also fair to note the ancillary benefits that they receive, such as higher profiles, public exposure, as well as advertising for their individuals programs, seminars, videos, etc.

[98] An interesting analogy that I will take further. Say, hypothetically, Gichin Funakoshi had died at age 32, leaving behind a handful of yellow belts, green belts and a couple of brown belts as students. Suddenly, these people were being looked to for information about Funakoshi's art. Say further that these students were eventually being recognized as masters of Funakoshi's art, even though most of them had only briefly trained with Funakoshi and even then irregularly. Put in that context, you get some idea of the dilemma Bruce Lee's art faces.

$6,000, a 76% drop from the previous year's already paltry earnings, and a drop of nearly 91% in just two years!

The shift in focus for the Bruce Lee Estate began to impact the Bruce Lee Educational Foundation as well. The most apparent indication was the change in status of Linda Lee Cadwell and Shannon Lee regarding its board of directors. At the advice of their lawyers, they could no longer serve as voting members on the board of the non-profit foundation because, with the profit-driven reorganization of the Bruce Lee Estate, there would be a conflict of interest.[99] Becoming non-voting board members was a simple legal maneuver that many fans mistakenly took to mean the Lee family had abandoned the Bruce Lee Educational Foundation. "They didn't leave," points out Steve Golden. "They just cannot be voting board members because of conflict of interest with their corporation. They still attend meetings and are a part of the organization."[100] Not so apparent at the time was that the Nucleus quietly signed over the rights to the name "Bruce Lee Educational Foundation" to Concord Moon.

The decision to hold the 2001 annual Bruce Lee Educational Foundation seminar in Holland was a disastrous one. Attendance was not what was expected. The previous year's seminar in Las Vegas drew over 400 people; the Holland seminar reportedly drew

---

[99] I feel particularly compelled to point out that evidence does seem to favor Linda Lee Cadwell's honest effort to make something positive of the Bruce Lee Educational Foundation. Although she has been accused (like the rest of the Nucleus members) of using the foundation to further her own self-interests, I was told by John Little (while he was still director of the foundation) that both he and she invested their own money into the foundation without an expectation of return. This is confirmed by foundation tax records which identify a $10,000 loan from Linda Lee Cadwell made to the Bruce Lee Educational Foundation in the year 2000, a loan which she had to have known could not be repaid. In addition, page two of the Supplemental Schedule for the Bruce Lee Educational Foundation's 2000 tax return indicated donations in 1999 by John Little for $10,200 and Linda Lee Cadwell for $18,000. That same record also identifies a 1998 donation by Linda Lee Cadwell for the sum of $24,244. None of the tax records for the years 1998, 1999, and 2000 indicate any donations to the foundation made by other members of the Nucleus, although I do know that many often spent their own money attending the meetings and seminars. Therefore, the suggestion that all Nucleus members (and Mrs. Cadwell in particular) are less than magnanimous with regards to the foundation is simply incorrect. By all appearances Linda Lee Cadwell honestly wanted to do justice to her late husband's memory, often giving and sacrificing above and beyond what is generally known.

Additionally, even her ex-husband and chief critic, Tom Bleecker, admitted that Linda Lee Cadwell was not profit-driven. On an AOL Internet forum, Bleecker noted, "I can still recall back in the late 80s when I was married to Linda, her constantly telling me that she wanted no part in the Bruce Lee business. And she was sincere. She wasn't putting anything on. At one point she even raised the notion of giving the lion's share away to charity."

[100] An example of Shannon Lee and Linda Lee Cadwell's continued involvement in the background of the foundation can be found in the last issue of the foundation newsletter, which Shannon Lee reportedly had to edit and compile herself.

less than 200. That, coupled with the fact that the logistics of the European location increased operating costs, seriously damaged the already unstable financial situation of the Bruce Lee Educational Foundation, which depended (in large part) on the annual seminar for its operating capital.

"We lost money in Holland," says Tim Tackett. "They promised 500 students but we didn't get enough to pay our expenses. All teachers ended up paying their own way."

James Ter Beek, one of the organizers of the Holland seminar, has a different perception of what went wrong. "One of the biggest problems that we faced was the lack of publicity. Since it was officially announced in Las Vegas that the seminar would be held in the Netherlands, four *Bruce Lee* magazines were published and none of them contained an announcement about the seminar.

"We also did not know about the problems with John Little and the fact that *Warrior's Journey* had its European premiere one month before the seminar was a matter of very bad timing. Can you imagine how much more people we would have had if the premiere would have been at the seminar?"

On August 9, 2001, following the Lee family's move to become non-voting members of the foundation's board, Shannon Lee called a meeting in Los Angeles of the remaining board members at which she and her mother made a suggestion. The two suggested that Shannon Lee and Concord Moon were in better positions to protect the trademarked name and logo of the Jun Fan Jeet Kune Do Nucleus and that the board should sign the names over to her. "They are willing, through their corporation (Concord Moon), to legally enforce the trademarks," said Steve Golden shortly after the meeting, "whereas the Bruce Lee Educational Foundation does not have the time or money to do so." Shannon Lee told the board members that she would protect the names and continue to allow the board of directors to use them. Shannon Lee's husband, Ian Keasler, presented the board members with four legal contracts, already prepared in advance, which she asked them to sign, relinquishing rights to the names and organization over to her. When someone in the group suggested that they should have a lawyer look over the details of the wordy documents, Shannon Lee reportedly assured them that it was no big deal and that they would receive a license to use the name and trademark. "What's the matter," Linda Lee Cadwell was said to have added, "Don't you trust us?" No one wanted to say no. Although there was some immediate concern among the board members about such a move, the Lee family mentioned no restrictions and the board chose to accede to Shannon Lee and Linda Lee Cadwell's wishes and the transfer of trademark ownership was made. "We signed over the names because they said that their company had the resources to go after those who were misusing them," noted Tim Tackett. "They want the rights to the name Bruce Lee and Jun Fan as that is Bruce's name. We probably made a mistake with turning over the name Jun Fan Jeet Kune Do."[101]

About the same time, the Bruce Lee Educational Foundation began holding small and more frequent regional seminars on the West Coast of the United States. Publicly, this was done to "spread the art of Bruce Lee". Privately, this was being done in an effort to generate revenue for the cash-strapped foundation. It was little help, though; the first such event reportedly drew less than 30 people, even though it featured the majority of the Nucleus members and an appearance by Shannon Lee. That's about the average attendance of a single instructor hosting a seminar - one who doesn't have the pedigree of being a direct student of Bruce Lee.

By early 2002, the members of the board of the Bruce Lee Educational Foundation were trying to determine if it is even feasible for the struggling foundation to remain in existence. "At the present time we're trying to earn money to remain solvent," said Tim Tackett. "The expense of the newsletter was killing us, so we are making it into a normal newsletter. We also cut our rate for one year to 25 dollars. We are having more regional seminars and, by having our yearly seminar in Los Angeles, we hope to earn enough to stay in business."

---

[101] Some members of the Nucleus are less than educating about the details of the Bruce Lee Educational Foundation's business. When I contacted Richard Bustillo and asked him about the decision to sign over the trademarked names to the Bruce Lee Estate, Bustillo feigned ignorance. "What rights and names?" he asked. When pressed further about the financial situation of the foundation, Bustillo became uncooperative. "Our financial situation is confidential," said Bustillo. "We have no intention to dissolve." Likewise, Nucleus member Steve Golden also refused to answer questions about the financial status of the foundation, calling it "confidential information". Whether it is a matter of ignorance or simply an unwillingness to provide the information, their statements that the financial situation of the Bruce Lee Educational Foundation is confidential are not true. As a tax exempt charitable foundation under section 501(c)(3) of the Internal Revenue Service code, the Bruce Lee Educational Foundation's financial dealings are open to public scrutiny; to say that they are confidential is to violate IRS statutes. On the other hand, I should mention that when I contacted the Bruce Lee Educational Foundation through their main office, administrative secretary Tammy Ledda was very pleased to provide the required records on their financial situation.

In addition, the Bruce Lee Educational Foundation would thereafter focus solely on martial arts training and phased out the philosophical and historical aspects of their previous efforts. "We will concentrate on the martial aspect instead of all aspects of Bruce's life," says Steve Golden. "That was our choice, not Linda's or Shannon's."

While Shannon Lee and Linda Lee Cadwell had promised to go after the people who were abusing the name and trademarks of the Bruce Lee Educational Foundation and the Jun Fan Jeet Kune Do Nucleus, they decided in very short order that the people whom they would go after were the very board members who most recently signed over those rights to them. In a letter sent to all current Nucleus members dated February 9, 2002, Shannon Lee and her legal team wrote: "It has come to our attention that the Foundation is not complying with the terms of the Trademark License from Concord Moon to the Foundation dated August 9, 2001. As you know, under the License, the Foundation is supposed to obtain written consent from Concord Moon in all instances where the Trademarks and/or the name and likeness of Bruce Lee are used. From emails I have received, it is clear that the Foundation is not doing this, but rather telling us either after you have already made the decision to use the marks and the name and likeness, or after you have actually used them. You must obtain Concord Moon's consent for all use of the marks and name and likeness (which includes announcements, press releases and the like) prior to their release. We want to avoid a situation where we are forced to take more formal action under the terms of the License."[102]

In response to the letter from Concord Moon, and as a sign of protest, Bruce Lee Educational Foundation Chairman Richard Bustillo resigned. "This is to tender my resignation from the Bruce Lee Educational Foundation, as Chairman, effective immediately February 11, 2002," wrote Bustillo in his resignation letter. "I am confident that you will adjust in my absence for the betterment of our Foundation."

The rhetoric from Concord Moon concerning the Nucleus escalated over the coming weeks. On March 11, 2002, arguing that the Nucleus members had mismanaged the foundation into a state of debt that might "tarnish" the good name of Bruce Lee[103], Shannon's lawyers sent a legal letter to the Nucleus members

---

[102] Source: http://www.imbacademy.com/news-resign.html

[103] Including the loan Linda Lee Cadwell made to the foundation a few year's before.

terminating the license granted them and ordering them to cease using the names and trademarks of the Bruce Lee Educational Foundation and the Jun Fan Jeet Kune Do Nucleus.

The Nucleus members were also informed (much to their surprise) that legal language buried in the contracts they signed on August 9, 2001 also enjoined them, individually, from engaging in any Bruce Lee-related event or enterprise without the permission of Shannon Lee and Concord Moon. Broadly interpreted, the restriction could even be extended to something as innocuous as a martial art magazine interview that referenced Lee.

Most of the remaining Nucleus members, disenfranchised by the turn of events and fed up with what they felt was a betrayal of their long-term commitment to the Lee family, resigned from the now nameless organization. By early summer of 2002, only Ted Wong and Taky and Andy Kimura remained (out of a desperate desire to clean the debt the foundation had generated in Bruce Lee's name). By July of 2002, the Bruce Lee Educational Foundation and the Jun Fan Jeet Kune Do Nucleus were no more.

"For me," says Doug Klinger, "I think the Nucleus has accomplished the obvious. They have given the world a more accurate picture of the *actual* art that Bruce Lee was teaching, training and perpetuating in his lifetime. From a historical martial art standpoint, this is a milestone."

HOW DID BRUCE LEE DIE?

Over the years there has been much speculation concerning the death of Bruce Lee. Many people have questioned the official finding that his death was accidental and natural. I have long been a defender of that point of view, but, due to recent experiences, I am compelled to enter the discussion questioning whether Bruce Lee's death was accidental...or an act of murder.

The reader must be warned: I cannot say that the following theory concerning Lee's death is accurate or not – only that it deserves to be told. Like a lawyer presenting a case, in presenting a theory the theory is your client and you have to argue its case, assembling the evidence that may support it. I have done so in this instance, but I want to remind readers that it remains unproven, and I myself am not sure of its validity.

In order to balance the supposition in this chapter, I have enlisted the aid of a panel of Bruce Lee authorities. The panel includes myself, Bey Logan (author of *Hong Kong Action Cinema*, former editor of *Combat* and *Impact* magazines, and commentator on the *Hong Kong Legends* DVD series), Spanish Bruce Lee historian Marcos Ocaña, Tom Bleecker (*Unsettled Matters* author and Linda Lee Cadwell's ex-husband), and Patrick Strong, a student and friend of Bruce Lee's. Their comments appear footnoted throughout the chapter.

"This is the guy you need to tell your story to," said Lou Ferrigno, star of the 1970s television series *The Incredible Hulk*. Lou, a friend of mine, was introducing me to Edwin Neal, star of the classic 1970s cult horror film, *The Texas Chainsaw Massacre*. Lou knew that I was a Bruce Lee scholar and he was eager to introduce me to Neal, whom Lou claimed had a story to tell me about Lee.

After brief introductions, we began talking about Bruce Lee. I told Neal about my experience in the field of studying Lee's life and philosophy. He seemed quite happy to meet someone with experience on the subject.

"How did Bruce Lee die?" Edwin Neal abruptly asked me. It was a common question that I am often asked when the subject of Bruce Lee is brought up, so I thought nothing of it. I just chambered up the uniform response.

"Cerebral edema," I replied by rote, "brought on by an allergic reaction to a headache tablet."

Neal shook his head. "No way," he said. "That is *not* how Bruce Lee died."

The Hitchhiker's Story

I had expected Edwin Neal's story to be another anecdotal tale of meeting the late martial arts master. I was not prepared for what Edwin Neal revealed to me. His story was complicated and disturbing, and it began with the production of *The Texas Chainsaw Massacre*.

The Texas Chainsaw Massacre was a low-budget horror film that launched the career of director Tobe Hooper. Neal, like the rest of the cast and many of the crew, had deferred his salary for the film in exchange for a percentage of the profits. All the major distributors initially rejected the shocking film. When a small independent distributor, Bryanston Pictures, came forward with a generous offer, the producers of the film gladly entered into an agreement with them.

The film went on to be a smash independent hit, a genuine cult phenomenon of the 1970s. It is reportedly the most profitable independent feature film ever made. None of the actors and crewmembers in the production, however, were compensated for their efforts.

"Months went by with nothing," recalls Neal. "Finally, after nine months, we got a check for less than $30."

While the film was garnering fame and money, the principles involved in its production were shut out of the profits by Bryanston Pictures, who manipulated the books (industry trade publications were reporting the film made $12 million in its first year of release while Bryanston was claiming $1 million in its bookkeeping), sold the international rights to foreign distributors without the legal authority to do so, and printed and distributed unauthorized and unaccounted copies of the film to theaters worldwide.

By 1975, the cast and crew of *Texas Chainsaw Massacre* were boiling with anger and frustration over the clear swindling on the part of Bryanston Pictures and the mismanagement of the production company. They all wanted answers and demanded legal recourse. Edwin Neal, the most vocal and confrontational member of the cast and crew, met with representatives of Bryanston Pictures and demanded answers. The men in business suits laughed at him. When he responded that he was going to sue them, one of the men pulled back his suit jacket to reveal a holstered gun.

"Go ahead and sue us," the man told Edwin Neal, with deadly seriousness. Neal had just received his first lesson in dealing with the Mafia. *Don't threaten them. Ever.*

The Colombo Connection

Louis "Butchie" Peraino loved the movies and fantasized about being involved in the industry. Peraino did not grow up in Hollywood, though: he was the son of Anthony "Big Tony" Peraino, whose father Giuseppe "The Clutching Hand" Peraino was murdered during the Castellammarese gangland war in 1930. Louis Peraino and brother Joseph represented the third generation of the Peraino family's service to the Colombo crime family, one of the most notorious mafia organizations in New York history.

In the late 1960s, the Perainos spearheaded the Colombo crime family's growing business in pornographic stag films. Louis Peraino established a front company, All-State Film Labs, to process and distribute the hardcore 8mm films.

The Perainos entered the mainstream film distribution business on the basis of the film *Deep Throat*. Producer Gerard Damiano shared the rights to *Deep Throat*, the film that launched the porn industry, through their jointly-owned Damiano Productions until the Perainos "made him an offer he couldn't refuse". With the profits from the hardcore porn film, Louis "Butchie" Peraino (along with his older brother Joseph) launched Bryanston Pictures, setting up shop in Hollywood and financing several independent films.

Bryanston Pictures, established in July 1971, was a Louis Peraino vanity project which served as wish-fulfillment for the wannabe film mogul and as a front for the Peraino family's criminal activity. Bryanston's media brochure selectively outlined its shady origins, speaking admirably of how it all began: "Mr. Peraino combined a hobby and a deep interest in cinema techniques by forming his own motion-picture processing laboratory All-State Film Labs, specializing in processing and editing facilities and high-speed animation..."

"The Perainos made so much money on *Deep Throat* that they went out to Hollywood, California and they developed their own legitimate motion picture studio called Bryanston Films," said Bill Kelly, a retired FBI agent who spent his career fighting the organized crime and pornography racket. "They bought up something like nine scripts, they hired a whole lot of technical people, camera men, directors, technicians of various kinds. But they never really made a movie (even though they spent all this money out there). However, they did go into the national distribution of a number of very violent but not obscene motion picture films."[104]

One of the violent films that the Perainos would distribute, fatefully, was Bruce Lee's first directorial effort, *Way of the Dragon.*[105]

The Way of the Dragon

In 1972 Bruce Lee formed a partnership with Golden Harvest executive Raymond Chow. Concord Productions was to be the means by which Bruce Lee took control of his professional future. Instead, it may have led to his death.

The first picture Concord completed was *Way of the Dragon* (called *Return of the Dragon* in the United States). Written by, directed by, and starring Bruce Lee, the film was most notable for its climactic fight scene between Bruce Lee and Chuck Norris. Shot in Rome, the film was Lee's attempt at creating a production that had a Western appeal to it. Lee and Raymond Chow were eager to get the film distributed in the United States, where they both stood to make a substantial profit and Lee could make an impression on the executives in Hollywood (with whom he was currently negotiating to do a Hollywood feature).

Unfortunately for Bruce Lee and Raymond Chow, no major distributor in the United States was interested in distributing the film. Under Chow's direction, and without the consent of Bruce Lee, Concord Productions entered into an agreement with Bryanston Pictures to distribute the film in the United States.

Bruce Lee was reportedly furious with Raymond Chow over *Way of the Dragon.* Part of his anger stemmed from Chow's unilateral decision-making in what was supposed to be an equal partnership; Lee was also furious over Chow's distribution deals

---

[104] Source: "Interview of Bill Kelly", Court TV. Transcript.

[105] TOM BLEECKER: It isn't unusual for film companies and distributors to be involved with a number of mafias. Such companies are good vehicles for money laundering. Point in fact, Steven Segal was involved with such a company and recently ended up being a government witness against the mob. Also, Brandon Lee's last film was financed by a well known mafia film company that was filing Chapter 11.

and the fact that Concord's books did not reflect the money that *Way of the Dragon* had earned at the box office.[106]

It was clear that Bruce Lee was deeply concerned about the financial situation surrounding *Way of the Dragon*. Linda Lee, in her book *The Bruce Lee Story*, recalls that Bruce Lee was still facing mounting insecurity concerning his financial situation: "The reason for this was that the money we were spending was being advanced to us from Concord Productions on the strength of profits that were not yet realized from *Way of the Dragon*. That made it doubly important that *Way* be successful. And so while some stresses in Bruce's life were decreasing, other tensions were accelerating."[107]

Murder Most Foul

Edwin Neal, rattled by his meeting with the Perainos and fearful of whom he was dealing with, went to the FBI. In consultation with an FBI agent, Neal claims the agent showed him a "stack of photographs of people whom the Perainos had killed. According to Neal, the agent also told him that "Bruce Lee was killed by the Perainos because he was planning to sue them."[108]

Neal said that when Bryanston failed to come through with the up-front money they agreed to give Concord for the distribution rights to *Way of the Dragon*, Bruce Lee threatened to take them to court.

If this is true, Louis "Butchie" Peraino's response to the threat of litigation was likely the same as his response to a similar threat by Robert Kuhn, one of the attorneys for the Texans with a stake in the original production of *The Texas Chainsaw Massacre*:

> "There were these guys just standing around if you want people to think you have guys who might hurt them. We said, 'Well, if you don't give us an accounting right now and let us look at your books, then we are going to sue.' And Lou [Peraino] said, 'Don't sue me.'"

---

[106] TOM BLEECKER: Adrian and Linda's concerns over Chow's accounting really had little, if anything, to do with Bryanston. Rather, their main focus was directed at verbal contracts that Chow had made with Bruce prior to Bruce's death. Moreover, the accounting discrepancies had to do with Chow's payments to the Triad, of which Bruce probably knew very little.

[107] Source: page 129 of the book, *The Bruce Lee Story*, by Linda Lee. Ohara Publications, Santa Clarita, California. Copyright 1989 Linda Lee.

[108] PAT STRONG: The part about the FBI agent telling the actor about Bryanston killing Bruce rings hollow.

Kuhn repeated Peraino's response slowly and menacingly, "There's only one meaning it could have had in my mind," Kuhn said, "and that was, 'If you do, I'm going to hurt you.'"[109]

Noted FBI agent Bill Kelley: "Well, when you're dealing with people in the Gambino family and Colombo family, you're naturally in danger. These guys will kill you along with some of the others, some of the California people."

Unlike Edwin Neal and the cast and crew of *The Texas Chainsaw Massacre*, Bruce Lee had the fame and finances to pursue a spirited legal fight against Bryanston, which Lee reportedly informed Bryanston he intended to do – regardless of their threats against him.[110] It was for that reason, Edwin Neal was told, that Louis "Butchie" Peraino put out a contract on Bruce Lee's life.[111]

Ed Neal believes, based on what he was told, that the Perainos paid the Chinese Triads to fulfill a contract on Bruce Lee. If true, the method seems clear: poisoning, most likely the poisoning of Lee's marijuana and hashish supply. It would explain the mysterious fit and coma that Bruce Lee experienced on May 10, 1973, when, at the Golden Harvest studios, he inexplicably began vomiting, fell into convulsions, and then spent several hours in a coma before recovering. The vomiting, convulsions, and the coma are all classic symptoms of poisoning; a simple Google search of the combined three terms yields scores of websites on poisoning, most relating to herbs and plants. It is likely that the Triads, who had succeeded in infiltrating all levels of the Hong Kong film industry, had access to Bruce Lee's drug supply, and contaminated his supply before or after it was in his possession.[112]

---

[109] Source: *CFQ* magazine, Volume 16, issue four. 1986.

[110] In a report on the Perainos that appeared in the *Los Angeles Times* in 1982, an unnamed movie producer recalled a business meeting with Louis Peraino, saying "I didn't know if I was negotiating for my picture or my life. There were threats made against me... My nose was threatened, my ears..." For the same report, a *Los Angeles Times* reporter called a studio executive to ask him about his experiences with the Perainos. "No way," the executive told the reporter. "As far as I'm concerned, this phone call never happened."

[111] PATRICK STRONG: The amount owed to Bruce from Bryanston was very little when compared to the amount of money at stake through the rest of Raymond Chow's faulty, at best, negotiations. From what Tom Bleecker told me, Bruce talked with attorneys about the monies owed to him by Bryanston, but never filed a lawsuit.

[112] BEY LOGAN: For the record, I explained my own 'death of Bruce Lee' theory, on camera, for a Turner CNX channel special I produced for the UK. Basically, it goes like this:

1. Bruce Lee was a habitual cannabis user, with no apparent ill effects from the drug.

It is equally likely that the Triads succeeded in fulfilling the contract on Bruce Lee's life on July 20, 1973, when Bruce Lee once again fell into a mysterious coma. Just like the first incident, Lee's coma and edema were preceded by ingestion of hashish. Unlike the first incident, Bruce Lee never recovered.[113]

If this were true, why then would Linda Lee remain silent? Surely she would have exposed this murder for what it was, wouldn't she? Not really. If the American mafia had indeed killed Bruce Lee, his family would also potentially be in the crosshairs of their proverbial guns. Her silence may have been the only way to ensure the safety of herself and her children. It would also explain the bizarre press statement Linda Lee made shortly after Bruce Lee's funeral, when she said: "Although we do not have a final autopsy report, I hold no suspicion of anything other than natural death. I myself do not hold any person or people responsible for his death. Fate has ways we cannot change. The only thing of importance is that Bruce is gone and will not return."

Was Linda Lee's statement a secret message to Peraino and his mafia partners? Was this Linda Lee's way of assuring them that she intended to remain silent and the lives of her family should be spared? The fact that she made the peculiar move of publicly ruling out foul play so early in the investigation tends to

---

2. Someone started giving him 'tainted' cannabis and, while ingesting this at Golden Harvest, he suffered a seizure, and almost died.
3. He returned to the US, out of range of the tainted cannabis, and a medical check-up revealed he was in perfect health.
4. He returned to Hong Kong, where he once again ingested the tainted cannabis. He was at Ting Pei's apartment when the second attack happened, and so did not receive the appropriate attention in time, and died.
5. The Equagesic Ting Pei gave him is just a red herring.
6. The question is, was the substance that tainted the cannabis placed their accidentally or on purpose? If on purpose, what was the purpose? If Lee himself used the substance as an aphrodisiac or stimulant, then we can say he really did die from 'misadventure'. If not, then its murder.

All of the above is so evident from the facts, I can't believe that the matter is still being debated as widely as it is!

[113] JAMES BISHOP: Had Bruce Lee been in a quarrel with the mafia, would he not have suspected an attempt on his life after the first medical incident? Would he not have then modified his behavior, including the source of his hashish? From all accounts, Bruce Lee did not modify his behavior and even bragged to others that he had been given a clean bill of health. This suggests to me that he was not "looking over his shoulder" and draws doubts about this theory.

That being said, a member of the production team at Golden Harvest has stated that Bruce Lee kept his own drinking mug at his side at all times in the last few months of his life and would react violently when anyone would approach it. Clearly, he had some degree of fear of poisoning.

suggest there was something more under the surface of her statement.[114]

Rumors that Edwin Neal had heard seem to back-up this theory. "I had been told," says Neal, "that Bruce Lee had been knocked off and his widow went underground and refused to give interviews."[115]

This explanation would also explain Linda Lee's continued insistence to keep silent about the details surrounding his death, and her insistence on focusing on how Bruce Lee "lived" rather than how he "died". Perhaps the continued health of her family was dependent on her silence?

Endings

In 1974, *Daily Variety* declared Bryanston Pictures one of the hottest distributors in Hollywood. Bryanston was responsible for the North American distribution of three big independent hits: *Andy Warhol's Frankenstein*, *The Texas Chainsaw Massacre*, and Bruce Lee's *Way of the Dragon* (renamed *Return of the Dragon* to sound like a sequel to 1973's *Enter the Dragon*). Around the same time, the Perainos were suspected of ordering the mob murders of three people involved in an unpaid loan Bryanston had extended to their company. One victim was beaten to death, another was shot, and a car mysteriously struck the third. Also in 1974, Louis "Butchie" Peraino (along his father and uncle) was indicted by a federal grand jury in Memphis for transporting obscene materials across state lines.

On April 30, 1976, the Perainos were convicted on obscenity charges. A month later, Bryanston Pictures simply disappeared without notice - not even to its own employees. The Perainos left of trail of debts and bad business deals.

A few years later, according to FBI reports, a dispute over movie profits led Louis' father, Anthony, to request a hit on Anthony's own brother, Joseph. The head of the Colombo crime family, Carmine "The Snake" Persico, authorized the hit, and, on

---

[114] JAMES BISHOP: And maybe it is simply what it appears to be on the surface. As Sigmund Freud remarked about hidden meanings: "Sometimes a cigar is just a cigar."

[115] MARCOS OCAÑA: She wasn't precisely silent. Immediately after his death Linda gave an interview that was found recently. She was at her house on Cumberland and remembering her husband. This tape was discovered some time ago and is circulating around.

TOM BLEECKER: There is no doubt that during the immediate years following Bruce's death that Linda was scared. But I don't feel that she was frightened by Bryanston, but rather the Chinese Triads.

January 4, 1982, Salvatore Miciotta and Vincent "Jimmy" Angellino, soldiers for Colombo crime family, chased Joseph "Joe the Whale" Peraino and his son, Joseph Jr., down a street in residential Brooklyn. The Perainos pounded on the door of a home seeking entry but were struck from behind by a hail of bullets. "Joe the Whale" was seriously injured but survived; his son was hit six times in the head and killed. A retired nun, Veronica Zuraw, who lived in the home was also struck by the bullets and died.

Louis Peraino was eventually convicted in another obscenity case and spent a few years in prison. After his release, he continued in the porn business with Arrow Film and Video until his death in April 1999.

Unanswered Questions

Did Louis "Butchie" Peraino order the death of Bruce Lee? Has this information been kept a secret by the Lee family since his death? Or is this all just a fanciful confluence of coincidences and rumors? I cannot say with certainty, but the available corroborating evidence is compelling. Bruce Lee's production company had, for a fact, become involved with the American mafia. But without access to Concord's business and financial records, questions of exactly when Concord went into business with Bryanston Films remain unanswered. A cryptic reference in a letter Bruce Lee wrote to Ted Ashley in 1972 may offer a clue: "An independent, American producer here is in the process of negotiating with me to produce films in English for international release."[116] Was this independent producer Bryanston Pictures?[117] Could they have had an influence on the decision to film *Way of the Dragon* in Italy, the first time a Hong Kong production had ever been filmed in another country? Regardless of the answers, the accounting discrepancies that were frustrating Bruce Lee with *Way of the Dragon* bore an uncanny resemblance to the problems that plagued *The Texas Chainsaw Massacre*. Perhaps too uncanny to be coincidence.

---

[116] Source: Bruce Lee quoted on page 165 of the book *Letters of the Dragon*, edited by John Little, Published by the Charles E. Tuttle Publishing Company, Boston, copyright 1998 Linda Lee Cadwell.

[117] JAMES BISHOP: The independent American producer may also have been a reference to Andre Morgan, whom Bruce Lee came to know during that time.

Ultimately, the answer to the basic question of how Bruce Lee died may have gone to the grave with Bruce Lee and Louis Peraino.

CONCLUSION

I want to mention a particular occurrence that you might find interesting. It occurred at the Dragon Expo 2000, the Bruce Lee Educational Foundation's annual seminar held in Las Vegas in April 2000. The Nucleus (the board members of the foundation) debuted a disappointing painting that they had a professional artist do. As an artist, I found it absurd. I immediately recognized that it was done mechanically, likely using a silk-screen process, rather than being painted by human hands. A glorified photocopy. Worse still, they then sold posters of it for $50 a pop (needless to say, I didn't have "sucker" tattooed on my forehead and didn't purchase one).[118] The artist was on hand to sign copies of his work.

Later that night, a colleague, Sean Mick, and I were in the hotel near one of the restaurants when we overheard the artist on a pay phone talking to someone, saying, "Yes, it's true! You wouldn't believe it! All these goofy people standing in line for hours to have me sign posters of that silly painting."

Yes, he was absolutely right. They were goofy people, and he did accurately assess his artwork. Yet he underestimated what many of the "stars" of the Bruce Lee community came to realize a long time ago: put Bruce Lee's name or face on something and people will buy it, no matter how shoddy it is. It is the bedrock upon which they have built their little Bruce Lee empires, the knowledge that people will flock to them and join their training programs, buy their videos, their books, go to their seminars, and shower them with unadulterated adoration simply because of their association with Bruce Lee. They knew that they could print five-dollar posters of that "silly painting" and people would buy them at ten times their value.[119]

---

[118] The Bruce Lee Educational Foundation was reportedly going to auction the original painting off. However, tax records indicate that the original painting is still in the possession of the foundation and valued as a $7,261 asset.

[119] In another prime example, one of my colleagues (who is working on his own Bruce Lee project) contacted Bob Wall, Bruce Lee's co-star in two of his films (best known for his role as the villainous "Ohara" in *Enter the Dragon*) to ask Wall some questions about his relationship with Lee. The response he received to his email follows. Take note of how a request for information is responded to with a very sly (and commercial) *quid pro quo*: "Bob

One thing I don't want you to do, my readers, is simply "buy" what you have just read because it came from Bruce Lee. If you do get one thing of value from Bruce Lee, let it be to think for yourself, to question for yourself, and to decide for yourself what is of value to you. Don't be afraid to reject what your intuition tells you is wrong, even if it came from Bruce Lee, or any other authority, for that matter. Be your own guide. Be, as Krishnamurti called it, "A light unto yourself." Like the lame man throwing away his crutches, let loose of your reliance on authorities and find the strength to walk on your own. Be wary of authorities and anti-authorities as well, those who set themselves up as the authoritative response to the established authorities.

There is never really such a thing as objectivity. We never come to reporting with a blank slate. Everything is interpretation; in philosophy we call this hermeneutics. Our memories and current sense data are all subject to our emotions, our perceptions, and our desires. When listening to an authority on Bruce Lee or any other subject, always question their reasons for making their statements. It's a Rorschach test revealing more about the speaker than about the subject of his speech. Ask yourself the following questions:

- What is the desire of the audience they are addressing?
- What are their desires about the memory of the man that they are trying to paint?
- What is the personal history between the two? Was it equitable or was there strife?
- Does one story told by the same person contradict another? If so, which is correct? Is any correct?
- Is there a consensus statement from multiple sources?
- Did the person actually know the individual? How well did they know him? Did their

wanted to thank you for your email regarding the Bruce Lee project that you are working on. At this time, Mr. Wall receives a large amount of emails from people all over the world. Because of the sheer number he receives, he can only take the time to answer those emails he receives from members of WorldBlackBelt. Why not check out Mr. Wall's current project, WorldBlackBelt.com and become a member today! Membership is only $30.00 a year to part of the best online Martial Arts Community. Once you become a member, Mr. Wall will definitely get back to you and help you out with the input you desire. He makes it a point to answer each email he receives from members of WorldBlackBelt."

relationship with him relate to the testimony that they are giving?

- What is the personality of the speaker? Are they considered fair and equitable? Positive or negative?

Do not, however, deny the excellent opportunities and possibilities that can come of Bruce Lee's philosophy. While talking to John Little about Lee's philosophy, he said that the opportunity to do good was what it was all about. He's right - that kind of making a difference, of creating something positive, planting a seed in the world, holding the hand of a person who has fallen, that's why I do what I do. That's why I find value in Bruce Lee's philosophy; because I know what a powerful force for good it can be.

Last fall, I was approached by one of the crisis counselors at the college where I work. She was counseling a young college student who was depressed and suicidal. The girl was from Mexico, had no family in the United States other than one sister and had recently broken up with her boyfriend. She was despondent with no support system to help her. She had already made one suicide attempt. The counselor had been working with this young lady for some weeks, and she was concerned that there was no progress being made; she seriously believed that the girl would make another suicide attempt. The distressed young lady had expressed an interest in philosophy. The counselor knew of my work in philosophy and humanistic psychology, and this gave the counselor the idea that I might be able to help the student on a philosophical level. (I should point out that the counselor and I had had many discussions on philosophy and psychology, and I had, in fact, counseled the counselor on her own family affairs.) The crisis counselor came to my office asking for my help.

I agreed to meet with the student and she sent the girl down to my office. I spoke to the girl at length about her philosophical interests, recommending several uplifting philosophical works that would give her a more positive perspective. I told her about Bruce Lee's philosophy, and this in particular struck a resonant chord with the young lady. I told her about Taky Kimura's experiences in the internment camps, his self-esteem problems afterwards, and how Bruce Lee addressed those problems for him and helped him too see his own value as a person. This really hit home for her, because, as a stranger in a strange land, part of her problems was related to this. Then I told her how upset Taky Kimura was at the failure of his marriage and the advice that Lee gave him that helped him get past the pain of the breakup. Again, these were the things she needed to hear at that moment because she had just gone through her own painful breakup.

When I was done with her, she went back to talk to her counselor. Not long after that, her counselor came to me very excited. She told me that, after the student talked to me, it was the first time she had seen the girl smile since she had been working with her, and that there was a definite change in her attitude. After a follow-up meeting with the young lady a few days later, the counselor came to me again to tell me that the girl had really improved, thanks to the things I told her, and that she feels she is on the road to emotional recovery.

It is immensely gratifying when you can make such a difference in another human being's life. I can't begin to explain it, but I know that Taky Kimura understands of what I am saying. That's what it is all about. The licensed crisis counselor was unable to make inroads with this young lady's problems, yet I was through the wisdom that Bruce Lee and Taky Kimura have shared with me and so many others.

In my own experience, I must say that the effort to use Bruce Lee as a teacher on a wider scale has failed. While there are many that have learned valuable life experiences from Bruce Lee, most of his fans seem to miss even the most obvious lessons to be gleaned from his memory.

Particularly in the areas of multiculturalism, racism, and prejudice, Bruce Lee enthusiasts that I believed were enlightened by his message of "one family" have surprised me with unexpected statements that fly in the face of what he believed. Some of the instructors in his art carry prejudices against other races, including, ironically, the Chinese. Instead of perpetuating Bruce Lee's inclusive worldview, they continue to perpetuate old hatreds.[120] Other more general fans have shocked me with their bitter statements toward homosexuals and various minority groups. On one Bruce Lee Internet forum some fans have even openly supported terrorism.

---

[120] Especially among themselves. There is one relatively common thread among Jeet Kune Do instructors, whether they learned directly from Bruce Lee or from his heirs: that they alone seem to "get it" to the exclusion of everyone else. The other instructor in Bruce Lee's art never seems to know what he or she is talking about; everyone seems to think they do. The instructors are constantly questioning the legitimacy of each other, making them all seem unqualified to represent Lee or his art.

While this would seem to cry out for action on the part of those in control of Bruce Lee's memory, sadly, for the majority of the first-generation instructors in Bruce Lee's martial art, the philosophy is a threat to their livelihood. It seems they are more concerned with what the Bruce Lee can do to promote their individual martial art schools and seminar schedules than what they can actually do to promote Bruce Lee and do something positive for other people. They prefer to maintain a strict martial art interpretation of Bruce Lee's legacy because that is what sells "real estate" for them, in the sense of "real estate" being memberships in their training schools.[121]

Such an approach only reinforces the limited view most people have of Bruce Lee. Fans still see Bruce Lee as a vehicle for violence, a sad indictment of Bruce Lee regardless of whether the violence is righteous or not. The following messages left by Internet fans on a tribute page for the late Bruce Lee are a good barometer of how Bruce Lee is remembered.

"If a tree fell in the forest, would it make a sound?" asked one fan who did not leave his name. "Of course not, because no one would hear you kicking it down."

"Bruce Lee, you were the best actor and martial artist," wrote Vicky Kizas. "You inspired me and others to learn martial arts by watching your movies and thank you for inspiring me to kick ass."

Mark Williams wrote, "Bruce, I first saw you on *Batman* as *Kato* you could have kicked everybody's ass on the show but they wouldn't let you."

An anonymous fan left the most memorable entry. "Next time you see Osama Bin Laden or Saddam Hussein, spare a thought for those they have hurt and land a few well-placed kicks and punches to their mouths, please."[122]

Bruce Lee is the king of the cult of violence. A recent article from Agence France Presse, a French news agency, featured an article on a young Palestinian Bruce Lee fan:

> Osama al-Kalban, 14, writhing in bed from a bullet wound to his upper right leg, dreams about kung fu legend Bruce Lee one minute and becoming a martyr the next.
> "I will someday," he says, expressing his wish to die hurling stones at Israeli soldiers, the activity he and hundreds

---

[121] I know for a fact that instructors in Bruce Lee's art often squabble like little children over the tiny hills or fiefdoms they control in the Bruce Lee valley, fighting amongst themselves and even threatening each other when they perceive that another has "crossed" their seminar turf.
[122] Source: findagrave.com.

> of others joined last Friday and Saturday in demonstrations marking the one year anniversary of the Palestinian uprising or intifada.
>
> But dodging Israeli bullets also competes for Osama's attention with karate classes, watching Bruce Lee videos and kung fu fights with his friend Mohammed by their homes in Khan Yunis in the southern Gaza Strip.
>
> "I pretend I'm Bruce Lee," Osama smiles.[123]

This is the product of the Bruce Lee martial myth, perpetuated by his students, his family, and by the merchandisers and magazines. It is the product of the salesmanship of violence without rationale or conscience. It is an example of an opportunity to teach (in ways much more meaningful) never taken.

This will only complicate matters for fans that are trying to justify the time they devote to Bruce Lee. Lester San Jose, a Bruce Lee fan and high school student, struggles with his family's narrow perception of Lee. "What upsets me is that whenever my mother sees me purchasing a Bruce Lee magazine, she somewhat grimaces. Most people believe that Bruce Lee was just some martial arts actor and they tell me, 'What is he going to teach you that is beneficial to your well-being?'"

Thalia, a Bruce Lee fan who wrote to me, sees a different side to Bruce Lee. "I am a dedicated fan of Bruce Lee and Bruce Lee taught me that life has no guarantees, but if you believe in yourself and work hard you can achieve whatever you desire." She included a poem in his memory:

> "Freedom"
>
> Freedom means not being controlled by others or something outside yourself.
> Freedom means self-control...
> Not pointless self-indulgence...
> Not pointless self-denial.
> It means following your own path
> As you discover it.

"Bruce Lee used to say that no matter how much you know, you will always be a learner," says Angela Zaballa, a teacher. "This is very much one of my personal philosophies, particularly in psychology."

---

[123] Source: article titled "Palestinian Kids Want to Die Throwing Stones at Israeli Soldiers" from *Agence France Presse*, October 2, 2001.

She continues: "'Don't think, *feel*,' was a phrase that Bruce Lee used to say, a phrase that I think is an important one for people to consider in the kind of busy, materialistic society we live in. So many people think and act without seeming to analyze how they feel about things. Bruce Lee was a man of vision who believed in his passions and pursued them. As a result, most of his dreams were realized before his death."

Even those who knew Bruce Lee reflect upon his memory with differing perspectives. "Bruce was inspirational to his students because he showed them what was inspirational in the arts," said Joe Hyams, author of the book *Zen in the Martial Arts*. "But, he was not a good teacher. It was monkey see-monkey do. In short, he showed us the way (not *tao*) that something should be done by personal example. Since he was so good and so fast it was impossible for me to imitate his moves. Also, his English was not very good, and he often spoke in parables."

A surprising statement coming from a man whose whole best-selling book, *Zen in the Martial Arts*, was predicated on Lee's parables. Hyams fell into the trap that many of Bruce Lee's students fell into: an inability to interpret Lee's words. It's a trap that comes, not from language or cultural differences, but from differences in perception and cognitive thinking, as well as "psychic blockage", a self-imposed inability to comprehend.

The problem in interpreting Bruce Lee's words is in seeing things from an "either/or" viewpoint. Bruce Lee's personal and martial philosophy was predicated on duality. It was deeply influenced by Taoism, which is itself a philosophy of complementary dualities. People tend to look at things from a Western mind-set, in which things have to be rationalized and cast in stone. Thus, what Bruce Lee personally practiced in the martial arts becomes the "style" of Jeet Kune Do that cannot be altered and is the answer for all things and all situations.[124]

It was Bruce Lee's goal for his students to find their own way. As he said: "Man, the creating individual, is more important than any established style." It was his hope that they transcended mere technique, which he taught, and for it to become an intrinsic part of their being. At that point they would be able to express themselves freely, openly, and honestly. He knew that the

---

[124] Bruce Lee recognized that all human beings share the same basic physiognomy, and because of that there would be certain universally efficient ways of doing things. But, at the same time, he recognized that a human being must be liberated from all forms of conditioning, because conditioning is a form of prison for the conditioned. A conditioned man is a man who can be predicted, a man who can be intercepted, and a man who cannot evolve, as a fighter or as a human being.

greatest weapon that a person can have in their arsenal is self-knowledge.

Bruce Lee's greatest contribution to philosophy was not as a philosopher but rather as an ambassador of philosophy; someone who did what we all should do: seek for ourselves and grow as rationalizing organisms.

"I was born disabled," wrote Sean, a Bruce Lee fan. "You [Bruce Lee] gave me the inspiration to help me adapt to life. Now, I can do anything without any hands or assistance. Thank You!"

I have been rather turned off by most of what I've seen in Bruce Lee's martial art of Jeet Kune Do, people who just don't seem to get it or are only looking at a piece of the truth and blinded (usually by choice or their own rigidity) to the rest. As Bruce Lee stated, there is no partial segment of a totality. Yet I find that a great number of the self-professed "Jeet Kune Do" men train solely because they want to "kick ass", or they think that just because Bruce Lee's expression of the martial arts worked so well for him, it will make them supermen. They concentrate only on the most superficial aspects of the art and exclude the internal lessons that must be learned and that Lee stressed. As Lao Tzu said:

> "The wise person chooses what is real
> And looks beneath the surface,
> Chooses the fruit and not the flower
> Not reacting, but responding
> In harmony with Tao."

Or, as Jun Fan Jeet Kune Do Nucleus member Chris Kent put it, when asked about the future of Bruce Lee's art, "I think it all depends on how it is handled. It could go to one extreme and become a solidified and concretized style or go to the other extreme and become a sort of catch-all martial art, both of which would be wrong. Or it could be what it is supposed to be, a martial art and philosophy which offers each individual a prescription for their own personal growth."[125]

Ultimately, Bruce Lee shied away from offering a roadmap to mastery of the martial arts because he knew that crystallizing what is essentially formless would only lead to stagnation and decay. Here again is the Western mentality problem: Lee speaks of a circle with no circumference and yet, to the Western mind, a circle

---

[125] Source: Article titled "Chris Kent: Last of the Backyard Breed Breaks the Code of Silence" from *Martial Arts Legends Magazine*, February 1999. Published by CFW Publications.

must have a circumference, or else it cannot be a circle; it cannot exist. Because of that, here we are, thirty years after Bruce Lee's death, and still there is constant pressure in the United States to "shape water" - in other words, to nail down what is and isn't Jeet Kune Do. Bruce Lee was right: giving it a name has hurt the process because by doing so the process has become a product, the "gospel truth, which cannot be changed". Stone decays, glass breaks; that which continues to grow and change endures because it remains strong and capable of overcoming the challenges of today.

APPENDIX:
BRUCE LEE'S PERSONAL LIBRARY

The following is a list of known books that Bruce Lee owned or read. I compiled this list with the help of my colleague, Doug Klinger, and additional assistance from Marcos Ocaña, for the primary purpose of researching and tracking Lee's sources. This list was compiled using references made to Bruce Lee's library in publications, books cited as being a part of his library, personal responses from those who knew Lee, and examination of photographs of Bruce Lee in his library with books in the background. The latter involved painstaking examination of the photographs to identify whole or partial book authors and/or titles and then going through rare book collections and search engines to make positive identifications of the books. In addition, recognition of certain passages in Bruce Lee texts as verbatim the work of other authors yielded many additional titles that Bruce Lee clearly drew from.

If the official tally of 2,500 books in Bruce Lee's personal library is correct, then this list, the most comprehensive list ever available on Bruce Lee's personal library, still represents less than sixteen percent of his collection. It should be pointed out, however, that the official tally also includes multiple copies of books, such as the Tao Te Ching, the I'Ching and Joe Louis' How to Box, as well as at least one encyclopedia collection. In addition, it has been estimated that roughly 500 of the books were Chinese-language books.

Note: Although not considered part of the official tally, a few verified magazine and periodical publications have been included in this list. Also, it might be argued that some of these books are not in Bruce Lee's library as it stands today (Doug Klinger's own recent discovery at a Vancouver used book store of a book marked, signed, and annotated by Bruce Lee indicates that Bruce Lee did not keep all of the books that came into his possession). However, they have been *included because they contain passages that Bruce Lee quoted verbatim from, indicating that he at one time had possessed and read them.*

- *Acupuncture: The Ancient Chinese Art of Healing and How It Works Scientifically* by Felix Mann
- *Advanced Karate* by Mas Oyama
- *The Age of Reason* by Stuart Hampshire
- *An Affair of the Heart* by Adele Davis
- *Aikido* by Kisshamaru Ueshiba
- *Aikido: The Art of Self Defense* by K. Tohei
- *The Amazing Results of Positive Thinking* by Norman Vincent Peale
- *The Analects of Confucius* by Confucius (translated by Arthur Waley)
- *Application of Measurement to Health and Physical Education* by H.H. Clarke
- *Arms for Living* by Gene Tunney
- *The Art of Keeping Fit* by the editors of Esquire Magazine
- *The Art of War* by Sun Tzu
- *The Art of Worldly Wisdom* by Baltasar Gracian
- *As a Man Thinketh* by James Allen
- *The Athlete In The Making* by Jesse Feiring Williams, M.D., and Eugene White Nixon, M.A.
- *Atlas of Man* by William H. Sheldon, C. Wesley Dupertius and Eugene McDermott
- *At the Feet of the Master* by Jiddu Krishnamurti
- *Be Fit For Life* by Kaare Rohdal, M.D.
- *A Beginner's Book of Gymnastics* by Barry Johnson
- *Beneath The Wheel* by Herman Hesse
- *Better Boxing* by LaFond and Menendez
- *Body and Mind in Harmony: Tai Chi Chuan-An Ancient Chinese Way of Exercise to Achieve Health and Tranquillity* by Sophia Delza
- *Bodybuilding: The Official Training Textbook of the British Amateur Weightlifting Association* by John Barrs
- *The Book* by Alan Watts
- *The Book of Fencing* by Kass
- *The Book of Five Rings* by Miyamoto Musashi
- *The Book of Tao* translation by F.J. MacHovec
- *Boxing* by Edwin L. Haislet

- *British Boxing* by Denzil Batchelor
- *Buddhism* by Christmas Humphreys
- *Bokuden Ikun Sho* by Tsukahara Budoken
- *Bud Wilkinson's Guide to Modern Physical Fitness* by Bud Wilkinson
- *Building Our Own Rainbows* by Harry and Joan Mier
- *Bushido: The Soul of the Samurai* by Nitobe Inazo
- *Candles In the Sun* by Emily Lutyens
- *Canon of Judo* by Kyuzo Mifune
- *C. G. Jung and Hermann Hesse: A Record of Two Friendships* by Miguel Serrano
- *Championship Fighting: Explosive Punching and Aggressive Defense* by Jack Dempsey
- *Championship Judo* by Trevor Leggett and K. Watanabe
- *Change: Eight Lectures on the I'Ching* by Hellmut Wilhelm
- *The Chinese Classics: The Book of Documents* translated by James Legge
- *The Chinese Classics: The Book of Odes* translated by James Legge
- *The Chinese Classics: I Ching* translated by James Legge
- *The Chinese Classics: Record of Rites* translated by James Legge
- *The Chinese Classics: Spring and Autumn Annals* translated by James Legge
- *Chinese Gung Fu: The Philosophical Art of Self-Defense* by Bruce Lee
- *Chinese Philosophy in Classical Times* translated and edited by E.R. Hughes
- *Chuang Tzu* by Chuang Tzu
- *The Chung Yung or the Centre, the Common* translated by Leonard A. Lyall
- *The Civilization of China* by Herbert Giles
- *Client-Centered Therapy* by Carl Rogers
- *Combat Training of the Individual Soldier and Patrolling* published by the US Department of the Army
- *Come Away* by Jiddu Krishnamurti
- *Commentaries on Living: First Series* by Jiddu Krishnamurti
- *Commentaries on Living: Second Series* by Jiddu Krishnamurti
- *Commentaries on Living: Third Series* by Jiddu Krishnamurti
- *Commentaries on Zen* by D.T. Suzuki
- *The Complete Amateur Boxer* by Bohun Lynch

- *The Complete Kano of Jujitsu* by Hancock H. Irving and Katsukona Higashi
- *The Complete Physique Book* by David Webster
- *Concentration: A Guide to Mental Mastery* by Mouni Sadhu
- *Conjectures and Refutations* by Karl Jaspers
- *Contest Judo* by Charles Yerkow
- *Controlled Exercise for Physical Fitness* by J.R. Peebler
- *Creative Selling* by Charles Lohse
- *Crisis in Consciousness: Commentaries on Love, Life and Death and Other Matters* by Robert Powell
- *Discourse on the Method* by René Descartes
- *Dynamic Aikido* by Gozo Shioda
- *Dynamic Judo: Throwing Techniques* by Kazuzo Kudo
- *Dynamic Judo: Grappling Techniques* by Kazuzo Kudo
- *Dynamic Self-Defense* by Sam H. Alred
- *Dynamic Thinking* by Melvin Powers
- *Education and the Significance of Life* by Jiddu Krishnamurti
- *Efficiency of Human Movement* by Marion Ruth Broer
- *Elements of Style* by Strunk and White
- *Encyclopedia Britannica 14th Edition: Volume I*
- *Encyclopedia Britannica 14th Edition: Volume II*
- *Encyclopedia Britannica 14th Edition: Volume III*
- *Encyclopedia Britannica 14th Edition: Volume IV*
- *Encyclopedia Britannica 14th Edition: Volume V*
- *Encyclopedia Britannica 14th Edition: Volume VI*
- *Encyclopedia Britannica 14th Edition: Volume VII*
- *Encyclopedia Britannica 14th Edition: Volume VIII*
- *Encyclopedia Britannica 14th Edition: Volume IX*
- *Encyclopedia Britannica 14th Edition: Volume X*
- *Encyclopedia Britannica 14th Edition: Volume XI*
- *Encyclopedia Britannica 14th Edition: Volume XII*
- *Encyclopedia Britannica 14th Edition: Volume XIII*
- *Encyclopedia Britannica 14th Edition: Volume XIV*
- *Encyclopedia Britannica 14th Edition: Volume XV*
- *Encyclopedia Britannica 14th Edition: Volume XVI*
- *Encyclopedia Britannica 14th Edition: Volume XVII*
- *Encyclopedia Britannica 14th Edition: Volume XVIII*
- *Encyclopedia Britannica 14th Edition: Volume XIX*
- *Encyclopedia Britannica 14th Edition: Volume XX*
- *Encyclopedia Britannica 14th Edition: Volume XXI*
- *Encyclopedia Britannica 14th Edition: Volume XXII*

- *Encyclopedia Britannica 14th Edition: Volume XXIII*
- *Encyclopedia Britannica 14th Edition: Yearbook*
- *English Grammar and Composition* (author unknown)
- *Enthusiasm Makes the Difference* by Norman Vincent Peale
- *The Essence of Buddhism* by P. Lakshmi Narasu
- *Essential Karate* by Mas Oyama
- *Ethics* by Baruch Spinoza
- *Faith is the Answer* by Norman Vincent Peale
- *Fencing* by Hugo and James Castello
- *Fencing* by Muriel Bower and Torao Mori
- *Fencing With the Electric Foil* by Roger Crossnier
- *Fencing With the Epee* by Roger Crossnier
- *Fencing With the Sabre: Instruction and Technique* by Roger Crossnier
- *Fighting and Boxing* (author unknown)
- *The Fighting Man* by Jack Coggins
- *Figure Improvement and Body Conditioning Through Exercise* by Earl Wallis and Gene Logan
- *The Fireside Book of Boxing* edited by W.C. Heinz
- *The First and Last Freedom* by Jiddu Krishnamurti
- *Fit All the Way* by Camp
  - *The Flight of the Eagle* by Jiddu Krishnamurti
- *Freedom from the Known* by Jiddu Krishnamurti
- *Functional Isometric Contraction* by Bob Hoffman
- *Fundamental Training on Martial Arts* by Tsai Lung-Yun
- *Fun in the Water* (Author Unknown)
- *Gentleman's Art of Self-Defense*
- *Genuine Tai Chi: Lee's Modified Tai Chi for Health* by Lee Ying Arn
- *Gestalt Therapy: Excitement and Growth in the Human Personality* by Federick Perls, M.D., Ralph F. Hefferline, Ph.D., and Paul Goodman, Ph.D.
- *Gestalt Therapy Now* by Joen Fagan and Irma L. Shepherd
- *Gestalt Therapy Verbatim* by Fritz Perls
- *Get Fit: The Champion's Way* by Brian Corrigan and Alan R. Morton
- *A Gold Orchid: The Love Poems of Tzu Yeh* by Tzu Yeh
- *Good English: How to Speak and Write It*
- *Gorgias* by Plato
- *Gray's Anatomy*
- *The Great Philosophers* by Karl Jaspers

- *Greek Temples, Theaters and Shrines* by H. Berve, etc. al.
- *The Green Berets* by Robin Moore
- *Grow Rich While You Sleep* by Ben Sweetland
- *Grow Rich! With Peace of Mind* by Napoleon Hill
- *A Guide to Confident Living* by Norman Vincent Peale
- *Hagakure: The Book of the Samurai* by Yamamoto Tsunetomo
- *The Handbook of Judo* by Gene LeBell and L.C. Coughran
- *Handbook of Progressive Gymnastics* by Tom DeCarlo
- *Handbook of Proverbs* by Henry George Bohn
- *The Hand is My Sword* by Robert A. Trias
- *Happiness Begins Before Breakfast* by Harry and Joan Mier
- *Help For Your Aching Back!* By Harvey Kopell, M.D.
- *Helping Yourself With Self-Hypnosis* by Frank S. Caprio and Joseph R. Berger
- *The Hero With a Thousand Faces* by Joseph Campbell
- *The Historical Aspect of the Study of Human Constitutional Types* by Wilbur Marion Krogman in <u>Ciba Symposia</u> December, 1941
- *A History of Chinese Philosophy* by Fun Yu-lan, translated by Derk Bodde
- *The Holy Bible*
- *Honor Blackman's Book of Self-Defense* by Honor Blackman with Joe and Doug Robinson
- *How I Raised Myself From Failure to Success in Selling* by Frank Bettger
- *How to Box* by Joe Louis (two copies)
- *How to Make Movies* by Robert Ferguson
- *How to Relax: Scientific Body Control* by William H. Miller
- *I Can: The Key to Life's Golden Secrets* by Ben Sweetland
- *The I'Ching or Book of Changes* translation by Carry F. Baynes and R. Wilhelm
- *The I Ching* translation by Richard Wilhelm
- *If The Shoe Fits* by Harry and Joan Mier
- *If the War Goes On: Reflections On War and Politics* by Hermann Hesse (translated by Ralph Manheim)
- *I Will* by Ben Sweetland
- *Illustrated Guide to the Takedown in Wrestling* by Robert L. Brown and Thomas E. Robertson
- *An Illustrated History of the Olympics* by Richard Schaap
- *The Immortal Friend* by Jiddu Krishnamurti
- *The Impossible Question* by Jiddu Krishnamurti

- *The Indian Mind: Essentials of Indian Philosophy and Culture* edited by Charles A. Moore
- *An Inquiry Concerning Human Understanding* by David Hume
- *Integral Yoga Hatha* by Swami Satchidananda
- *Instructions to Young Boxers* (author unknown)
- *Introduction to Logic* by Irving M. Copi
- *Introduction to Saint Thomas Aquinas* edited by Anton C. Pegis
- *An Introduction to Zen Bhuddism* by D.T. Suzuki
- *Introduction to Zen Training* by Omori Sogen
- *Ironman Magazine* (quantity unknown, but he was a subscriber)
- *Islam* (author unknown)
- *Isometric and Isotonic Exercises* (author unknown)
- *Jesus and Krishnamurti: Their Lives and Teachings* by Harriet Tuttle Bartlett
- *Jiu Jitsu* by Frederick Paul Lowell
- *Journey to the East* by Herman Hesse
- *Judo* by Eric Dominy
- *Judo* by Wolfgang Hofmann
- *Judo* by Kiyoshi Kobayashi
- *Judo Combination Techniques* by Teizo Kawamura
- *Judo for the West* by G.R. Gleeson
- *Judo For Young Men* by Tadao Otaki and Donn Draeger
- *Judo On the Ground: the Oda (9th Dan) Method Katamawaza* by E. J. Harrison
- *Judo Throws and Counters* by Eric Dominy
- *Judo Training Methods: A Sourcebook* by Takahiko Ishikawa and Donn Draeger
- *Karate: The Art of Empty Hand Fighting* by Hidetaka Nishiyama and Richard C. Brown
- *Karate Basics* (author unknown)
- *Karate-Do: Nyumon* by Gichin Funakoshi
- *Kenpo Karate: Law of the Fist* by Ed Parker
- *The Key to Judo* by Chikashi Nakanishi
- *The Key to Nutrition* by Carlson Wade
- *Kill Or Get Killed* by Col. Rex Applegate
- *The Koran*
- *Language, Truth and Logic* by A.J. Ayers
- *Let's Cook It Right* by Adele Davis
- *Let's Eat Right to Keep Fit* by Adele Davis

- *Lets Get Well* by Adele Davis
- *Life Ahead* by Jiddu Krishnamurti
- *Life in Freedom* by Jiddu Krishnamurti
- *Living Issues in Philosophy* by Harold Titus
- *Living Zen* by Robert Linssen
- *The Logic of Preference* by G.H. Von Wright
- *The Magic of Personality Power: Your Guide to Business and Social Success* by Gyula Denes
- *The Magic of Thinking Big* by David J. Schwartz
- *The Magic Power of Self-Image Psychology: The New Way to a Bright, Full Life* by Maxwell Maltz
- *Man: A Constitutional Investigation* by William A. Tucker and William A. Lessa in the <u>Quarterly Review of Biology</u> September, 1940
- *A Man Must Fight* by Gene Tunney
- *Mas Oyama's Karate: As Practiced in Japan* by Bobby Lowe
- *The Master Key To Riches* by Napoleon Hill
- *Masterpieces of World Philosophy* by L. Frank N. Magill
- *The Matter of Zen: A Brief Account of Zazen* by P. Wienphahl
- *Maxims and Reflections* by Johann Wolfgang Von Goethe
- *The Mechanics of Atheletics* by Geoffrey H.G. Dyson
- *The Medical Implications of Karate Blows* by Brian C. Adams
- *Meditations* by René Descartes
- *Mencius* by Leonard A. Lyall
- *The Method of Zen* by Eugen Herrigel
- *Modem Weight Training* by Oscar Heidenstam
- *Modern Kung-Fu Karate: Iron, Poison Hand Training* by James Yimm Lee
- *More Playboy's Party Jokes* by the editors of Playboy Magazine
- *Muir's Thesaurus of Truths* by Leo J. Muir
- *The Muscles of the Body and How to Develop Them* by Athletic Publications
- *Muscular Arms and Shoulders* by Harry B. Paschall
- *Musings of a Chinese Mystic: Selections from the Philosophy of Chuang Tzu* introduction by Lionel Giles
- *The Mystic Path To Cosmic Power* by Vernon Howard
- *My Study of Judo* by G. Koizumi
- *Myths To Live By* by Joseph Campbell
- *The Naval Aviation Physical Training Manual* (1943)

- *The New Art of Living* by Norman Vincent Peale
- *New Dimensions of Yoga* by Yogi Raushan Nath
- *The NFL Guide to Physical Fitness* (1965)
- *Noble and Manly: The History of the National Sporting Club* by Guy Deghy
- *Notes to Myself* by Hugh Prather
- *The Odes of Confucius* translated by Kramer Byna
- *On Becoming a Person* by Carl Rogers
- *On Fencing* by Nadi Aldo
- *The Only Revolution* by Jiddu Krishnamurti
- *On Sudden Illumination* by Master Hui Hai
- *The Other Side of the Mind* by Clement Stone
- *Overload Circuit Training* by John E. Nulton
- *Pa Kua: Chinese Boxing for Fitness and Self-Defense* by Robert W. Smith
- *A Passionate State of Mind* by Eric Hoffer
- *Peng Pu Chuan* (author and exact title unknown)
- *The Philosophers of China* by Clarence Burton Day
- *Philosophical Works* edited by J.M.Robertson
- *Philosophy* by Bertrand Russell
- *Physical Activity in Modern Living* by Wayne Van Huss, John Friedrich, Robert Mayberry, Roy Miemeyer, Herbert Olson, and Janet Wessel
- *Physical Combat* (author unknown)
- *Physical Conditioning Exercises for Sports and Healthful Living* by George T. Stafford and Ray O. Duncan
- *Physical Culture* (author unknown)
- *Physical Fitness and Dynamic Health* by Thomas Kirk Cureton, Jr.
- *Physiology of Exercise* by Laurence Morehouse and Augustus Miller
- *A Pictorial History of Boxing* by Sam Andre and Nat Fleischer
- *Pictorial History of Philosophy* by Dagobert Runes
- *Playboy Magazine* (reportedly four boxes worth)
- *Playboy's Party Jokes* by the editors of Playboy Magazine
- *Platform Sutra* by Eno Daikan Zenji
- *Poems That Live Forever*, compiled by Hazel Feldman
- *Power in Athletics* by Glenn Clark
- *The Power of Positive Thinking* by Norman Vincent Peale
- *Practical Combat* (author unknown)

- *Practical Karate Book Four: Defense Against Armed Assailants* by Donn F. Draeger, Masatoshi Nakayama
- *Practical Karate Book One: Fundamentals* by Donn F. Draeger, Masatoshi Nakayama
- *Practical Karate Book Three: Defense Against Multiple Assailants* by Donn F. Draeger, Masatoshi Nakayama
- *Practical Karate Book Two: Against the Unarmed Assailant* by Donn F. Draeger, Masatoshi Nakayama
- *The Practice of Zen* by Chang Chen Chi
- *The Prophet* by Kahlil Gibran
- *Psycho-Cybernetics* by Maxwell Maltz
- *Psychotherapy East and West* by Alan Watts
- *Psycho-Yoga: The Practice of Mind Control* by B. Edwin
- *Pure and Applied Gymnastics* by Albert D. Munrow
- *The Range of Philosophy* by Harold Titus and Maylon Hepp
- *Rational Limbering* by Zelia Raye
- *The Recognition of Reason* by Edward Pols
- *Reference Book of Gymnastics Training for Boys* by the Board of Education (His Majesty's Stationary Office)
- *The Red Badge of Courage* by Stephen Crane
- *The Relationship of Extreme Somatypes to Performance in Motor and Strength Tests* by Frank D. Sills and Peter W. Everett in <u>Research Quarterly</u> May, 1953.
- *Right and Left Hand Fencing* by L.F. Terrone
- *Ring Magazine* (quantity unknown, but he was a subscriber)
- *Rocky Marciano's Best of Boxing and Bodybuilding* by Rocky Marciano
- *Roget's Thesaurus*
- *Rosshalde* by Herman Hesse (translation by Ralph Manheim)
- *The Samurai Sword: A Handbook* by John M. Yumoto
- *The Sayings of Chuang Tzu* by Chuang Tzu
- *Scientific Basis of Athlete Training* by Laurence E. Morehouse, Ph.D. and Philip J. Rasch
- *The Screwtape Letters* by C. S. Lewis
- *The Search* by Jiddu Krishnamurti
- *Secret Fighting Arts of the World* by John Gilbey
- *Secrets of Chinese Karate* by Ed Parker and James Woo
- *Secret of the Golden Flower* by Tung-Pin Leu
- *Secrets of Judo: A Text for Instructors and Students* by Jiichi Watanabe and Lindy Avakian
- *Secrets of Shaolin Temple Boxing* by Robert W. Smith

- *Self Defense or the Art of Boxing (9th Edition)* by Professor Ned Donnelly
- *Selected Verse* by Johann Wolfgang Goethe, translated by David Luke
- *Selling Water By the River: A Manual of Zen Training* by Jiyu Kennett
- *Sense and Sensitivity in Gymnastics* by Allen
- *Shin Buddhism* by D. T. Suzuki
- *Shorinji Kempo: Philosophy and Techniques* by Doshin So
- *A Short History of Chinese Philosophy: A Systematic Account of Chinese Thought From It's Origins to the Present Day* by Dr. Fun Yu-Lan
- *Siddhartha* by Herman Hesse
- *Sign of the Times* by Thomas Carlyle
- *Slimnastics* by Pamela Nottidge
- *The Song of Life* by Jiddu Krishnamurti
- *A Source Book In Ancient Philosophy* edited by Charles. M. Blakewell
- *A Source Book In Chinese Philosophy* by Wing-Tsit Chan
- *The Spirit of Chinese Philosophy* by Fung Yu-Lan
- *The Spirit of Zen* by Alan Watts
- *The Sport of Judo* by Kiyoshi Kobayashi and Harold E. Sharp
- *Sports Illustrated Book of Fencing* by Sports Illustrated.
- *Standing Judo: The Combinations and Counterattacks* by Mikonosuke Kawaishi
- *The Status Seekers* by Vance Packard
- *The Story of Civilization Volume I: Our Oriental Heritage* by Will Durant
- *The Story of Civilization Volume II: The Life of Greece* by Will Durant
- *The Story of Civilization Volume III: Caesar and Christ* by Will Durant
- *The Story of Civilization Volume IV: The Age of Faith* by Will Durant
- *The Story of Civilization Volume V: The Renaissance* by Will Durant
- *The Story of Civilization Volume VI: The Reformation* by Will Durant
- *The Story of Civilization Volume VII: The Age of Reason Begins* by Will Durant
- *The Story of Civilization Volume VIII: The Age of Louis XIV* by Will Durant

- *The Story of Civilization Volume IX: The Age of Voltaire* by Will Durant
- *The Story of Civilization Volume X: Rousseau and Revolution* by Will Durant
- *The Story of Oriental Philosophy* by L. Adam Beck
- *The Story of Philosophy* by Will Durant
- *Strength and How to Obtain It* by Eugen Sandow
- *Successful Wrestling: Its Bases and Problems* by Arnold William Umbach
- *Success Through a Positive Attitude* by W. Clement Stone and Napoleon Hill
- *Succeed and Grow Rich Through Persuasion* by Napoleon Hill
- *The Success System That Never Fails* by Clement Stone
- *Success Through a Positive Mental Attitude* by Clement Stone
- *Summa Theologica* by Saint Thomas Aquinas
- *Tai Chi Chuan and I Ching* by Da Liu
- *Tai Chi: The Supreme Ultimate Exercise for Health, Sport and Self-Defense* by Man-Ching Chen and Robert W. Smith
- *Tai Chi for Health* by Edward Maisel
- *A Taoist Notebook* by Edward Herbert
- *Tao Te Ching* by Lao Tzu
- *Tao, the Great Luminant* translation by Evan Morgan
- *Teach Yourself Logic* by A.A. Luce
- *The Technique of Film Making* (author unknown)
- *Techniques of Aikido* by Thomas H. Makiyama
- *The Textbook of Ju-Jitsu As Practiced in Japan* by Sada Kazu Uyenishi
- *The Textbook of Yoga Psychology* by Ramamurti S. Mishra, M.D.
- *The Texts of Taoism* translated by James Legge
- *Theory and Practice of Fencing* by Julio Martinez Castello
- *Think and Grow Rich* by Napoleon Hill
- *Think On These Things* by Jiddu Krishnamurti
- *This Is It* by Alan Watts
- *This Is Karate* by Mas Oyama
- *This Is Kendo* by Junzo Sasamori and Gordon Warner
- *This Matter of Culture* by Jiddu Krishnamurti
- *The Tibetan Book of The Dead*
- *Tibetan Yoga* by Bernard Bromage

- *Training for Great Strength: An Introduction to the Science of Strength and BodyBuilding by Means of Progressive Weight Lifting* by Chas T. Trevor
- *Translations From The Chinese* by Arthur Waley
- *Translations From The Chinese* by Lin Yu-Tang
- *The True Believer* by Eric Hoffer
- *The Undiscovered Self* by Carl Jung
- *The Unfettered Mind : Writings of the Zen Master to the Sword Master* by Takuan Soho
- *The Urgency of Change* by Jiddu Krishnamurti
- *U.S. Army Boxing Manual* by the United States Army
- *The U.S. Navy Boxing Manual* by the United States Navy
- *The Varieties of Human Physique* by W.H. Sheldon, S.S. Stevens and W.B. Tucker
- *The Viking Book of Aphorisms* edited by W.H. Auden
- *Wake Up Your Mind* by Alex Osborn
- *Walk On!* by Christmas Humphreys
- *War Without Weapons* by Philip Goodhart
- *The Way of Action* by Christmas Humphreys
- *The Way of Chinese Painting: It's Ideas and Techniques* by Mai-Mai Sze
- *The Way of Chuang Tzu* translation by Thomas Merton
- *The Way of Karate: Beyond Technique* by George E. Mattson
- *The Way of Life* (Tao Te Ching) by Lao Tzu, translation by R.B. Blakney
- *The Way of Zen* by Alan Watts
- *Weightlifting* by Tackle
- *Weightlifting and Weight Training* by George Kirkley
- *Weight Training for Athletics* by Oscar State
- *What the Buddha Taught* by Walpola Rahula
- *What Is Karate* by Mas Oyama
- *Wing Chun* by James Lee
- *Winning Personal Recognition* by Charles B. Roth
- *The Wisdom of China and India* by Lin Yu-Tang
- *The Wisdom of the Chinese* edited by Brian Brown
- *The Wisdom of Confucius* translated by Epiphanius Wilson
- *The Wisdom of Lao-Tse* edited and translated by Lin Yu-Tang
- *Wisdom of the West* by Bertrand Russell
- *The World of Literature* (author unknown)
- *The World of Philosophy* (author unknown)
- *The Works of Mencius* translated by James Legge

- The Works of Plato
- *The Works of Shakespeare* by William Shakespeare
- The Works of Socrates
- *The World of Zen* by Nancy Ross
- *The World's Religions* by Huston Smith
- *Yoga Practice* (author unknown)
- *Yogic Exercises* (author unknown)
- *You Are the World* by Jiddu Krishnamurti
- *You Can Learn to Speak* by Royal L. Garff
- *Your Personal Handbook of Self Defense* by Gene LeBell and L. C. Coughran
- *Yourself and Zen* (author unknown)
- *You Too Can Work Wonders* by Harry and Joan Mier
- *Zen and American Thought* by Van Meter Ames
- *Zen and Japanese Culture* by D.T. Suzuki
- *Zen and Reality* by Robert Powell
- *Zen Buddhism and Psychoanalysis* by Daisetz T. Suzuki
- *Zen Comes West* by Christmas Humphreys
- *Zen Dictionary* by Ernest Wood
- *Zen for the West* by Sohaka Kogata
- *Zen in the Art of Archery* by Eugen Herrigel
- *Zen: Poems, Prayers, Sermons, Anecdotes, Interviews* edited by Lucien Stryk
- *Zen, Taoism and Oriental Philosophy* (author unknown)
- *The Zen Teaching of Huang Po: On the Transmission of the Mind* by John Blofeld

APPENDIX:
ADDITIONAL BRUCE LEE MISATTRIBUTIONS

The following citations are all wrongly attributed to Bruce Lee. This is a constantly growing list, as I am discovering more and more cases of misattribution in my research. This only includes passages for which I have been able to find the original source, although I strongly believe this merely scratches the surface. I am absolutely certain several more passages in such Bruce Lee books as Tao of Jeet Kune Do, *Artist of Life, and* Striking Thoughts *are not original to Bruce Lee for various deductive reasons: archaic grammar usage, terminology and explanatory text that I have found referring to other belief systems (especially Buddhism), and a writing style that is different than Lee's (explanations of ideas in a manner that leads me to suspect that some were taken, particularly, from a textbook). In addition, Lee was also in the habit of translating Chinese texts into English for his own personal use. It is safe to assume that at least some of that has been mistaken for his words as well and is doubly difficult to ascertain. I should also mention that, as these are my own personal discoveries, this list may not include other discoveries made over the course of time by other individuals.*

"Our Grand business is not to see what lies dimly at a distance, but to do what lies clearly at hand." Attributed to Bruce Lee in the book *Striking Thoughts*, page 31; these are actually the words of Thomas Carlyle from the book *Sign of the Times*, first published in 1836.

"The end of man is action, and not thought, though it be of the noblest. In this world there are a lot of people who cannot touch the heart of the matter but talk merely intellectually (not emotionally) about how they would do this or do that; talk about it, but yet nothing is ever actualized or accomplished." Attributed to

Bruce Lee on page 32 of *Striking Thoughts*. This is also by Carlyle, from *Sign of the Times.*

"He who knows himself best, esteems himself least." Attributed to Bruce Lee on page 375 of the book *Jeet Kune Do: Commentaries on the Martial Way*. Henry George Bohn, a 19th century English writer, publisher, and translator, is the real author of this quote.

"If you want to know the value of money, try and borrow some." Bruce Lee's handwritten notes in the possession of a private collector. The real author is Benjamin Franklin.

"Associate yourself with men of good quality if you esteem your own reputation for 'tis better to be alone than in bad company." Attributed to Bruce Lee on an Internet forum in a scanned copy of one of Bruce Lee's notes provided to the forum by his brother, Robert Lee. This quote is from George Washington, first president of the United States.

"Success is the journey, not a destination." Attributed to Bruce Lee on page 126 of *Striking Thoughts*. This is by Ben Sweetland, a self-help and motivational author.

"Better to have loved and lost, than to have never loved at all." Bruce Lee's handwritten notes in the possession of a private collector. The real author is Saint Augustine.

"The work of conservation is shown to be a continuous actualization and differentiation of form. One does not allow oneself to be influenced by outward success or failure, but confident in one's strength, one bides one's time." Attributed to Bruce Lee on page 33 of *Striking Thoughts*. This is actually from Richard Wilhelm's translation of the *I Ching.*

"SET me whereas the sun doth parch the green
Or where his beams do not dissolve the ice;
In temperate heat, where he is felt and seen;
In presence prest[1] of people, mad, or wise;
Set me in high, or yet in low degree;
In longest night, or in the shortest day;
In clearest sky, or where clouds thickest be;
In lusty youth, or when my hairs are gray:
Set me in heaven, in earth, or else in hell,

In hill, or dale, or in the foaming flood ;
Thrall, or at large, alive whereso I dwell,
Sick, or in health, in evil fame or good,
    Her's will I be; and only with this thought
    Content myself, although my chance be nought."
Bruce Lee's handwritten notes in the possession of a private
collector. The real author is Henry Howard, the Earl of Surrey.

"Any idea that is constantly held in the mind and emotionalized
begins at once to clothe itself in the most convenient and
appropriate physical form that is available." Attributed to Bruce
Lee on page 369 of the book *Jeet Kune Do: Commentaries On the
Martial Way*. This is actually paraphrased from page 19 of Alan
Watts' *This Is It*, which goes: "As water seeks the course of least
resistance, so the emotions clothe themselves in the symbols that
lie most readily at hand."

"A woman is like your shadow; follow her, she flies; fly from her,
she follows." Bruce Lee's handwritten notes in the possession of
a private collector. The real author is Nicholas Chamfort.

"Patience is the art of hoping." Bruce Lee's handwritten notes in
the possession of a private collector. The real author is the
Marquis de Vauvenarques.

"The good life is a process, not a state of being. It is a direction,
not a destination. The good life constitutes a direction selected by
the total organism, when there is psychological freedom to move
in any direction." Attributed to Bruce Lee on page 379 of *Jeet
Kune Do: Commentaries on the Martial Way*. This is from page
186 of Carl Rogers' book, *On Becoming a Person*.

"We are told that talent creates its own opportunities. But it
sometimes seems that intense desire creates not only its own
opportunities, but its own talents." Attributed to Bruce Lee on
page 115 of *Striking Thoughts*. This is aphorism 18 of Eric
Hoffer's *A Passionate State of Mind*.

"You can never invite the wind, but you must leave the window
open." Attributed to Bruce Lee on page 379 of *Jeet Kune Do:
Commentaries on the Martial Way*. This is actually from
Krishnamurti's book, *Freedom From the Known*.

"Optimism is a faith that leads to success." Attributed to Bruce Lee on page 120 of *Striking Thoughts.* This is actually a statement by Helen Keller.

"To tolerate is to insult." Attributed to Bruce Lee on page 375 of *Jeet Kune Do: Commentaries on the Martial Way.* This is actually the words of the German poet Johann Wolfgang von Goethe, from his book *Maxims and Reflections.*

"True thusness is the substance of thought, and thought is the function of true thusness. There is no thought except that of the true thusness. Thusness does not move, but its motion and function are inexhaustible." Attributed to Bruce Lee on page 42 of *Striking Thoughts.* This is actually a statement by Wing-Tsit Chan on page 435 of *A Source Book in Chinese Philosophy.*

"I'll not willingly offend, nor be easily offended. What's amiss I'll stop to mend, and endure what can't be mended." Attributed to Bruce Lee on page 375 of *Jeet Kune Do: Commentaries on the Martial Way.* This is, from all places, taken from a 19th century hymnal titled, "Though I'm now in younger days", published in Isaac Watts' book *Divine and Moral Songs*, first published in 1866.

"Would that we could at once paint with the eyes! In the long way from the eye through the arm to the pencil, how much is lost." Attributed to Bruce Lee on page 138 of *Striking Thoughts.* Gotthold Lessing, an 18th century German philosopher and dramatist, is the real author of this statement.

"Not failure, but low aim, is the crime. In great attempts it is glorious even to fail." Attributed to Bruce Lee on page 121 of *Striking Thoughts.* This is actually a statement by Cassius Longinus, a Roman General and statesman best known for being one of the conspirators who murdered Julius Caesar.

"Thoughts are things, in the sense that thought can be translated into its physical equivalent." Attributed to Bruce Lee on page 122 of *Striking Thoughts.* This one is actually Napoleon Hill, likely from his book *Think and Grow Rich.*

"Wisdom does not consist of trying to wrest good from evil but in learning to 'ride' them as a cork adapts itself to the crests and troughs of waves." Attributed to Bruce Lee on page 8 of *The Tao *of Jeet Kune Do.* This is actually Alan Watts, from his book *This Is It.*

"The perfection of art is to conceal art." Attributed to Bruce Lee on page 138 of *Striking Thoughts.* Marcus Fabius Quintilianus, a Roman rhetorician wrote this in his *Instituto Oratoria.*

"The individual is of first importance, not the system. Remember that man created method and not that method created man, and do not strain yourself in twisting into someone's preconceived pattern, which unquestionably would be appropriate for him, but not necessarily for you." Attributed to Bruce Lee on page 153 of *Striking Thoughts.* This is from Krishnamurti's *Education and the Significance of Life* (1953).

"In Buddhism there is no place for using effort. Just be ordinary and nothing special. Eat your food, move your bowels, pass water, and when you're tired go and lie down. The ignorant will laugh at me, but the wise will understand." Attributed to Bruce Lee on page 161 of *Striking Thoughts.* This is actually a statement by Ch'an Buddhism (Zen) master Lin-Chi, quoted by Alan Watts in *Beat Zen, Square Zen and Zen* (1959); reprinted in the book *This Is It,* which is where Bruce Lee came to find it.

"I respect faith, but doubt is what gets you an education." Attributed to Bruce Lee on page 123 of *Striking Thoughts.* Wilson Mizner, an American dramatist, wrote this.

"What do I live on? My faith in my ability that I'll make it. Faith makes it possible to achieve that which man's mind can conceive and believe. It is a well-known fact that one comes, finally, to believe whatever one repeats to one's self, whether the statement be true or false. If a man repeats a lie over and over, he will eventually accept the lie as truth. Moreover, he'll *believe* it to be the truth. Every man is what he is because of the dominating thoughts which he permits to occupy his mind." Attributed to Bruce Lee on page 124 of *Striking Thoughts.* This is from Napoleon Hill's *Think and Grow Rich.*

"A purpose is the eternal condition of success." Attributed to Bruce Lee on page 126 of *Striking Thoughts.* The real author is Theodore T. Munger, from his book *The Freedom of Faith.*

"An assertion is Zen only when it is itself an act and does not refer to anything that is asserted in it." Attributed to Bruce Lee on page 163 of *Striking Thoughts*. This is a paraphrasing of a statement by Zen master Mumon.

"To meditate means to realize the imperturbability of one's original nature. Meditation means to be free from all phenomena, and calmness means to be internally unperturbed. There will be calmness when one is free from external objects and is not perturbed." Attributed to Bruce Lee on page 166 of *Striking Thoughts*. This is from Wing Tsit Chan's *A Source Book in Chinese Philosophy*.

"To know oneself is to study oneself in action with another person. Relationship is a process of self-revelation. Relationship is the mirror in which you discover yourself -- to be is to be related." Attributed to Bruce Lee on page 181 of *Striking Thoughts*. Bruce Lee borrowed this from Krishnamurti's book *The First and Last Freedom*.

"When I have listened to my mistakes, I have grown." Attributed to Bruce Lee on page 189 of *Striking Thoughts*. This is actually a quote by Hugh Prather in his book *Notes to Myself*.

"Truth is a pathless road. A road that is not a road. It is total expression that has no before or after. How can there be methods and systems by which to arrive at something that is living? To that which is static, fixed, dead, there can be a way, a definite path, but not to that which is living." Attributed to Bruce Lee on page 208 of *Striking Thoughts*. This is paraphrased from Krishnamurti, particularly from his historic speech dissolving the Order of the Star, in which he stated that, "Truth is a pathless land."

"Nothing is less sincere than our mode of giving and asking advice. He who asks seems to have deference for the opinion of his friend, while he only aims to get approval of his own and make his friend responsible for his action. And he who gives repays the confidence supposedly placed in him by a seemingly disinterested zeal, but he seldom means anything by his advice but his own interest or reputation. When a man seeks your advice he generally wants your praise." Attributed to Bruce Lee on page 131 of *Striking Thoughts*. These are the words of Philip Dormer Chesterfield, an 18th century English statesman and author.

"There is a powerful craving in most of us to see ourselves as instruments in the hands of others and thus free ourselves from the responsibility for acts which are prompted by our own questionable inclinations and impulses. Both the strong and the weak grasp at this alibi. The latter hide their malevolence under the virtue of obedience: they acted dishonorably because they had to obey orders. The strong, too, claim absolution by proclaiming themselves the chosen instrument of a higher power -- God, history, fate, nation, or humanity." Attributed to Bruce Lee on page 174 of *Striking Thoughts*. This is actually sociologist Eric Hoffer, from his book *True Believer.*

"We acquire a sense of worth either by realizing our talents, or by keeping busy, or by identifying ourselves with something apart from us -- be it a cause, a leader, a group, possessions, and the like. Of the three, the path of self-realization is the most difficult. It is taken when other avenues to a sense of worth are more or less blocked." Attributed to Bruce Lee on page 177 of *Striking Thoughts*. This is a mixture of aphorisms 30 and 35 in Eric Hoffer's *A Passionate State of Mind.*

"Self-conquest is the greatest of victories. Mighty is he who conquers himself." Attributed to Bruce Lee on page 180 of *Striking Thoughts*. This is a statement by Lao Tzu, this translation of which appeared in Herbert Giles' *The Civilization of China* (1911).

"The Usefulness of a cup is in its emptiness." A statement Bruce Lee made to a letter writer responding to his "Liberate Yourself From Classical Karate" article in *Black Belt* magazine; it has since been quoted frequently as being Bruce Lee. It is actually from verse 11 of the *Tao Te Ching.*

"We judge ourselves by what we feel capable of doing, while others judge us by what we have already done." Bruce Lee's handwritten notes in the possession of a private collector. The real author is Henry Wadsworth Longfellow.

"It is later than you think! Know yourself!" Attributed to Bruce Lee on page 181 of *Striking Thoughts*. This is based on two common phrases in Latin: *Memento Mori*, literally, "Remember to Die", is often loosely translated as, "It is later than you think." It is a reminder that death is always creeping up on you. The second,

"Know Yourself", is (of course) immediately recognizable as "Know Thyself", or *Nosce Te Ipsum*. It is a declaration of introspection attributed to both Plato and the Oracle at Delphi.

"Sorrows are our best educator. A man can see further through a tear than a telescope." Attributed to Bruce Lee on page 100 of *Striking Thoughts*. This is actually from *Muir's Thesaurus of Truths* by Leo J. Muir, a book of quotations published in 1937.

"Loneliness is only an opportunity to cut adrift and find yourself. In solitude you are least alone. Make good use of it." Attributed to Bruce Lee on page 101 of *Striking Thoughts*. This is actually Anne Shannon Moore, a turn-of-the-century American journalist and novelist. This could be from Muir's book of quotations, although it is also possible that he actually owned one of Moore's books.

"Aim at perfection in everything, though in most things it is unattainable; however, they who aim at it, and persevere, will come much nearer to it than those whose laziness and despondency make them give it up as unattainable." Attributed to Bruce Lee on page 117 of *Striking Thoughts*. This is actually the words of Lord Chesterfield, likely taken from Muir's book of quotations.

"What you habitually think, largely determines what you will ultimately become." Attributed to Bruce Lee on page 120 of *Striking Thoughts*. This is actually one of Anne Landers' many aphorisms.

"If you think you are beaten, you are; If you think you dare not, you don't. If you'd like to win, but think you can't It's almost a cinch you won't If you think you'll lose, you're lost, For out in the world we find Success begins with a fellow's will; It's all in the state of mind.

"If you think you're outclassed, you are. You've got to think high to rise. You've got to be sure of yourself before you can ever win a prize. Life's battles don't always go to the stronger or faster man; but sooner or later the man who wins is the one who thinks he can." Attributed to Bruce Lee on page 375 of *Jeet Kune Do: Commentaries on the Martial Way*. This is actually a poem by D. Wintle, "The Man Who Thinks He Can" in the book *Poems That Live Forever*, comp. Hazel Feldman 1965.

"In summer we sweat; in winter we shiver." Quoted by Bruce Lee on page 46 of the book, *Words of the Dragon.* Lee identified it as part of a Zen parable. It comes from Alan Watts' book, *This Is It.*

"In the landscape of spring, there is neither better nor worse. The flowering branches grow naturally; some long, some short." Quoted by Bruce Lee in response to a letter made to a reader responding to his "Liberate Yourself From Classical Karate" article in *Black Belt* magazine; it has since been quoted frequently as being Bruce Lee, even though Lee identified it as a Zen saying. It was taken by Lee from Alan Watts' book, *This Is It.*

"Never trouble trouble til trouble troubles you." Attributed to Bruce Lee on page 375 of *Jeet Kune Do: Commentaries on the Martial Way.* This is actually a very old saying from colonial America.

"Live content with small means; seek elegance rather than fashion. Be worthy, not respectable, wealthy, not rich; study hard, think quietly, talk gently, act frankly; bear all cheerfully, do all bravely, await occasions, hurry never. In a word, let the spiritual, unbidden and unconscious, grow up through the common." Attributed to Bruce Lee on page 78 of the book, *Striking Thoughts.* This is a prose piece titled "My Symphony" by a 19th century clergyman named William Henry Channing. The last line, which is left off of the Bruce Lee quote, is: "This is to be my symphony."

"The additive process is merely a cultivation of memory, which becomes mechanical. Learning is never cumulative, it is a movement of knowing that has no beginning and no end." Attributed to Bruce Lee on page 33 of *Striking Thoughts.* I found this listed on the Krishnamurti Foundation of America's website, quoted from a book titled *Book of Life,* although I believe the book is a compilation of previous Krishnamurti writings, so it is likely that Bruce Lee picked it up from another book by Krishnamurti.

The entire page 89 of the Bruce Lee book *Artist of Life,* titled "Hesse on Self-Will", is Hesse verbatim, quoted from the book *If the War Goes On: Reflections on War and Politics* by Herman Hesse, translated by Ralph Manheim (1970); Farrar, Straus and Giroux. Pages 79-85.

All of the following misattributions come from Gestalt Therapy Verbatim **by Fritz Perls (1969); Real People Press.**

"The meaning of life is that it is to be lived, and it is not to be traded and conceptualized and squeezed into a pattern of systems."

> *Gestalt Therapy Verbatim*, page 3.
> Attributed to Bruce Lee in several instances, including *Striking Thoughts*, page (coincidentally) 3.

The following are also taken from Striking Thoughts**:**

"The ego boundary is the differentiation between the self and the otherness. If the ego boundary is a fixed thing (which it is not) then it again becomes a character, or an armor, like the turtle."

> *Gestalt Therapy Verbatim*, page 7/ *Striking Thoughts*, page 56

"Inside the Ego Boundary there is cohesion, love, cooperation. Outside the Ego Boundary there is suspicion, strangeness, unfamiliarity."

> *Gestalt Therapy Verbatim*, page 8/ *Striking Thoughts*, page 56

"The enemy of development is this pain phobia - the unwillingness to do a tiny bit of suffering. As you feel unpleasant you interrupt the continuum of awareness and you become phobic - so therapeutically speaking we continue to grow by means of integrating awareness/attention."

> *Gestalt Therapy Verbatim*, page 52/ *Striking Thoughts*, page (another coincidence) 52

The following selections from Artist of Life **are so large and extensive that I will not repeat them here. Instead I will refer to page and paragraph to cite the passages, which are copied verbatim from** Gestalt Therapy Verbatim**.**

Pages 71-72 of *Artist of Life*, titled "Notes on Gestalt Therapy" are copied from the following pages of *Gestalt Therapy Verbatim* (in the order in which they appear in *Artist of Life*): pages 6, 2-3, 3, 4, 7.

Pages 73-74 of *Artist of Life*, titled "The Relationship of the Organism to Its Environment" are copied from the following pages of *Gestalt Therapy Verbatim* (in the order in which they appear in *Artist of Life*): pages 7l, 8, 8, 8-9, 7, 10, 11, 11, 14, 14, 14, 15.

Pages 75-76 of *Artist of Life*, titled "Three Types of Philosophy" are copied from the following pages of *Gestalt Therapy Verbatim* (in the order in which they appear in *Artist of Life*): pages 15-16.

Pages 77-78 of *Artist of Life*, titled "Self-Regulation Versus External Regulation" are copied from the following pages of *Gestalt Therapy Verbatim* (in the order in which they appear in *Artist of Life*): pages 16-17.

Page 79-80 of *Artist of Life*, titled "The Top Dog and the Underdog" are copied from the following pages of *Gestalt Therapy Verbatim* (in the order in which they appear in *Artist of Life*): pages 17-19.

Page 83 of *Artist of Life*, titled "Thinking is Rehearsing" is copied from the following page of *Gestalt Therapy Verbatim*: page 28.

Page 84 of *Artist of Life*, titled "Learning" is copied from the following page of *Gestalt Therapy Verbatim*: page 25.

Appendix:
Additional Discoveries

In an effort to make this book the most comprehensive resource for Bruce Lee misattributions, I have included the following collection of additional discoveries by other researchers. As I want to give them credit for making the discoveries as well as crediting the original author, I have separated these from my own discoveries and duly noted the researchers who identified them.

Kip Brockett discovered the following misattributions:

"...It is a constant, rapid shifting of ground, seeking the slightest closing which will greatly increase the chances of hitting the opponent." Attributed to Bruce Lee in *The Tao of Jeet Kune Do*. This was taken from the *Sports Illustrated Book of Fencing*.

"With all the training thrown to the wind, with a mind perfectly unaware of its own working, with the self vanishing nowhere, anybody knows where, the art of Jeet Kune Do attains its perfection." Attributed to Bruce Lee in *The Tao of Jeet Kune Do*. This is paraphrased from the writings of Yagyu Tajima no kami Munenori (1571-1646), a Japanese swordsman.

"Approach Jeet Kune Do with the idea of mastering the will. Forget about winning and losing; forget about pride and pain. Let your opponent graze your skin and you smash his flesh; let him smash into your flesh and you fracture his bones; let him fracture your bones and you take his life! Do not be concerned with your escaping safely- lay your life before him!" Attributed to Bruce Lee in The Tao of Jeet Kune Do; paraphrased from the *Hagakure: The Book of the Samurai* by Yamamoto Tsunetomo.

"The first stage is the primitive stage. It is a stage of original ignorance in which a person knows nothing about the art of combat...he simply blocks and strikes instinctively..."

"The second stage- the stage of sophistication, or mechanical stage- begins when a person starts his training. He is taught the different ways of blocking, striking, ...Unquestionably, he has gained the scientific knowledge of combat, but unfortunately his original self and sense of freedom are lost, and his action no longer flows by itself...his mind tends to freeze at different movements..."

"The third stage- the stage of artlessness, or spontaneous stage- occurs when, after years of serious and hard practice, the student realizes that after all, gung fu is nothing special..." Taken from the essay titled "The Three Stages of Cultivation" attributed to Bruce Lee in the book *Warrior Within*; this is paraphrased from D.T. Suzuki's book *Zen and Japanese Culture.*

"The primary purpose of JKD is kicking, hitting and applying bodily force. Therefore, the use of the on-guard position is to obtain the most favorable position for the above-mentioned." Attributed to Bruce Lee in *The Tao of Jeet Kune Do*; this is (with minor name changes) from *Boxing* by Edwin L. Haislet.

"To hit or to kick effectively, it is necessary to shift weight constantly from one leg to the other. This means perfect control of body balance. Balance is the most important consideration in the on-guard position." Attributed to Bruce Lee in *The Tao of Jeet Kune Do*; this is also from Haislet's *Boxing.*

"In Western boxing, the head is treated as if it were a part of the trunk, generally, with no independent action of its own. In close-in fighting, it should be carried vertically, with the point of the chin pinned to the collarbone and the side of the chin held against the inside of the lead shoulder..." Attributed to Bruce Lee in *The Tao of Jeet Kune Do*; from Haislet's *Boxing.*

"The point of the chin is not tucked into the lead shoulder except when angling the head back in an extreme defensive position. Tucking the point of the chin into the lead shoulder turns the neck into an unnatural position, takes away the support of the muscles and prevents straight bone alignment. It also tenses the lead shoulder and arm, preventing free action and causing fatigue." Attributed to Bruce Lee in *The Tao of Jeet Kune Do*; from Haislet's *Boxing.*

"With the chin dropped and pinned tight to the collarbone, the muscles and bone structure are in the best possible alignment and only the top of the head is presented to the opponent, making it impossible to be hit on the point of the chin." Attributed to Bruce Lee in *The Tao of Jeet Kune Do*; from Haislet's *Boxing*.

"The on-guard position is that position most favorable to the mechanical execution of all the total techniques and skills. It allows complete relaxation yet, at the same time, gives a muscle tonus most favorable to quick reaction time." Attributed to Bruce Lee in *The Tao of Jeet Kune Do*; from Haislet's *Boxing*.

"Ducking is dropping the body forward under swings and hooks (hands or feet) directed at the head..."

"Ducking is used as a means of escaping blows and allowing the fighter to remain in range for a counter attack. It is just as necessary to learn to duck swings and hooks as it is to slip straight punches. Both are important in counterattacks." Attributed to Bruce Lee in *The Tao of Jeet Kune Do*; from Haislet's *Boxing*.

"Rolling nullifies the force of a blow by moving the body with it. Against a straight blow, the movement is backward. Against hooks, the movement is to either side. Against uppercuts, it is backward and away." Attributed to Bruce Lee in *The Tao of Jeet Kune Do*; from Haislet's *Boxing*.

"Give up thinking as though not giving it up. Observe techniques as though not observing." Credited to Bruce Lee under the heading, "On Zen", in the *Tao of Jeet Kune Do*, the words of Yagyu Tajima no kami Munenori (1571-1646), taken from D.T. Suzuki's book *Zen and Japanese Culture*.

"I'm moving and not moving at all. I'm like the moon underneath the waves that ever go on rolling and rocking." Credited to Bruce Lee under the heading, "On Zen", in the *Tao of Jeet Kune Do*, the words of Yagyu Tajima no kami Munenori (1571-1646), taken from D.T. Suzuki's book *Zen and Japanese Culture*.

"Let yourself go with the disease, be with it, keep company with it-this is the way to be rid of it." Credited to Bruce Lee under the heading, "On Zen", in the *Tao of Jeet Kune Do*, the words of

Yagyu Tajima no kami Munenori (1571-1646), taken from D.T. Suzuki's book *Zen and Japanese Culture.*

"Turn into a doll made of wood: it has no ego, it thinks nothing, it is not grasping or sticky. Let the body and limbs work themselves out in accordance with the discipline they have undergone." Credited to Bruce Lee under the heading, "On Zen", in the *Tao of Jeet Kune Do*, the words of Yagyu Tajima no kami Munenori (1571-1646), taken from D.T. Suzuki's book *Zen and Japanese Culture.*

The following discoveries were first identified by Robert Colet:

"We are those kata, we are those classical blocks and thrusts, so heavily conditioned are we by them." Attributed to Bruce Lee in the *Tao of Jeet Kune Do.* This is taken, with minor changes, from Krishnamurti's *Freedom From the Known.*

"You cannot see a street fight in its totality, observing it from the viewpoint of a boxer, a kung-fu man, a karateka, a wrestler, a judo man and so forth. You can see clearly only when style does not interfere." Attributed to Bruce Lee in the *Tao of Jeet Kune Do.* This is taken, with changes, from Krishnamurti's *Freedom From the Known.*

"Fighting is not something dictated by your conditioning as a kung fu man, a karate man, a judo man or what not." Attributed to Bruce Lee in the *Tao of Jeet Kune Do.* This is taken, with changes, from Krishnamurti's *Freedom From the Known.*

"The man who is really serious, with the urge to find out what truth is, has no style at all. He lives only in what is." Attributed to Bruce Lee in the *Tao of Jeet Kune Do.* This is taken, with minor changes, from Krishnamurti's *Freedom From the Known.*